A-Level Year 1 & AS

Physics

Exam Board: OCR B (Advancing Physics)

Revising for Physics exams is stressful, that's for sure — even just getting your notes sorted out can leave you needing a lie down. But help is at hand...

This brilliant CGP book explains **everything you'll need to learn** (and nothing you won't), all in a straightforward style that's easy to get your head around. We've also included **exam questions** to test how ready you are for the real thing.

There's even a free Online Edition you can read on your computer or tablet!

How to get your free Online Edition

Go to **cgpbooks.co.uk/extras** and enter this code...

3303 0209 1923 7801

This code only works for one person. If somebody else has used this book before you, they might have already claimed the Online Edition.

CGP

A-Level revision? It has to be CGP!

Published by CGP

Editors:
Emily Garrett, David Maliphant, Rachael Marshall, Sam Pilgrim, Frances Rooney, Charlotte Whiteley, Sarah Williams and Jonathan Wray.

Contributors:
Tony Alldridge, Jane Cartwright, Peter Clarke, Mark A. Edwards, Barbara Mascetti, John Myers and Andy Williams

ISBN: 978 1 78294 296 2

With thanks to Ian Francis for the proofreading.
With thanks to Jan Greenway for the copyright research.

NASA's Earth Observatory image on page 22 using Landsat data from the U.S. Geological Survey Courtesy of USGS/NASA

www.cgpbooks.co.uk

Clipart from Corel®
Printed by Elanders Ltd, Newcastle upon Tyne.

Based on the classic CGP style created by Richard Parsons.

Contents

The Scientific Process

'How Science Works' is all about the scientific process — how we develop and test scientific ideas. It's what scientists do all day, every day (well, except at coffee time — never come between a scientist and their coffee).

*Scientists Come Up with **Theories** — Then **Test Them**...*

Science tries to explain **how** and **why** things happen — it **answers questions**. It's all about seeking and gaining **knowledge** about the world around us. Scientists do this by **asking** questions, **suggesting** answers and then **testing** their suggestions to see if they're correct — this is the **scientific process**.

1) **Ask** a question about **why** something happens or **how** something works. E.g. what is the nature of light?
2) **Suggest** an answer, or part of an answer, by forming a **theory** (a possible **explanation** of the observations) — e.g. light is a wave. (Scientists also sometimes form a **model** too — a **simplified picture** of what's physically going on.)
3) Make a **prediction** or **hypothesis** — a **specific testable statement**, based on the theory, about what will happen in a test situation. For example, if light is a wave, it will interfere and diffract when it travels through a small enough gap.
4) Carry out a **test** — to provide **evidence** that will support the prediction (or help to disprove it). E.g. Young's double-slit experiment (p.58-59).

The evidence supported Quentin's Theory of Flammable Burps.

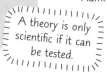

A theory is only scientific if it can be tested.

*...Then They **Tell** Everyone About Their **Results**...*

The results are **published** — scientists need to let others know about their work. Scientists publish their results in **scientific journals**. These are just like normal magazines, only they contain **scientific reports** (called papers) instead of the latest celebrity gossip.

1) Scientific reports are similar to the **lab write-ups** you do in school. And just as a lab write-up is **reviewed** (marked) by your teacher, reports in scientific journals undergo **peer review** before they're published.
2) The report is sent out to **peers** — other scientists that are experts in the **same area**. They examine the data and results, and if they think that the conclusion is reasonable it's **published**. This makes sure that work published in scientific journals is of a **good standard**.
3) But peer review **can't guarantee** the science is **correct** — other scientists still need to **reproduce** it.
4) Sometimes **mistakes** are made and bad work is published. Peer review **isn't perfect** but it's probably the best way for scientists to self-regulate their work and to publish **quality reports**.

*...Then **Other Scientists** Will **Test** the Theory Too*

Other scientists read the published theories and results, and try to **test the theory** themselves. This involves:

- Repeating the **exact same experiments**.
- Using the theory to make **new predictions** and then testing them with **new experiments**.

*If the **Evidence** Supports a Theory, It's **Accepted** — **for Now***

1) If all the experiments in all the world provide good evidence to back it up, the theory is thought of as **scientific 'fact'** (for now).
2) But it will never become **totally indisputable** fact. Scientific **breakthroughs or advances** could provide new ways to question and test the theory, which could lead to **new evidence** that **conflicts** with the current evidence. Then the testing starts all over again...

And this, my friend, is the **tentative nature of scientific knowledge** — it's always **changing** and **evolving**.

The Scientific Process

So scientists need evidence to back up their theories. They get it by carrying out experiments, and when that's not possible they carry out studies. But why bother with science at all? We want to know as much as possible so we can use it to try and improve our lives (and because we're nosy).

Evidence Comes From Controlled Lab Experiments...

1) Results from **controlled experiments** in **laboratories** are **great**.
2) A lab is the easiest place to **control variables** so that they're all **kept constant** (except for the one you're investigating).

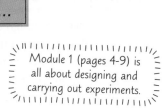

Module 1 (pages 4-9) is all about designing and carrying out experiments.

...That You can Draw Meaningful Conclusions From

1) You always need to make your experiments as **controlled** as possible so you can be confident that any effects you see are linked to the variable you're changing.
2) If you do find a relationship, you need to be careful what you conclude. You need to decide whether the effect you're seeing is **caused** by changing a variable (this is known as a **causal relationship**), or whether the two are just **correlated**. There's more about drawing conclusions on page 9.

"Right Geoff, you can start the experiment now... I've stopped time..."

Society Makes Decisions Based on Scientific Evidence

1) Lots of scientific work eventually leads to **important discoveries** or breakthroughs that could **benefit humankind**.
2) These results are **used by society** (that's you, me and everyone else) to **make decisions** — about the way we live, what we eat, what we drive, etc.
3) All sections of society use scientific evidence to make decisions, e.g. politicians use it to devise policies and individuals use science to make decisions about their own lives.

Other factors can **influence** decisions about science or the way science is used:

Economic factors

Society has to consider the **cost** of implementing changes based on scientific conclusions — e.g. the cost of reducing the UK's carbon emissions to limit the human contribution to **global warming**.

Scientific research is often **expensive**. E.g. in areas such as astronomy, the Government has to **justify** spending money on a new telescope rather than pumping money into, say, the **NHS** or **schools**.

Social factors

Decisions affect **people's lives** — e.g. when looking for a site to build a **nuclear power station**, you need to consider how it would affect the lives of the people in the **surrounding area**.

Environmental factors

Many scientists suggest that building **wind farms** would be a **cheap** and **environmentally friendly** way to generate electricity in the future. But some people think that because **wind turbines** can **harm wildlife** such as birds and bats, other methods of generating electricity should be used.

So there you have it — how science works...

Hopefully these pages have given you a nice intro to how science works, e.g. what scientists do to provide you with 'facts'. You need to understand this, as you're expected to know how science works yourself — for the exam and for life.

Planning and Implementing

Science is all about getting good evidence to support (or disprove) your theories, so scientists need to be able to spot a badly designed experiment, interpret the results of an experiment or study, and design their own experiments too...

You Might have to **Design an Experiment** to Answer a **Question**

1) You might be asked to design a physics experiment to **investigate** something or answer a question.
2) It could be a **lab experiment** that you've seen before, or something **applied**, like deciding which building material is best for a particular job.
3) Either way, you'll be able to use the physics you know and the skills in this topic to figure out the best way to investigate the problem.

A **Variable** is Anything that has the Potential to **Change** in an Experiment

1) First, you need to identify your **independent** and **dependent variables**:

> The **independent** variable is the thing you **change**.
> The **dependent** variable is the thing you **measure**.

Example 1: If you're investigating how changing the potential difference across a component affects the current through it, the **independent variable** is the **potential difference**, and the **dependent variable** is the **current**.

2) Apart from the independent and dependent variables, **all other variables** should stay the same during your experiment. If not, you can't tell whether or not the independent variable is responsible for any changes in your dependent variable, so your results won't be **valid** (p.8). This is known as **controlling variables**. It might be worth **measuring control variables** that are likely to change during your experiment to check that they really are under control.

Example 1 (continued): In the example above, you need to use the same **circuit components**, and keep the **temperature** of the apparatus **constant** — e.g. by letting the circuit cool down between readings.

Example 2: If you're investigating the value of **acceleration due to gravity** by dropping an object and timing its fall, **draughts** in the room could really mess up your results. Picking an object that is more **resistant** to being blown about (like a ball-bearing) will help make your results more **precise** and therefore more **valid** (p.8).

Select Appropriate **Apparatus** and **Techniques**

1) You need to think about what **units** your measurements of the independent and dependent variables are likely to be in before you begin (e.g. millimetres or metres, milliseconds or hours).
2) Think about the **range** you plan on taking measurements over too — e.g. if you're measuring the effect of increasing the force on a spring, you need to know whether you should increase the force in steps of 1 newton, 10 newtons or 100 newtons. Sometimes, you'll be able to **estimate** what effect changing your independent variable will have, or sometimes a **pilot** ('trial') **experiment** might help.
3) Considering your measurements before you start will also help you choose the most appropriate **apparatus** and **techniques** for the experiment:

> There's a whole range of apparatus and techniques that could come up in your exam. Make sure you know how to use all the ones you've come across in class.

Examples:
- If you're measuring the length of a **spring** that you're applying a force to, you might need a **ruler**. If you're measuring the diameter of a **wire**, you'd be better off with a set of **callipers**.
- If you're measuring the extension of a wire, and the extension may be small, you'll need to use a long piece of wire. If it's **too long** to suspend vertically from a clamp, you'll need to use a pulley like on p.44.
- If you're measuring a **time interval**, you could use a **stopwatch**. If the time is **really short** (for example if you're investigating acceleration due to gravity), you might need to use something more sensitive and responsive (see next page), like **light gates**.

4) Whatever apparatus and techniques you use, make sure you use them **correctly**. E.g. if you're measuring a length with a ruler, make sure your eye is level with the point where you're taking the measurement.
5) While you're planning, you should also think about the **risks** involved in your experiment and how to manage them — e.g. if you're investigating a material that might snap, wear safety goggles to protect your eyes.

Planning and Implementing

Be Aware of **Sensitivity** and **Response Time**

$$\textbf{sensitivity} = \frac{\textbf{change in output}}{\textbf{change in input}}$$

1) An instrument's **sensitivity** is a measure of how much the quantity it's measuring needs to change by for the change to be detected.
2) You can calculate sensitivity using the equation on the right. It's the ratio of **change in output** (the change shown on your measuring device) to **change in input** (the change in the quantity the device is measuring).
3) The **response time** of an instrument is how long it takes for the output to change after a change in input.
4) The **quality** of your data will be **poor** if the response time is **too long** or the sensitivity **too low**. You need to make sure that the sensitivity and response time of your equipment are **appropriate** for what you're measuring.

Figure Out how to **Record** your Data Before you **Start**

Before you get going, you'll need a **data table** to record your results in.

1) It should include space for the **independent** and **dependent variables**. Specify the **units** in the headers, not within the table itself.
2) Your table needs room for repeated measurements. You should aim to **repeat** each measurement at least **three times**. Repeated measurements can reduce the effect of random errors in your results (see p.12) and makes spotting **anomalous** results, like this one, much easier.
3) Include space in your table for any data processing you need to do, e.g. calculating an **average** from repeated measurements, or speed from measurements of distance and time.
4) Usually, your data will be **quantitative** (i.e. you'll be recording numerical values). Occasionally, you may have to deal with **qualitative** data (data that can be observed but not measured with a numerical value). It's still best to record this kind of data in a table to keep your results **organised**, but the layout may be a little **different**.

	Current / A			
P.d. / V	Trial 1	Trial 2	Trial 3	Average
1.00	0.052	0.047	0.050	0.050
1.50	0.790	0.075	0.079	0.077
...	...	...	...	...

You Could be Asked to **Evaluate** An **Experimental Design**

If you need to evaluate an experimental design, whether it's your own or someone else's, you need to think about the same sorts of things that you would if you were designing the experiment yourself:

- Does it **actually test** what it sets out to test?
- Is the method **clear** enough for someone else to follow?
- Apart from the **independent** and **dependent variables**, is everything else **properly controlled**?
- Are the **apparatus** and **techniques appropriate** for what's being measured? Will they be used correctly?
- Have enough **repeated measurements** been planned?
- Is the experiment going to be conducted **safely**?

Practice Questions

Q1 Why should you control all the variables (other than the dependent and independent variables) in an experiment?

Q2 What do you need to consider when selecting your apparatus?

Q3 What is meant by sensitivity and response time? How is sensitivity calculated?

Q4 Why should you take repeated measurements in an experiment?

Exam Question

Q1 A student is investigating the effect of light level on the resistance of an LDR (light-dependent resistor). The student connects the LDR to a power supply, and measures the resistance of the LDR at various distances from a light source using a multimeter.

a) State the independent and dependent variables for this experiment. [1 mark]

b) State two variables that the student needs to control in order to ensure his results are valid. [2 marks]

The best-planned experiments of mice and men...

...often get top marks. The details of planning and carrying out an experiment will vary a lot depending on what you're investigating, but if all this stuff is wedged in your brain you shouldn't go far wrong, so make sure you've got it learned.

Analysing Results

You've planned an experiment, and you've got some results (or you've been given some in your exam). Now it's time to look into them a bit more closely...

Check for **Anomalous Results** and do any **Calculations** You Need to **First**

1) Before you calculate anything, check for any **anomalous results**. If there's something in the results that's **clearly wrong**, then don't include it in your calculations — it'll just **muck everything up**. Be careful though, you should only exclude an anomalous result if you have **good reason** to think it's wrong, e.g. it looks like a decimal point is in the **wrong place**, or you suspect that one of the control variables **changed**. And you should talk about any anomalous results when you're evaluating the experiment (pages 8-9).
2) For most experiments, you'll at least need to calculate the mean (average) of some **repeated measurements**:

$$\textbf{mean (average) of a measurement} = \frac{\textbf{sum of your repeated measurements}}{\textbf{number of repeats taken}}$$

In class, you could use a spreadsheet to process your data (and plot graphs), but it's important that you know how to do it by hand for the exam.

3) Calculate any quantities that you're interested in that you haven't **directly measured**.

You should try to give any values you calculate to the **same number of significant figures** as the data value with the **fewest significant figures** in your calculation, **or one more** where it's sensible. If you give your result to too many significant figures, you're saying your final result is more **precise** than it actually is (see p.8).

Present Your Results as a **Scatter Graph**

If you need to use your graph to measure something, select axes that will let you do this easily (e.g. by measuring the gradient or the intercept, see the next page).

Make sure you know how to plot a graph of your results:

1) Usually, the **independent variable** goes on the ***x*-axis** and the **dependent variable** goes on the ***y*-axis**. Both axes should be **labelled** clearly, with the quantity and **units**. The **scales** used should be sensible (i.e. they should go up in sensible steps, and should spread the data out over the full graph rather than bunching it up in a corner).

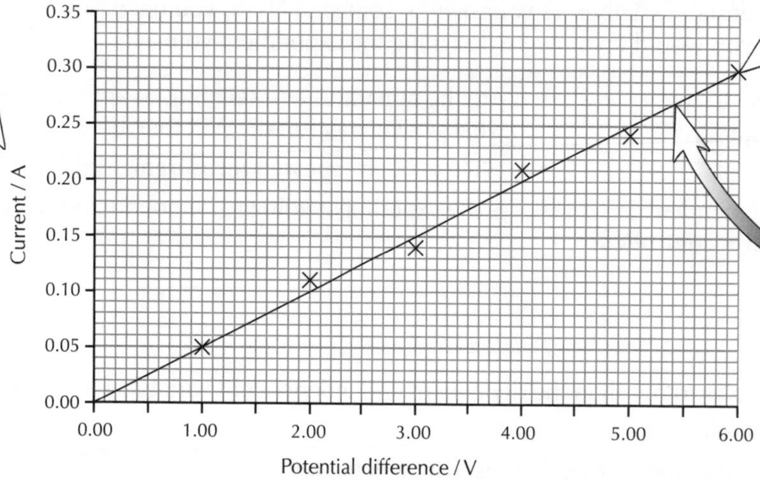

2) Plot your points using a **sharp pencil**, to make sure they're as **accurate** as possible.
3) Draw a **line of best fit** for your results. Around **half** the data points should be above the line, and half should be below it (you should ignore anomalous results). Depending on the data, the line might be **straight**, or **curved**.

Graphs can Show Different Kinds of **Correlation**

Remember, correlation does not necessarily mean cause — p.3.

The **correlation** describes the relationship between the variables. Data can show:

Positive correlation:

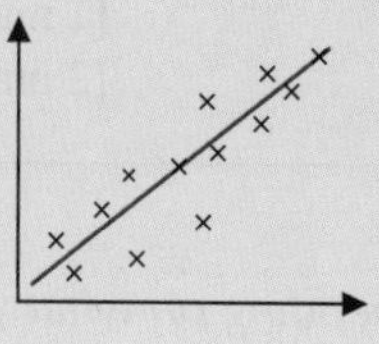

As one variable increases the other increases.

Negative correlation:

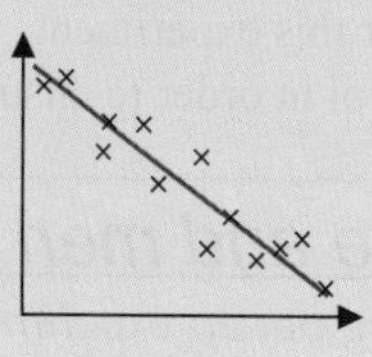

As one variable increases the other decreases.

No correlation:

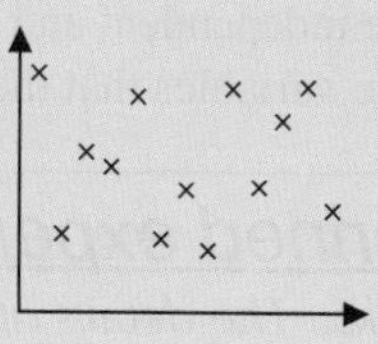

No relationship between the variables.

Analysing Results

You Might Need to Find a **Gradient** or **Intercept**

If the line of best fit is **straight**, then the graph is **linear**. This means if one variable changes by a given amount, the other variable will always change by the **same multiple** of that amount. The **line of best fit** for a linear graph has the **equation**: $y = mx + c$

Where m is the **gradient** of the line and c is the **y-intercept**.

If the line of best fit goes through the origin (c is 0), you can say the variables are **directly proportional** to each other: $y \propto x$

$\propto$ just means 'is directly proportional to'.

Example: This graph shows displacement against time for a motorbike travelling west. Find the bike's velocity.

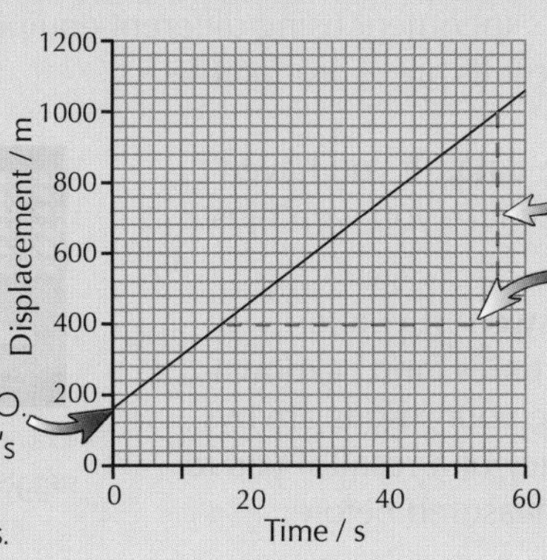

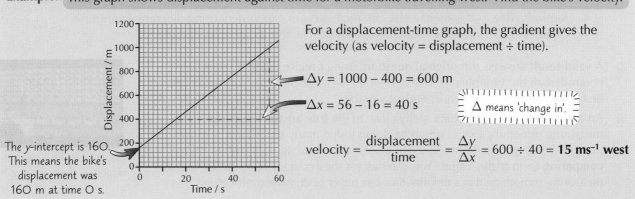

The y-intercept is 160. This means the bike's displacement was 160 m at time 0 s.

For a displacement-time graph, the gradient gives the velocity (as velocity = displacement ÷ time).

$\Delta y = 1000 - 400 = 600$ m

$\Delta x = 56 - 16 = 40$ s

Δ means 'change in'.

velocity = $\dfrac{\text{displacement}}{\text{time}} = \dfrac{\Delta y}{\Delta x} = 600 \div 40 =$ **15 ms^{-1} west**

If a graph has a **curved** line of best fit, you can find the gradient at a given point on the line by drawing a **tangent** to the curve (see page 83). It's sometimes helpful to choose axes that turn a curved graph into a straight one instead:

Example:

For a given power, the graph of **intensity** against the **area** that the power is applied over looks like this:

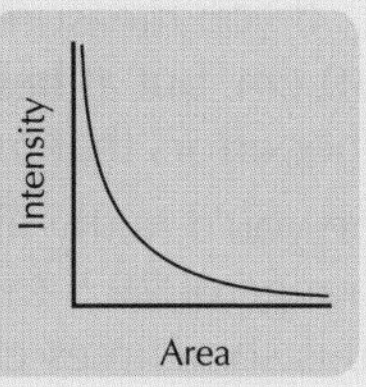

If you plot intensity against **1 ÷ area**, the graph looks like this:

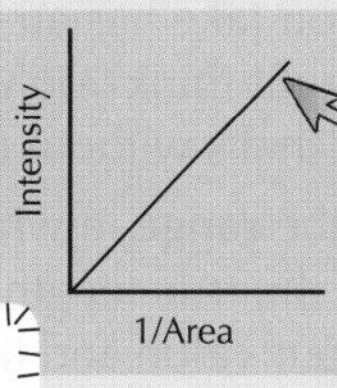

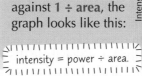

intensity = power ÷ area.

The **gradient** is:
intensity ÷ (1 ÷ area)
= intensity × area
= power (p.15)

Practice Questions

Q1 Describe what you should do with anomalous results when processing data.

Q2 How do you calculate an average of repeated results?

Q3 Sketch a graph showing a negative correlation.

Exam Question

Q1 An engineer is investigating the performance of a prototype car with a new kind of environmentally-friendly engine. The data below shows the speed of the car, going from stationary to over 70 kilometres per hour. (In this question, you may use the formula: acceleration = change in speed ÷ time taken to change speed.)

Time / s	0	2	4	6	8	10	12	14	16
Speed / km per hour	0	3	8	24	36	52	66	69	71

a) Draw a graph showing speed against time for this data. [4 marks]

b) State the times between which the graph is linear. [1 mark]

c) Using the graph, calculate the maximum acceleration of the car. [4 marks]

My level of boredom is proportional to the time I've spent on this page...

This stuff can get a bit fiddly, especially measuring the gradient of a curved line, but for the most part it's not too bad, and you should have seen a lot of it before. So dust off your pencil sharpener, and get to work...

Evaluating and Concluding

Once you've drawn your graphs and analysed your results, you need to think about your conclusions.

Evaluate the Quality of Your Results

Before you draw any conclusions, you should think about the quality of the results — if the quality's not great you won't be able to have much confidence in your conclusion. Good results are **precise**, **valid** and **accurate**.

1) The smaller the **range** that the repeats for each measurement are spread over, the more **precise** your data. A **precise** result is one that is **repeatable** and **reproducible**.

Precision is sometimes called reliability.

- **Repeatable** — **you** can **repeat** an experiment multiple times and get the **same results**. For experiments, doing more repeats enables you to assess how precise your data is — the **more repeats** you do, and the more **similar** the results of each repeat are, the more **precise** your data.
- **Reproducible** — if **someone else** can recreate your experiment using different equipment or methods, and gets the **same results** you do, the results are reproducible.

2) A **valid result** answers the **original question**, using **precise data**. If you haven't controlled all the variables, your results won't be valid, because you won't just be testing the effect of the independent variable.
3) An **accurate result** is one that's really close to the **true answer**. If you're measuring something like *g*, which has been tested many times, and is known to a good degree of certainty, you can assess how accurate your results are by **comparing** them to this value. You can't assess the accuracy of a result if you're measuring something that's **unknown** or has never been measured before.

David might have taken the suggestion that he repeat his experiment a bit far...

All Results have Some Uncertainty

1) **Every** measurement you take has an **experimental uncertainty**. If you measured a piece of string with a ruler marked in cm, you might think you've measured its length as 30 cm, but at **best** you've probably measured it to be 30 ± **0.5** cm. And that's without taking into account any other errors that might be in your measurement.
2) The ± sign gives you the **range** in which the **true** length (the one you'd really like to know) probably lies. 30 ± 0.5 cm tells you the true length is very likely to lie in the range of 29.5 to 30.5 cm. The maximum difference between your value and the true value (here 0.5 cm) is sometimes called the **margin of error**.
3) The smaller the uncertainty in a result or measurement, the smaller the range of possible values the result could have and the more precise your data can be. There are two measures of uncertainty you need to know about:

Absolute uncertainty — the **total uncertainty** for a measurement.
Percentage error — the uncertainty given as a **percentage** of the measurement.

There's more about different types of errors and how to do calculations with uncertainty on page 12.

Example: The resistance of a filament lamp is given as 5.0 ± 0.4 Ω. Give the absolute uncertainty and the percentage error for this measurement.

The **absolute uncertainty** is **0.4 Ω**.

To get the percentage error, just convert this to a percentage of the lamp's resistance: (0.4 ÷ 5.0) × 100 = **8%**

You can minimise percentage uncertainty by making sure that the thing you are measuring is large compared to the absolute uncertainty.

Significant Figures give Uncertainties

If no uncertainty is given for a value, the **assumed uncertainty** is **half of one increment** of the **last significant figure** that the value is **given** to. For example, 2.0 is given to 2 **significant figures**, and the last significant figure has an increment of 0.1, so you would assume an uncertainty of 0.05.

You should always assume the **largest** amount of uncertainty when doing an experiment, so keep an eye on the uncertainty when taking measurements and doing calculations (see p.12-13 for more on evaluating uncertainties).

Evaluating and Concluding

Draw **Conclusions** that Your Results **Support**

1) A conclusion **explains** what the data shows. You can only draw a conclusion if your data **supports** it.
2) Your conclusion should be limited to the **circumstances you've tested** it under — if you've been investigating how the current flowing through a resistor changes with the potential difference across it, and have only used potential differences between 0 and 6 V, you can't claim to know what would happen if you used a potential difference of 100 V, or if you used a different resistor.
3) You also need to think about how much you can **believe** your conclusion, by evaluating the quality of your results (see previous page). If you doubt the quality of your results, you can't form a **strong conclusion**.

Think About how the Experiment Could be **Improved**

Having collected the data, is there anything you think should have been done **differently**?
Were there any **limitations** to your method?

1) If the results aren't **valid**, could you change the experiment to fix this, e.g. by changing the data you're collecting?
2) If the results aren't **accurate**, what could have caused this?
   Systematic errors (p.12) can affect accuracy — are there any that you could prevent?
3) Are there any changes you could make to the **apparatus** or **procedure** that would make the results more **precise**?
   - The **less random error** (p.12) there is in the measurement, the more **precise** your results. **Increasing** the number of **repeats** could help to reduce the **effect** of random errors in your results.
   - By using the most **appropriate** equipment — e.g. swapping a millimetre ruler for a micrometer to measure the diameter of a wire — you can instantly cut down the **random error** in your experiment.
   - You can also use a **computer** to collect data — e.g. using light gates to measure a time interval rather than a stopwatch. This makes results more **precise** by reducing **human error**.
4) Are there any other ways you could have **reduced the errors** in the measurements?

Practice Questions

Q1 What is a valid result?

Q2 What is the difference between saying the results of an experiment are precise and saying that they are accurate?

Q3 What should you think about when you are trying to improve an experimental design?

Exam Questions

Q1 The resistance of a fixed resistor is given as 50.00 Ω.
According to the manufacturer, there is a 0.02% uncertainty in this value.
What is the minimum possible resistance of the resistor in Ω, to 2 decimal places?

A: 49.00 Ω B: 49.99 Ω C: 49.90 Ω D: 49.09 Ω [1 mark]

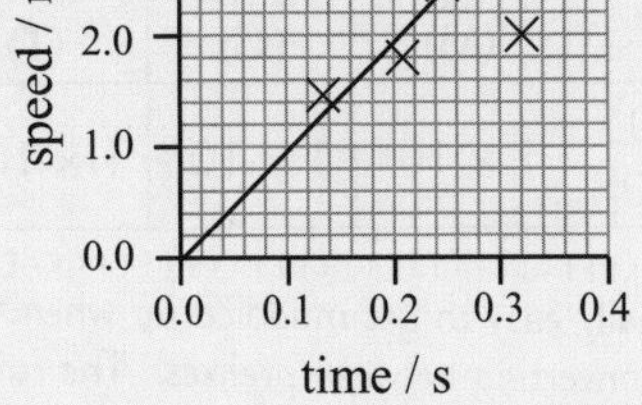

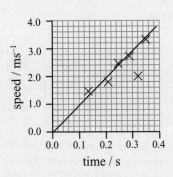

Q2 A student is investigating how the speed of a falling object is affected by how long it has been falling for. He drops an object from heights between 10 cm and 60 cm and measures its speed at the end of its fall, and the time the fall takes, using light gates. He plots a graph of the final speed of the object against the time it took to fall, as shown on the left.

a) Identify the anomalous result. [1 mark]

b) The student concludes that the speed of any falling object is always proportional to the time it has been falling for.
Explain whether or not the results support this conclusion. [2 marks]

In conclusion, Physics causes headaches...

Valid, precise, and accurate... you'd think they all mean the same thing, but they really don't.
Make sure you know the difference, and are careful about which one you use, or you'll be throwing marks away.

Quantities, Units and Graphs

Learning physics is a lot like building a house — both involve drinking a lot of tea. Also, both have important foundations — if you skip this stuff everything else is likely to go a bit wrong. So, here goes brick-laying 101...

A ***Physical Quantity*** has both a ***Numerical Value*** and a ***Unit***

1) Every time you measure something or calculate a quantity you need to give the **units**.
2) The **Système International** (S.I.) includes a set of **base units** for physical quantities from which lots of other units are derived. Here are the S.I. base units that you need to know:

Quantity	S.I. base unit
mass	kilogram, kg
length	metre, m
time	second, s
current	ampere, A
temperature	kelvin, K
amount of a substance	mole, mol

Kilograms are a bit odd — they're the only S.I. unit with a scaling prefix (see below).

You're more likely to see temperatures given in °C. To convert from °C to K, add 273.15.

Remembering how S.I. derived units are defined will help you make sure the other quantities in your equations are in the right units.

3) Many more units can be derived from these base units — e.g. newtons, N, for force are defined by $kg\,ms^{-2}$. The newton is an **S.I. derived unit**.
4) The S.I. derived units you'll need will be covered throughout the book and you need to remember them.
5) You also need to have a rough idea of the size of each S.I. base unit and S.I. derived unit in this book, so that you can **estimate quantities** using them.

Example: Pressure is measured in pascals (Pa). Use the formula pressure = force ÷ area to show that 1 Pa is equal to 1 $kg\,m^{-1}s^{-2}$.

Pressure = force ÷ area, so the units $Pa = \frac{N}{m^2}$

Force = mass × acceleration, so the units $N = kg \times ms^{-2} = kg \times m \times s^{-2}$

So the units of pressure can be written as $Pa = \frac{kg \times m \times s^{-2}}{m^2} = kg \times m^{-1} \times s^{-2} = \mathbf{kg\,m^{-1}s^{-2}}$

6) You might also have to **convert** between units using a **conversion factor**. For example, to convert an angle from **degrees** to **radians**, multiply by $\frac{\pi}{180}$. To get **back to degrees**, multiply by $\frac{180}{\pi}$. Radians are an S.I. derived unit, but you're **more likely** to see angles given in degrees in some areas of physics.

You'll be given 1 radian = 57.3° in your formula book, so if you get stuck you can use that.

Prefixes Let You ***Scale Units***

Physical quantities come in a **huge range** of sizes. Prefixes are scaling factors that let you write numbers across this range without having to put everything in standard form.

These are the prefixes you need to know:

prefix	**pico (p)**	**nano (n)**	**micro (μ)**	**milli (m)**	**centi (c)**	**deci (d)**	**kilo (k)**	**mega (M)**	**giga (G)**	**tera (T)**
multiple of unit	1×10^{-12}	1×10^{-9}	1×10^{-6}	0.001 (1×10^{-3})	0.01 (1×10^{-2})	0.1 (1×10^{-1})	1000 (1×10^{3})	1×10^{6}	1×10^{9}	1×10^{12}

Example: Convert 0.247 megawatts into kilowatts.

$1\text{ MW} = 1 \times 10^6\text{ W}$ and $1\text{ kW} = 1 \times 10^3\text{ W}$

So the scaling factor to move between MW and kW is:

$(1 \times 10^6) \div (1 \times 10^3) = 1 \times 10^3$.

So $0.247\text{ MW} = 0.247 \times 1 \times 10^3 =$ **247 kW**

It's really easy to get muddled up when you're converting between prefixes. The rule is, if you're moving to the right in the table above, your number should get smaller, and if you're moving to the left the number should get larger. If your answer doesn't match the rule, you've made a mistake.

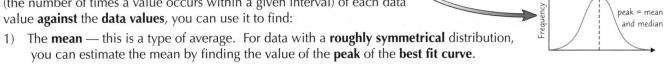

Quantities, Units and Graphs

You can find the *Mean, Median* and *Spread* from a *Frequency Plot*

After you've done an experiment and recorded data, you usually draw a **scatter graph** of the results (see page 6). But if you draw a **frequency plot** that shows the **distribution of data** by plotting the **frequency** (the number of times a value occurs within a given interval) of each data value **against** the **data values**, you can use it to find:

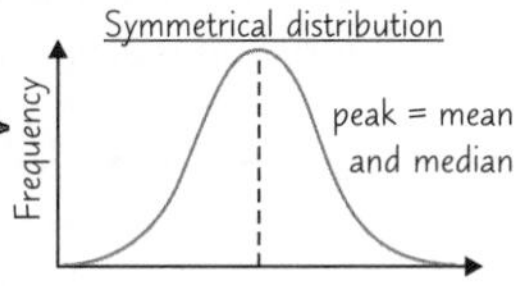

1) The **mean** — this is a type of average. For data with a **roughly symmetrical** distribution, you can estimate the mean by finding the value of the **peak** of the **best fit curve**.
2) The **median** — this is the **middle value** of your data. For a symmetrical distribution, this is the **same** as the mean.
3) The **spread** — this is how **wide** the distribution curve is and shows how spread out your data is. The easiest way to calculate the spread is by finding the **range**. But be careful to exclude any **anomalous** values that look **too high** or **too low** — these will give you an **incorrect range**.
4) The **range** — This is the **difference** between the **highest** data value and the **lowest** data value.

You can also find uncertainties from graphs — see p.13 for more.

Example: The graph shows a distribution of particle speeds. Estimate the mean, median and spread of the data.

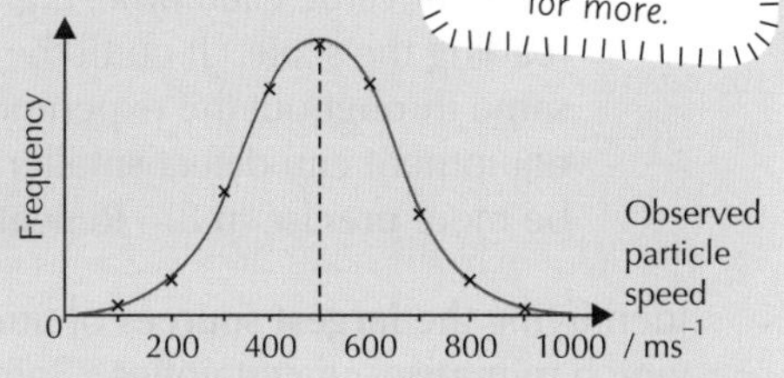

The best fit curve is roughly symmetrical, so the value of the peak is the mean and the median, and is **500 ms^{-1}**.

The spread can be estimated from the range: 980 – 20 = **960 ms^{-1}**.

All of these values can be **affected** by **anomalies** in your data. Page 6 shows you how to deal with anomalous results.

You could take the log of your data values and plot these values on normal axes instead.

Log Graphs Can be used for *Exponentials* and *Power Laws*

1) **Logarithm (log) graphs** allow you to plot **exponential** and **power law** relationships on smaller graphs. It's often **not practical** to plot exponential relationships on normal graphs — you'd need a **huge** sheet of paper, or you'd only see a **tiny part** of the relationship.
2) Log graphs are easily recognised because each **increment** on an axis represents an **equal factor** (e.g. **every grid line** could represent a **×10** increase). This factor is known as the **base** of the log.
3) You need to be **careful** when reading data points that are **between grid lines** — because the scale is **logarithmic**, the middle of a grid square is **not** the midpoint between the values of the adjacent grid lines.

Practice Questions

Q1 What are the S.I. units of mass, current and temperature?

Q2 What is meant by an S.I. base unit and an S.I. derived unit?

Q3 Which quantity best represents the magnitude of room temperature: 1×10^1 K , 1×10^2 K or 1×10^3 K?

Q4 What is π radians in degrees?

Q5 What is: a) 20 000 W in kilowatts, b) 2×10^{-6} W in milliwatts, c) 1.23×10^7 W in gigawatts?

Q6 How would you find the mean, median and spread from a frequency scatter graph with a symmetrical best fit line?

Exam Questions

Q1 Work done is measured in joules. Use the formula work done = force × distance to show that 1 joule is equal to 1 kg m^{2}s^{-2}. [2 marks]

Q2 The graph on the right shows the threshold of hearing (the minimum intensity of sound a person can hear) for a range of frequencies.

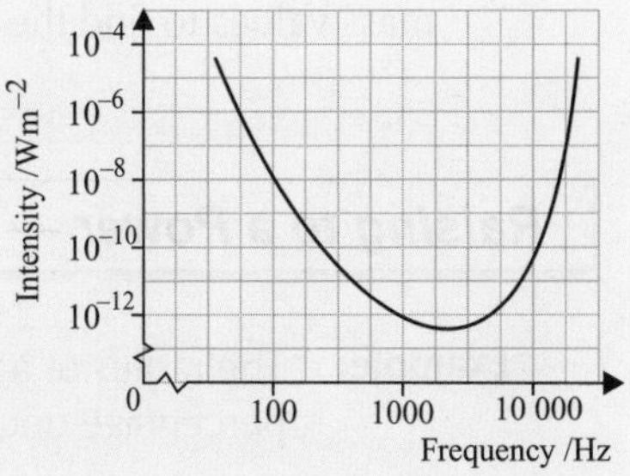

a) Explain how you can tell that the axes of the graph are logarithmic. [2 marks]

b) Estimate the minimum intensity (to the nearest power of 10) of a 100 Hz sound which could be heard by a human. [1 mark]

What's the S.I. base unit for boring...

Not the most exciting pair of pages these, I'll admit, but it's important that you have the basics down, or else you're leaving yourself open to simple little mistakes that'll cost you marks. So get cracking learning those S.I. units.

Measurements and Uncertainties

There are errors and uncertainties in every measurement. You need to know how to deal with them...

Uncertainty is Caused by *Random* and *Systematic Errors*

Every measurement you take has an experimental uncertainty (p.8) caused by two types of error:

1) **Systematic errors** (including **zero errors**) are the same every time you repeat the experiment (they shift all the values by the same amount). They may be caused by the **equipment** you're using or how it's **set-up**, e.g. not lining up a ruler correctly when measuring the extension of a spring. Systematic errors are really **hard to spot**, and they affect the **accuracy** of your results. It's always worth **checking your apparatus** at the start of an experiment, e.g. measure a few known masses to check that a mass meter is **calibrated** properly.

2) **Random errors** vary — they're what make the results a bit different each time you repeat an experiment. If you measured the length of a wire 20 times, the chances are you'd get a slightly different value each time, e.g. due to your head being in a slightly different position when reading the scale. It could be that you just can't keep controlled variables (p.4) exactly the same throughout the experiment. Using equipment with a **higher resolution** means that the equipment can detect smaller changes. This can reduce random error and so your results can be more **precise** (p.8). **Repeating measurements** can also reduce the effect of random errors.

Identifying the **largest sources** of uncertainty as far as possible is important when trying to design an experiment which minimises uncertainties. Sometimes all other smaller uncertainties are **dwarfed** by the largest one.

Sometimes You Need to *Combine Uncertainties*

You have to combine the uncertainties of different measured values to find the uncertainty of a calculated result:

Adding or *Subtracting* Data — *ADD* the *Absolute Uncertainties*

Example: A wire is stretched from 0.3 ± 0.1 cm to 0.5 ± 0.1 cm. Calculate the extension of the wire.

1) First subtract the lengths without the uncertainty values: 0.5 – 0.3 = 0.2 cm
2) Then find the total uncertainty by adding the individual absolute uncertainties: 0.1 + 0.1 = 0.2 cm
   So, the extension of the wire is **0.2 ± 0.2 cm**.

Multiplying or *Dividing* Data — *ADD* the *Percentage Uncertainties*

Example: A force of 15 N ± 3% is applied to a stationary object which has a mass of 6.0 ± 0.3 kg. Calculate the acceleration of the object and state the percentage uncertainty in this value.

1) First calculate the acceleration without uncertainty: $a = F \div m = 15 \div 6.0 = 2.5\ \text{ms}^{-2}$
2) Next, calculate the percentage uncertainty in the mass: % uncertainty in $m = \frac{0.3}{6.0} \times 100 = 5\%$
3) Add the percentage uncertainties in the force and mass values to find the total uncertainty in the acceleration: Total uncertainty = 3% + 5% = 8%
   So, the acceleration = **2.5 ms^{-2} ± 8%**

Raising to a Power — *MULTIPLY* the *Percentage Uncertainty* by the *Power*

Example: The radius of a circle is r = 40 cm ± 2.5%. What will the percentage uncertainty be in the area of this circle (πr^2)?

The radius will be raised to the power of **2** to calculate the area.
So, the percentage uncertainty will be 2.5% × 2 = **5%**

Percentage uncertainty (or percentage error) is covered on page 8.

Measurements and Uncertainties

Uncertainty Bars Show the Uncertainty of Individual Points

1) Most of the time, you work out the **uncertainty** in your **final** result using the uncertainty in **each measurement** you make.
2) When you're plotting a **graph**, you can show the uncertainty in **each measurement** by using **uncertainty** (error) **bars** to show the **range** the point is likely to lie in. E.g. the uncertainty bars on the graph on the right show the error in each measurement of the extension of an object when a force is applied.
3) You can have uncertainty bars for both the dependent and the independent variable.

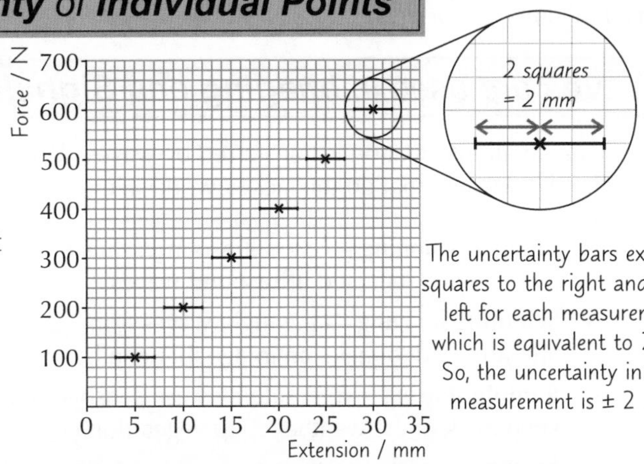

The uncertainty bars extend 2 squares to the right and to the left for each measurement, which is equivalent to 2 mm. So, the uncertainty in each measurement is ± 2 mm.

You Can Calculate the Uncertainty of Final Results from Lines of Worst Fit

Normally when you draw a graph you'll want to find the **gradient** or **intercept** (p.7). For example, you can calculate *k*, the **force constant** of the object being stretched, from the **gradient** of the graph on the right — here it's about 20 000 Nm^{-1}. You can find the **uncertainty** in that value by using **worst lines**:

1) Draw lines of best fit which have the **maximum** and **minimum** possible slopes for the data and which should go through all of the **uncertainty bars** (see the pink and blue lines on the right). These are the **worst lines** for your data.
2) Calculate the **worst gradient** — the gradient of the slope that is **furthest** from the gradient of the line of best fit. The blue line's gradient is about 21 000 Nm^{-1} and the pink line's gradient is about 19 000 Nm^{-1}, so you can use either here.
3) The **uncertainty** in the gradient is given by the **difference** between the **best gradient** (of the line of best fit) and the **worst gradient** — here it's 1000 Nm^{-1}. So this is the uncertainty in the value of the spring constant. For this object, the spring constant is 20 000 ± 1000 Nm^{-1} (or 20 000 Nm^{-1} ± 5%).
4) Similarly, the uncertainty in the **y-intercept** is just the **difference** between the **best** and **worst** intercepts (although there's no uncertainty here since the best and worst lines both go through the origin).

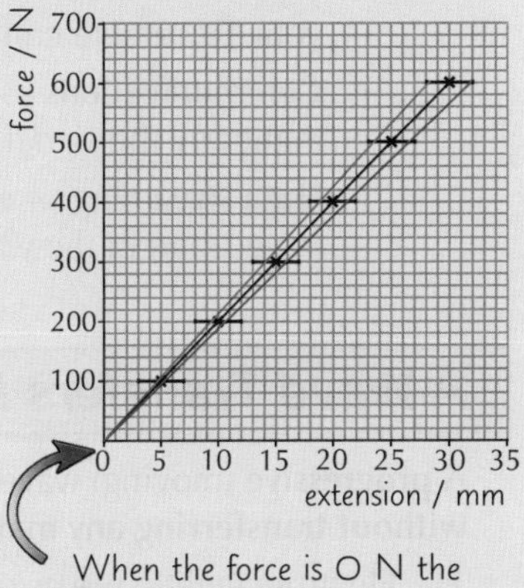

When the force is 0 N the extension is 0 mm — this is a measurement with no uncertainty.

Practice Questions

Q1 Give two examples of possible sources of random error and one example of a possible source of systematic error in an experiment. Which kind of error is least likely to affect the precision of the results?

Q2 Describe what uncertainty bars on data points on a graph show.

Q3 What are worst lines? How could you use them to find the uncertainty in the intercept of a graph?

Exam Question

Q1 A student is investigating the acceleration of a remote controlled car. The car has an initial velocity of 0.52 ± 0.02 ms^{-1} and accelerates to 0.94 ± 0.02 ms^{-1} over an interval of 2.5 ± 0.5 s.

a) Calculate the percentage uncertainty in the car's initial speed. [1 mark]

b) Calculate the percentage uncertainty in the car's final speed. [1 mark]

c) Calculate the car's average acceleration over this interval. Include the absolute uncertainty of the result in your answer. (acceleration = change in velocity ÷ time taken). [4 marks]

Physics is the meaning of life — of that, I'm 42% certain...

Uncertainties are a bit of a pain, but they're really important. Learn the rules for combining uncertainties, and how to read uncertainties from graphs using uncertainty bars and worst lines. Random and systematic errors are an exam favourite too, so make sure you know the difference, and how to minimise both in your experiments.

The Nature of Waves

This section's all about what happens when you take a picture with your mobile and send it to your mate Dave... with a few other minor details... it's all waves waves waves.

Waves are used in Imaging and Signalling

Pretty much all information is transferred by waves. Whenever you create an image or send a signal, it'll be waves that do the lackey work. Here are just a few examples of where they're used:

1) **Medical scanning** — e.g. ultrasound scans build up an image of a fetus by detecting reflected **ultrasound waves**.
2) **Scientific imaging** — e.g. light waves from stars and galaxies take billions of years to reach the Earth, and are used to make an image that can be recorded electronically.
3) **Remote sensing** — e.g. satellites use sensors to detect waves from distant objects to do things like keep track of the weather, map vegetation cover or even make very accurate elevation maps.
4) **Seeing** — anything you see, from stars to the cat being sick on your nicest pair of jeans, is thanks to millions of light waves hitting your retinas and forming an image.
5) **Heat cameras** sense infrared waves being emitted by the hot thing you're looking at. Infrared radiation is also the type of electromagnetic wave that carries the signal from your TV remote control to your telly to switch over to your favourite soap...
6) **Communications** — e.g. your mobile phone sends and receives **microwaves** that carry the signal containing that all-important text message.
7) **Data streaming** — e.g. when you stream music or videos over the internet, the data normally travels part of the way from a server to your home as a light wave through fibre optic cables.

A Wave Transfers Energy Away from its Source

A **progressive** (moving) wave carries **energy** and usually information from one place to another **without transferring any material**. Here are some ways you can tell waves carry energy:

1) Electromagnetic waves can cause things to **heat up**.
2) **X-rays** and **gamma rays** knock electrons out of their orbits, causing **ionisation**.
3) Loud **sounds** make things **vibrate**.
4) **Wave power** can be used to **generate electricity**.
5) Since waves carry energy away, the **source** of the wave **loses energy**.

Smile, wave and transfer energy away from its source...

Here are all the bits of a Wave you Need to Know

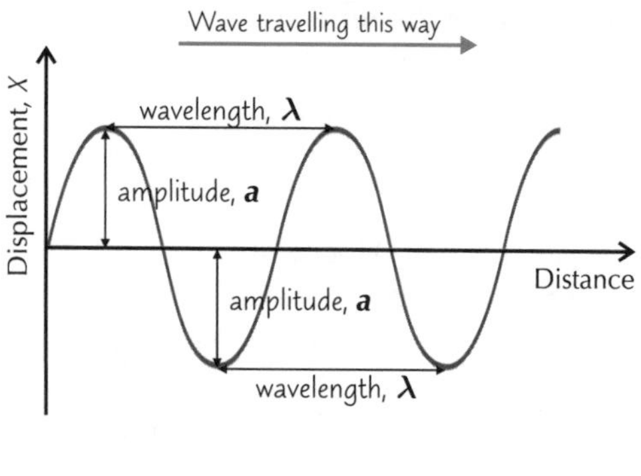

1) **Displacement**, X, metres — how far a **point** on the wave has **moved** from its **undisturbed position**.
2) **Amplitude**, a, metres — **maximum displacement**.
3) **Wavelength**, λ, metres — the **length** of **one whole wave**, e.g. from **crest** to **crest** or **trough** to **trough**.
4) **Period**, T, seconds — the **time taken** for a **whole vibration**.
5) **Frequency**, f, hertz — the **number** of **vibrations per second** passing a given **point**.
6) **Phase difference** — the amount by which **one** wave **lags behind** another wave. **Measured** in **degrees** or **radians**. See page 10.

The Frequency is the Inverse of the Period

$$\text{Frequency} = \frac{1}{\text{Period}} \qquad f = \frac{1}{T}$$

It's that simple.
Get the **units** straight: **1 Hz = 1 s^{-1}**.

The Nature of Waves

The Wave Equation Links Wave Speed, Frequency and Wavelength

1) **Wave speed** can be measured just like the speed of anything else:

$$\textbf{Wave speed } (v) = \frac{\textbf{Distance } (d)}{\textbf{Time } (t)}$$

2) You can use this equation to derive the **wave equation** (but thankfully you don't have to do that, you just need to be able to use it).

Speed of wave (v) = frequency (f) × wavelength (λ)

$$v = f\lambda$$

Remember, you're not measuring how fast a physical point (like one molecule of rope) moves. You're measuring how fast a point on the wave form moves.

All Electromagnetic Waves are Transverse Waves

1) **A transverse wave** is a wave where the **vibration** is at **right angles** to the wave's **direction** of travel.
2) All **electromagnetic waves** are **transverse**. Other examples of transverse waves are **ripples** on water and waves on **ropes**.

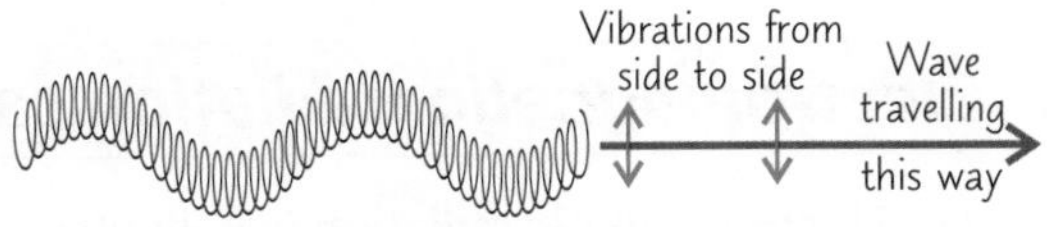

3) There are **two** main ways of **drawing** transverse waves:

1. Displacement against distance

They can be shown as **graphs of displacement** against **distance along the path of the wave.**

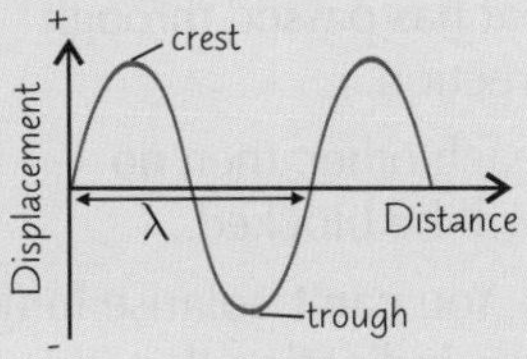

2. Displacement against time

Or, they can be shown as graphs of **displacement against time** for a point as the wave passes.

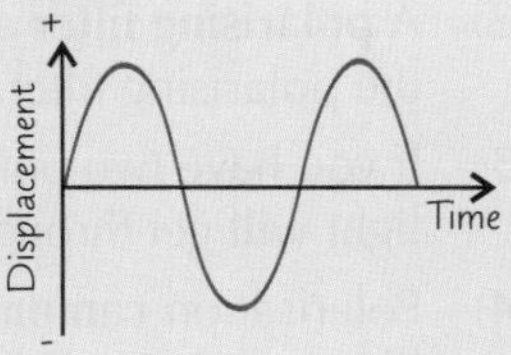

Both sorts of graph often give the **same shape**, so make sure you check out the label on the **horizontal axis**. Displacements **upwards** from the centre line are given a **+ sign**. Displacements downwards are given a **– sign**.

4) Not all waves are transverse, **sound** for example is a **longitudinal** wave — the vibrations are along the wave's direction of travel.

Intensity is a Measure of How Much Energy a Wave is Carrying

1) Intensity is the **rate of flow** of **energy** per **unit area** at **right angles** to the **direction of travel** of the wave — for example the amount of light energy that hits your retina per second.
2) It's measured in **watts per square metre** (Wm^{-2}).

$$\textbf{Intensity} = \frac{\textbf{Power}}{\textbf{Area}} \qquad I = \frac{P}{A}$$

Practice Questions

Q1 Give four examples of how waves can be used to generate images.

Q2 Write the equation that links the frequency and period of a wave.

Q3 Give one example of a transverse wave.

Q4 Describe the direction of vibrations in a transverse wave.

Exam Questions

Q1 A buoy floating on the sea takes 6.0 seconds to rise and fall once and complete a full period of oscillation. The difference in height between the buoy at its lowest and highest points is 1.2 m. Waves pass it at a speed of 3.0 ms^{-1}.

a) Calculate the wavelength of the waves. [2 marks]

b) State the amplitude of the waves. [1 mark]

Q2 A 10.0 W light beam is shone onto a screen. The beam covers an area of 0.002 m^2 on the screen. Calculate the intensity of the light beam on the screen. [1 mark]

ARRRGH... waves are everywhere — there's no escape...

Even just reading this sentence is one instance of using waves in signalling and imaging. A bunch of light waves are being reflected off the page and carrying the 'signal' to your eyes, which pass it on to the brain so you can see. Clever.

Polarisation

Polarisation is all about making a wave move up and down in only one direction. No, not that one direction.

A Polarised Wave Only Oscillates in One Direction

1) If you **shake a rope** to make a **wave**, you can move your hand **up and down** or **side to side** or in a **mixture** of directions — it still makes a **transverse wave**.
2) But if you try to pass **waves in a rope** through a **vertical fence**, the wave will only get through if the **vibrations** are **vertical**. The fence filters out vibration in other directions. This is called **polarising** the wave.

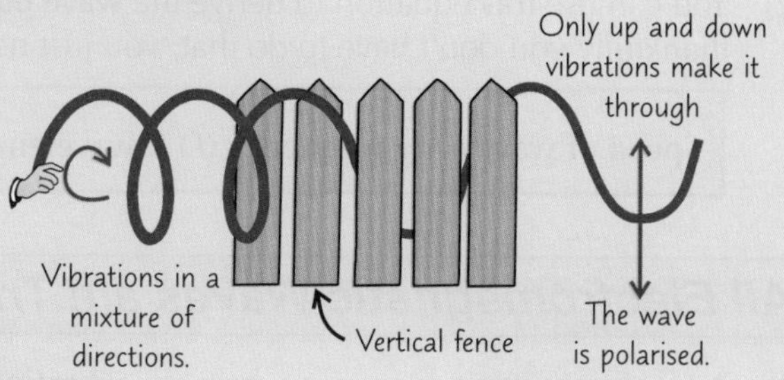

Electromagnetic Radiation can be Polarised

1) **Electromagnetic radiation** (e.g. light) is made up of two transverse waves vibrating in different directions. (The things vibrating are actually electric and magnetic fields.)
2) A **polarising filter** acts a bit like the fence. Light that has passed through the polarising filter will only be vibrating in one direction.
3) If you have two polarising filters at **right angles** to each other, then **no** light will get through as all directions of vibration will be blocked.
4) Polarisation **can only happen** for **transverse** waves. You **can't** polarise **longitudinal waves** like sound. The fact that you can polarise light is one **indication** that it's a transverse wave.

Liz was starting to think her polarising filter might be slightly too effective.

Investigate Polarisation of Light Using Two Polarising Filters

You can observe polarisation by shining unpolarised white light through two polarising filters.

1) Align the transmission axes of two **polarising filters** so they are both **vertical**. Shine unpolarised light on the first filter. Keep the position of the **first filter fixed** and **rotate** the second one.
2) Light that passes through the first filter will always be **vertically polarised**.
3) When the transmission axes of the two filters are **aligned**, **all** of the light that passes through the first filter also passes through the second.
4) As you rotate the second filter, the amount of light that passes through the second filter **varies**.

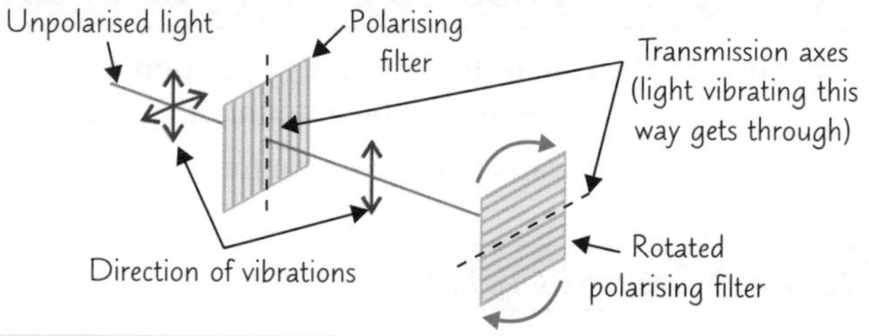

Just like vectors, you can think of the transmission axis of the rotating filter as having a **vertical** and **horizontal component**. The **larger** the **vertical component**, the **more** vertically polarised light will pass through the filter.

5) As the second filter is rotated, **less** light will get through it as the **vertical** component of the second filter's transmission axis **decreases**. This means the **intensity** of the light getting through the second filter will gradually **decrease**.
6) When the two transmission axes are at **45°** to each other, the intensity will be **half** that getting through the first filter. When they're at **right angles** to each other **no** light will pass through — the **intensity** is **0**.
7) As you continue turning, the intensity should then begin to **increase** once again.
8) When the two axes **realign** (after a 180° rotation), **all** the light will be able to pass through the second filter again.

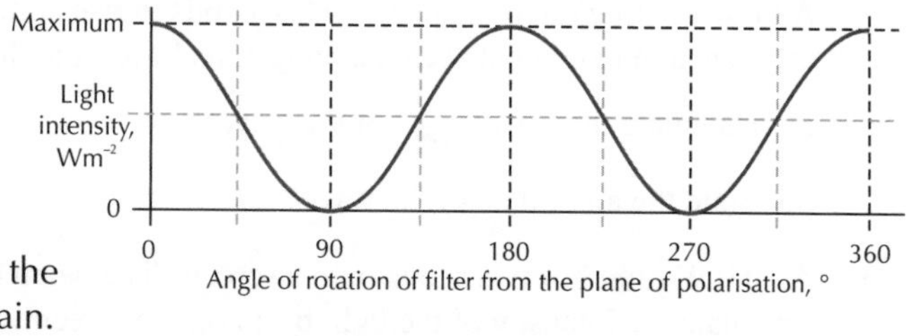

You come across polarising filters more often than you'd think. For example, **3D films** use polarised light to create depth — the filters in each lens are at right angles to each other so each eye gets a slightly different picture. **Polaroid sunglasses** also use polarising filters — reflected light is partially polarised so the sunglasses block this out to help prevent glare.

Polarisation

You Can Polarise Microwaves Using a Metal Grille

Polarising filters don't work on **microwaves** — their **wavelength** is too long. Instead, **metal grilles** (squares full of metal wires which are all aligned) are used to polarise them. You can investigate the polarisation of microwaves using a **microwave transmitter** and a **microwave receiver** linked to a **voltmeter**.

1) Place a metal **grille** between the microwave **transmitter** and **receiver** as shown below. (Handily, microwave transmitters transmit **polarised** microwaves, so you only need one metal grille.)
2) The intensity of microwaves passing through the grille is at a **maximum** when the direction of the vibration of the microwaves and the wires on the grille are at **right angles** to each other.
3) As you rotate the grille, the **intensity** of polarised microwaves able to pass through the grille **decreases**, so the reading on the voltmeter **decreases**.
4) When the wires of the metal grille are **aligned** with the direction of the polarised waves, **no signal** will be shown on the voltmeter.

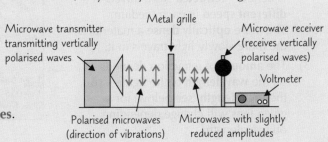

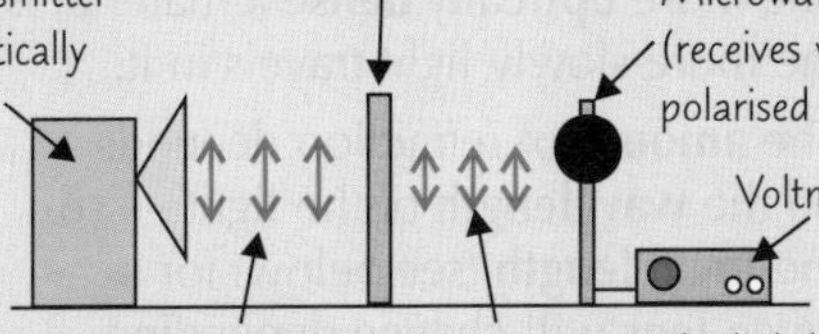

Make sure all of your electrical equipment is safely connected before you turn it on — microwave transmitters operate at very high voltages.

The **intensity** drops to **zero** when the wires are **aligned** with the **direction of polarisation** of the microwaves, because the grille is **absorbing their energy** (see below).
Be careful here — this is the **opposite effect** to polarising filters on the previous page, where aligning the polarising filter with the direction of vibrations gave the maximum intensity of waves passing through the filter.

1) The vibrating electric field of the microwave **excites** electrons in the metal grille.
2) The energy of the incoming microwaves is **absorbed** by the grille and **re-emitted** in **all directions**.
3) Only a few of those re-emitted waves are vibrating in the **direction** of the microwave receiver.
4) The microwave **receiver** only receives microwaves in **one plane**, so even if the **re-emitted** wave travels towards the receiver, it might not be picked up.
5) When the wires and vibrations of the waves are **aligned**, **more** electrons are excited than when they're at right angles to each other — all the energy is absorbed and the **intensity** reading drops to **zero**.
6) When the wires and vibrations are at **right angles** to each other, some electrons in the grille are still excited and so there is still a **small drop** in **intensity**.

Practice Questions

Q1 What is meant by a polarised wave? Why can't you polarise sound waves?

Q2 Describe an experiment that shows visible light can be polarised.

Q3 Explain why the intensity of vertically polarised microwaves passing through a metal grille will drop to zero when the grille is aligned with the direction of polarisation.

Exam Question

Q1 Two polarising filters are placed on top of each other and held in front of a source of white unpolarised light.

a) No light can be seen through the filters.
State the angle between the transmission axes of the two filters. [1 mark]

b) The filters are rotated so that the angle between their transmission axes is 45°.
Describe the difference in the intensity of the light once it has passed through both filters compared to the light once it has only passed through the first filter. [1 mark]

c) Give one use of polarising filters. [1 mark]

Forget polarisation, I need a mental filter...

...to stop me talking rubbish all the time. Polarisation isn't too bad once you get your head around it. It's just a case of filtering out different directions of wave vibrations. Make sure you really know it though as you'll have to be able to explain how both the experiments for polarising light and microwaves work. Doesn't that sound like a barrel of laughs.

Forming Images with Lenses

Astronomers use focal lengths, opticians use powers. Either way, you need to know how to deal with lens powers...

Refraction Happens when a Wave **Changes Speed** at a **Boundary**

1) When a ray of light meets a boundary between one medium and another, some of its energy is **reflected** back into the first medium and the rest of it is **transmitted** through into the second medium.
2) If the light meets the boundary at an angle to the normal, the transmitted ray is bent or "**refracted**" as it travels at a **different speed** in each medium. The more **optically dense** a material is, the more slowly light travels in it.
3) The **amount** of refraction depends on the **wavelength** of the light — so the **focal length** (see below) for a given lens will change depending on wavelength.

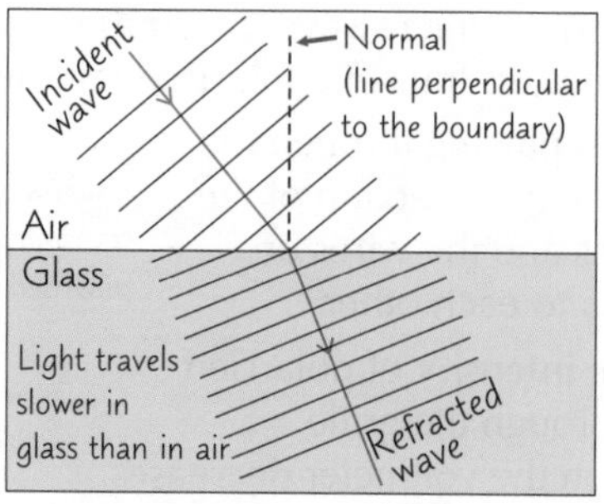

Steph wasn't quite sure this was what her teacher had meant when he asked her to demonstrate that rays bend in water.

Converging Lenses Change the **Curvature** of **Wavefronts**

1) **Lenses** change the curvature of wavefronts by **refraction**.
2) A lens **adds curvature** to waves as they pass through it. If waves are uncurved before passing through the lens, and parallel to the lens axis, they will be given spherical curvature, centred on the **focus** (or **focal point**) of the lens.
3) A converging lens curves the wavefronts by **slowing down** the light travelling through the middle of the lens more than light at the lens edges. All points on a wavefront take the **same amount of time** to get to the focus point.
4) The **focal length**, ***f***, is the distance between the **lens axis** and the **focus**.

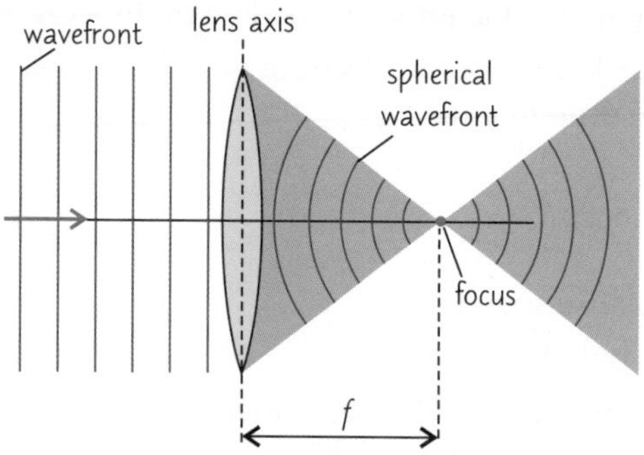

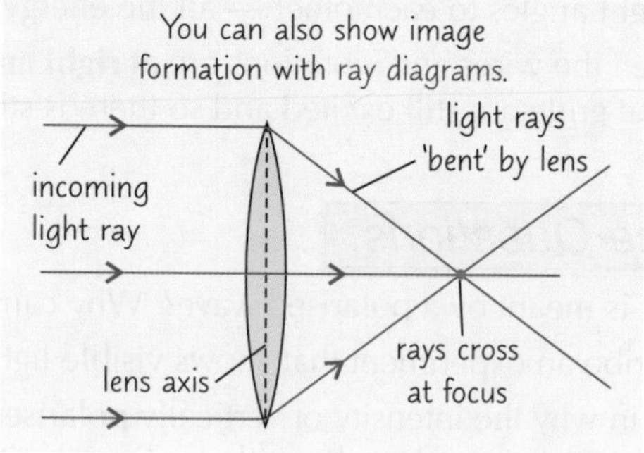

5) The **more powerful** (thicker) the lens, the more it will **curve** the wavefronts that travel through it — so the **shorter** its **focal length**.
6) The **power, *P*,** of a lens with focal length ***f*** metres is: $$P = \frac{1}{f}$$ where lens power is measured in **dioptres**, D.
7) The **curvature** of a wave is defined as: $$\text{curvature} = \frac{1}{\text{radius of curvature}}$$

So the **amount of curvature** a lens adds to a wave passing through it is $\frac{1}{f}$ — which is just the **power** of the lens.

The thicker the lens, the more curved its sides, so the more curvature it adds to a wave.

Forming Images with Lenses

You can use the Lens Equation to Find Where an Image Will be Formed

1) The distances between a lens, the image and the source are related to each other by **the lens equation**:

$$\frac{1}{v} = \frac{1}{u} + \frac{1}{f}$$

u = distance between object and lens axis,
v = distance between image and lens axis,
f = focal length.

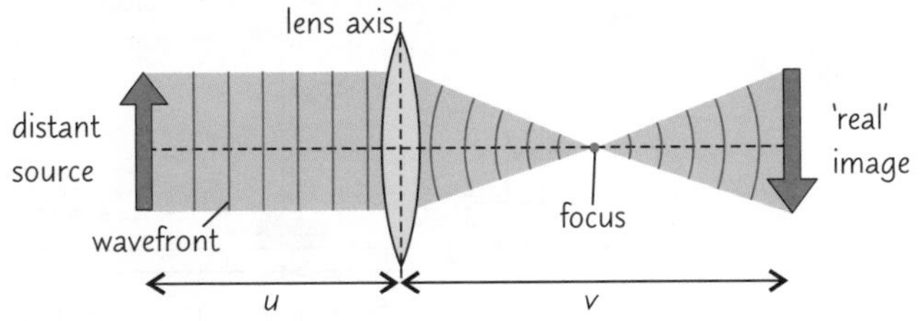

This equation assumes that the lens is thin. Thin converging lenses are used in glasses and contact lenses, magnifying glasses and microscopes.

2) You always measure the **distances** from the **lens axis**, and count distances to the **right** as **positive**, and distances to the **left** as **negative** — just like when you're drawing graphs.
3) The lens equation also tells you about **curvature**.

curvature after	=	curvature before	+	curvature added by lens
$\frac{1}{v}$	=	$\frac{1}{u}$	+	$\frac{1}{f}$

4) If you've got a **distant light source**, the wavefronts approaching a converging lens will be **flat** ($1/u = 0$). The converging lens will then give them a curvature of $1/f$. Easy.
5) If the source is at the **focus** of the lens, the wavefronts will start off **curved** with a **negative curvature** (because u is measured as a negative distance). This negative curvature is then cancelled out by the positive curvature added by the converging lens — so the wavefronts will be made **flat**.
6) For sources in between, the wavefronts before and after will be curved, and have a difference in curvature of $1/f$.
7) Don't forget that you can also draw all this in the form of **light rays** being '**bent**' by the lens. It's just a different way of thinking about it — you still use the lens equation in exactly the same way.

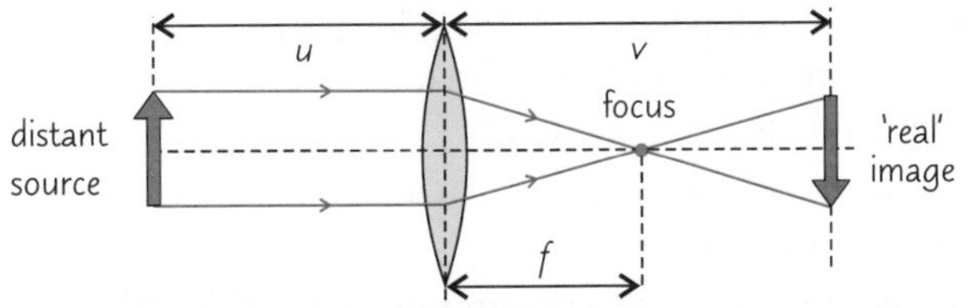

Example: An image of Mabel the cow is being projected onto a screen 80 cm from a 3.25 D lens. How far must the picture slide of Mabel be from the lens?

$P = \frac{1}{f} = 3.25$ D, $v = 80$ cm $= 0.8$ m.

Rearrange the lens equation: $\frac{1}{u} = \frac{1}{v} - \frac{1}{f} = \frac{1}{0.8} - 3.25$

$= 1.25 - 3.25 = -2$

$u = \frac{1}{-2} = -0.5$ m,

so the slide must be **0.5 m** from the lens.

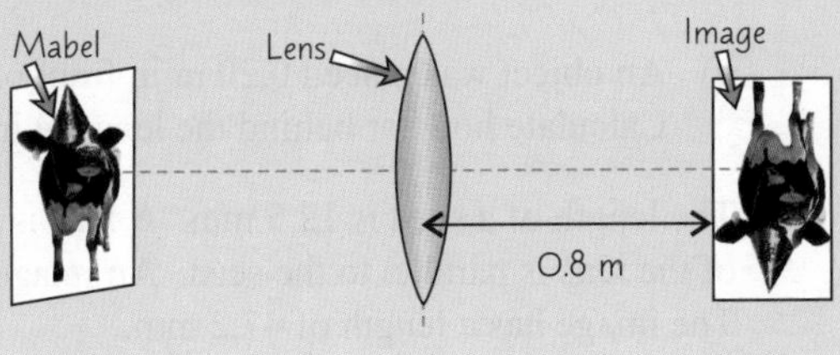

A Lens Can Produce a Magnified Image

There are a couple of ways of measuring the magnification of a lens.
You just need to know about the **linear magnification**.

The **linear magnification** of a lens is $m = \frac{\textbf{image height}}{\textbf{object height}}$, which is equal to $m = \frac{v}{u}$.

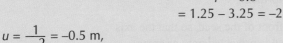

Forming Images with Lenses

Focus an Image on a Screen to Find the Power of a Converging Lens

You can determine the **focal length** of a thin converging lens by doing an experiment like this one...

1) Set up the equipment as shown, connecting the bulb to a low-voltage power supply.
2) Place the bulb exactly **0.200 m** away from the lens (i.e. u = 0.200 m) and turn on the power supply. Move the screen until you can see a clear picture of the filament on the screen.
3) Measure the **distance** between the **lens** and the **screen**. This is your value for v. Record u and v in a table, as shown below.
4) Repeat the experiment 5 or more times, for a range of different values of u. (Don't increase u so much that you can no longer see the image of the filament though.)
5) **Work out** $\frac{1}{u}$ and $\frac{1}{v}$ for each of your readings. **Add** them together to get $\frac{1}{f}$, which is the **power** of the lens.
6) Find the **average** of your values for $\frac{1}{f}$ and **divide** 1 by your answer to find the **focal length** f of your lens.

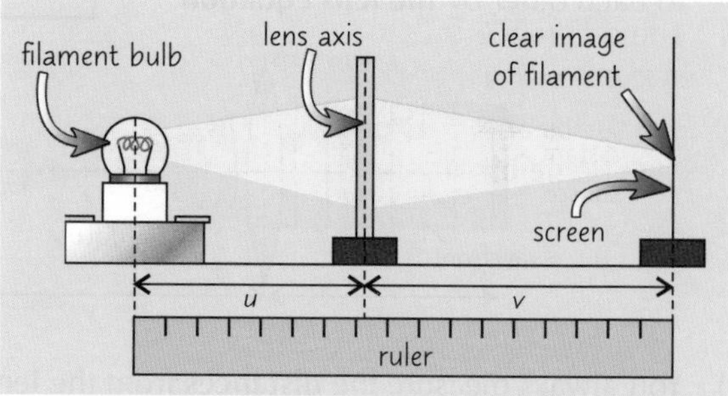

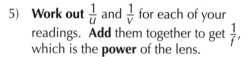

Distance from lamp to lens, u (metres)	Distance from lens to screen, v (metres)	$\frac{1}{u}$	$\frac{1}{v}$	Power, $\frac{1}{f}\left(=\frac{1}{u}+\frac{1}{v}\right)$
0.203	0.629	4.926...	1.589...	6.515...
...	...	...	...	...

Practice Questions

Q1 Define the focal length and power of a converging lens.

Q2 Describe what happens to wavefronts as they pass through a thin converging lens.

Q3 A wave passes through a thin converging lens with focal length f.
If the wavefronts have no curvature before entering the lens,
what is their curvature after passing through the lens?

Q4 Write an equation to show how the object distance (u), image distance (v) and focal length of a thin lens (f) are related.

Q5 Describe an experiment you could carry out to determine the focal length of a thin converging lens.

Exam Questions

Q1 a) Define the focus (focal point) of a converging lens. [1 mark]

b) An object was placed 0.20 m in front of a converging lens of focal length 0.15 m.
Calculate how far behind the lens the image was formed. [2 marks]

Q2 The length of a seed is 12.5 mm. A lens is placed in front of the seed, so that the axis of the lens is parallel to the seed. An image of the seed is projected onto a screen. The image has a length of 47.2 mm.

a) Calculate the linear magnification of the lens. [1 mark]

b) If the seed is 4.0 mm from the lens, calculate how far the screen is from the lens. [2 marks]

c) Calculate the power of the lens in dioptres. [2 marks]

By the power of Grayskull... I HAVE THE POWER...

This is all fairly straightforward — just a few formulas, a handful of diagrams and the odd practical to learn. But don't drop your guard — this topic is a great one for experiment-based questions in exams, so make sure you know how to deal with uncertainties and margins of error. *See page 12 for what you need to know on error analysis.*

Information in Images

Don't panic if waves are getting a bit too much for you — it's time for something completely different.

A Single Binary Digit is Called a Bit

1) The **binary number system**, like the **decimal** system, is a way of writing numbers.
2) The difference is that the **decimal** system uses **ten digits** (0-9) while the **binary** system only uses **two** (**0 and 1**). The table shows the first few values in each system.
3) The **zeros** and **ones** that make up binary numbers are called **binary digits** — a **single binary digit** is called a **bit**. A group of **eight bits** is called a **byte**.
4) So to get from **bits to bytes**, **divide** by **8**. To go from **bytes to bits**, multiply by **8**.

Decimal	Binary
0	0
1	1
2	10
3	11
4	100

In binary, 1 kilobyte is 1024 bytes, 1 megabyte is 1024 KB, and 1 gigabyte is 1024 MB.

$$\textbf{bits} = 8 \times \textbf{bytes} \quad \text{and} \quad \textbf{bytes} = \frac{\textbf{bits}}{8}$$

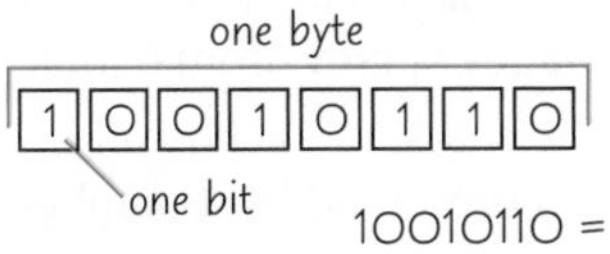

10010110 = 150

The Binary System is used to Store Data in Computer Memory

1) When you **save** a file on your computer, the computer stores the data as a **string of bits**.
2) The **number of bits** in a string (***b***) determines how many **alternatives** that string can represent. For example, a **single** bit has only **two** alternatives (0 and 1), while one **byte** (eight bits) has **256** alternatives. The number of alternatives **doubles** with each additional bit, which means:

$$\textbf{Number of alternatives} = 2^{\text{Number of bits}} \quad \textbf{or} \quad N = 2^b$$

3) The **number of bits** you need depends on how many **alternatives** you want:

$$\textbf{Number of bits} = \log_2(\textbf{Number of alternatives}) \quad \textbf{or} \quad b = \log_2 N$$

If yout calculator doesn't let you calculate $\log_2 N$ directly, you can do ($\log_{10} N \div \log_{10} 2$), which gives you the same thing.

4) For example, if you wanted to represent any letter of the **alphabet**, you'd need a string with **26 alternatives** — one for every letter. Substituting 26 into the **equation** gives $b = \log_2 26 \approx 4.7$ — so you'd need **five bits**.

Images Are Stored as Arrays of Binary Numbers

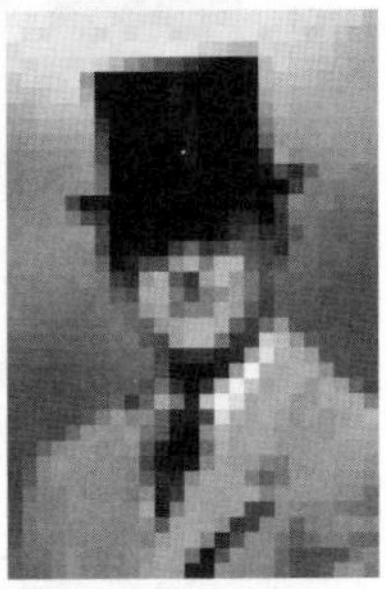

1) If you **zoom** in on part of a **digital photograph**, you'll see the individual **pixels** (single points that make up the image) — check out the example on the right.
2) When an **image** is stored in a digital camera (e.g. on a **memory card**) or on a **computer**, each pixel is represented by a **binary number**.
3) The **binary numbers** are stored in an **array**. This is a grid of numbers arranged so that the **location of** each **number** in the grid **matches** the location of the **pixel** in the photo.
4) The **value** of the binary number maps to (it gives) the **colour** of the corresponding **pixel**.
5) In **coloured images**, each pixel can be described by **three** binary numbers — one for each of the **primary colours** of light (**red**, **green** and **blue**). The **length** of the binary numbers used depends on **how many** colours are needed. On a typical PC display, each of the numbers for red, green and blue are 8-bits long, giving 256^3 = 16.8 million possible colours.

Image Resolution can mean Different Things

1) Usually **image resolution** refers to the **length** represented by **each pixel**. If an object of width 1.0 m is represented by 200 pixels in an image, then the resolution is 1.0 ÷ 200 = 0.005 metres per pixel.
2) The resolution of an image can also mean the **number of pixels** in the format **width × height** — for example the resolution of a **full HD telly** screen is 1920 × 1080.
3) Sometimes you might see resolution given in terms of **megapixels** — the **total number of pixels** in an image. For example, a **digital camera** that produces images of width 3790 pixels and height 2130 pixels has a resolution of 3790 × 2130 = 8 072 700 pixels or 8 megapixels in total.

Information in Images

The Amount of Information in an Image Depends on the Bits per Pixel

0	200	255
100	0	100
255	200	0

an array

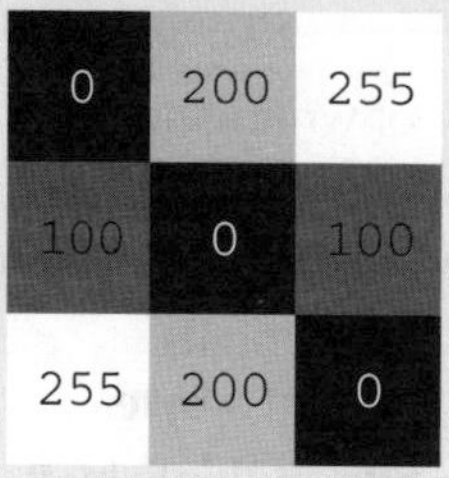

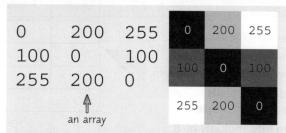

The **image** shown above can be made up of **256 shades** of grey, from 0 (black) to 255 (white).

The shade of each pixel (in the array on the left) is represented by a number between 0 and 255.

Each of these shade numbers is stored in memory as an **8-bit binary number**.

red (R) green (G) blue (B)

255, 255, 255

0,0,0	255,0,0	0,255,0
0,0,255	255,255,0	0,255,255
255,0,255	255,255,255	0,0,0

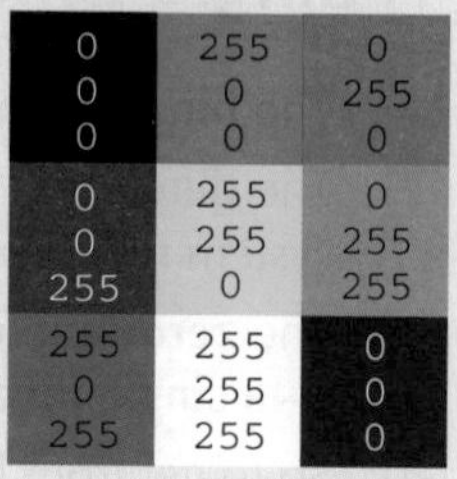

The colours in the image shown are made up of 3 numbers, each providing **256 possible shades** of red, green or blue.

This means there are 256 × 256 × 256 = **16.8 million** possible different RGB combinations in the image.

Each pixel needs **three different 8-bit binary numbers** in the array on the left — so each pixel requires 3 × 8 = **24 bits.**

The more **bits per pixel**, the **more information** is held by each pixel — and the **more pixels** there are in an image, the **more information** is held by the image. So the **total** amount of information in an image is given by:

total amount of information = number of pixels × bits per pixel

Multiplying by a Fixed Value Improves Contrast

The **values** of the binary numbers that make up an **image** determine how it looks — if you **change** the **values**, you **change** the **image**. Take a look at the example below to see what happens.

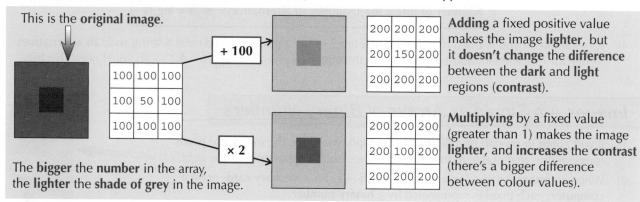

This is the **original image.**

100	100	100
100	50	100
100	100	100

The **bigger** the **number** in the array, the **lighter** the **shade of grey** in the image.

+ 100

200	200	200
200	150	200
200	200	200

Adding a fixed positive value makes the image **lighter**, but it **doesn't change** the **difference** between the **dark** and **light** regions (**contrast**).

× 2

200	200	200
200	100	200
200	200	200

Multiplying by a fixed value (greater than 1) makes the image **lighter**, and **increases** the **contrast** (there's a bigger difference between colour values).

Adding False Colour can Highlight Features

1) In the example above, a value of '**50**' in the array mapped to a **dark shade of grey** in the image, while a value of '**100**' mapped to a slightly **brighter shade**. But you could map '**2**' to a **dark shade of pink** and '**4**' to a **brighter shade** — or '**2**' to **orange** and '**4**' to **green**.
2) This process is called adding **false colour**. You can use **any** colours you like, but they're usually picked to **highlight certain features** — e.g. the **important features** could be made a really **bright** colour.
3) False colour images are often used in **remote sensing** of data. For example, a **thermal imaging camera** shows **heat** in colour instead of visible light. Satellites can be used to map **different parts** of the **electromagnetic spectrum** to red, green and blue to show features that **can't be seen** in **true colour** images.

You can transform an image by changing the colours that the values in its array map to — not the array itself.

A false colour satellite image of a river delta.

Information in Images

Replacing Pixels With the Median of their Neighbours Reduces Noise

60	100	60
20	220	60
60	60	20

→

60	100	60
20	60	60
60	60	20

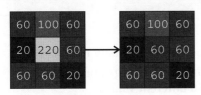

This array shows a bright spot in a uniform darker region — the spot is probably noise. Replacing the central value with the median of its value and the surrounding values reduces the brightness of the region.

1) **Noise** is **unwanted interference** affecting a signal. In images this is usually **bright** or **dark** spots on the picture.
2) One way you can get rid of **noise** is to **replace** each pixel with the **median** (see p.11) of itself and the eight pixels surrounding it.
3) The result is that any **'odd'** (i.e. very **high** or very **low**) values are **removed** and the image is made **smoother**.

Edge Detection Tells You if there is Something in your Image

1) If you're trying to work out if there is **something** in your **image** (rather than just a load of **noise**), using **edge detection** to find any **edges** can be a really **useful** first step.
2) The **Laplace rule** is a method of **finding edges**. To apply the rule, you **multiply** the value of a pixel by **four**, then **subtract** the value of the pixels immediately **above**, **below**, to the **left** and to the **right** of it. If the answer is negative, the pixel is treated as if its value is 0 (ie. it maps to the colour black).
3) Edge-detected images are usually then **inverted** so that **white becomes black** and vice versa.
4) The result is that any pixel **not** on an **edge** goes **white** — so you're left with **just** the **edges**.

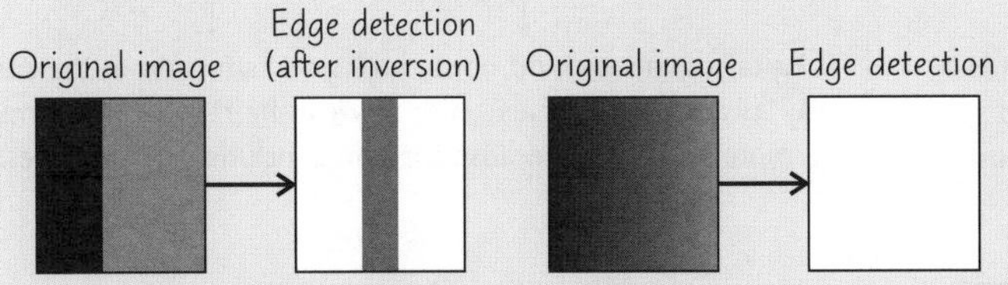

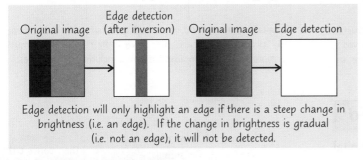

Edge detection will only highlight an edge if there is a steep change in brightness (i.e. an edge). If the change in brightness is gradual (i.e. not an edge), it will not be detected.

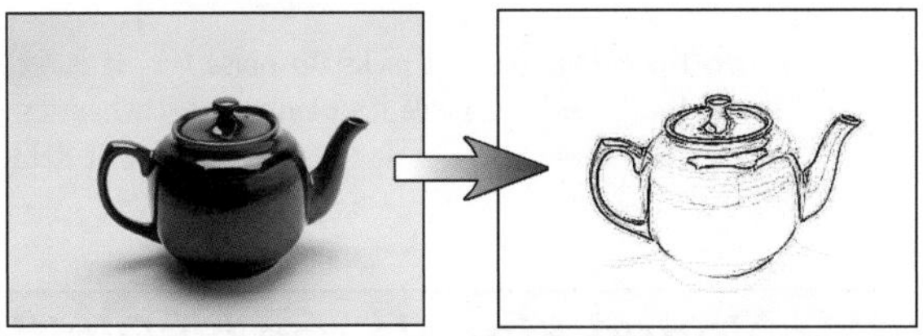

original image — image after edge detection

Practice Questions

Q1 What's the difference between a bit and a byte? Find the number of bits in 1024 bytes.

Q2 A string contains 3 500 000 different alternatives. What is the minimum number of bits required?

Q3 How can the brightness and contrast of an image be changed?

Q4 What is the Laplace rule used for? How do you apply it?

Exam Questions

Q1 A TV can display 65 536 different colours. It displays a still image of width 1920 pixels and height 1080 pixels.

a) Calculate the number of bytes required to store the colour of each pixel. *[2 marks]*

b) Calculate the total amount of information contained in the image in bits. *[1 mark]*

c) An image contains a 1.5 m^2 square that spans exactly a quarter of the available width. What is the resolution of the screen? *[2 marks]*

Q2 The diagram shows part of an array that describes an image. The image is made up of 256 shades of grey — 0 represents black and 255 represents white.

100	99	100
97	185	98
101	101	98

a) Sketch the image that this part of the array describes. *[1 mark]*

b) Describe how noise can be removed from digital images by finding a median value. *[1 mark]*

c) Apply this technique to the central value of the array shown. *[1 mark]*

All this talk of bytes is making me a megabit hungry — mmm, tasty bites...

It doesn't matter how many attempts you take, or how many filters you apply — all your selfies are really just a long list of ones and zeroes (unless you actually print them out on paper). Now — everybody say cheeeese...

Digital and Analogue Signals

You've just seen how information can be stored digitally, but what if you want to send that information? And what if the information isn't digital to start with? So many questions — read on to find out the answers.

Analogue Signals Vary Continuously

1) **Digital signals**, like the images on the previous three pages, are represented by **binary numbers**.
2) The **values** that a **digital signal** can take depend on the **number of bits** used — e.g. a **one bit** signal can only take the values **0 and 1**, but a **one byte** signal can take **256 different values**.
3) **Analogue signals** are **not limited** in the values they can take — they **vary continuously**. For example, **speech** is an **analogue signal** — the **sound waves** produced **vary continuously** over a range of **loudness** and **frequency**.

Digital Signals Are Resistant to the Effects of Noise

When you **transmit** an electronic signal it will pick up **noise** (interference) from **electrical disturbances** or other **signals**. The receiver needs to be able to **reconstruct** the **original signal** from the **noisy signal** if they're to get an **accurate representation** of what was sent. This is **much easier** with **digital** than analogue signals because the **number of values** a digital signal can take is **limited**.

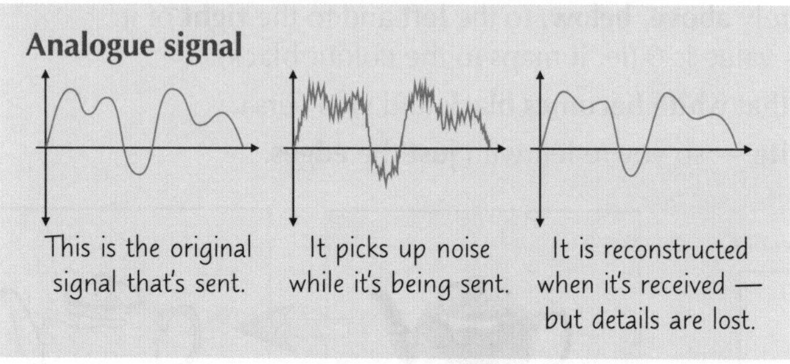

Analogue signal
This is the original signal that's sent.
It picks up noise while it's being sent.
It is reconstructed when it's received — but details are lost.

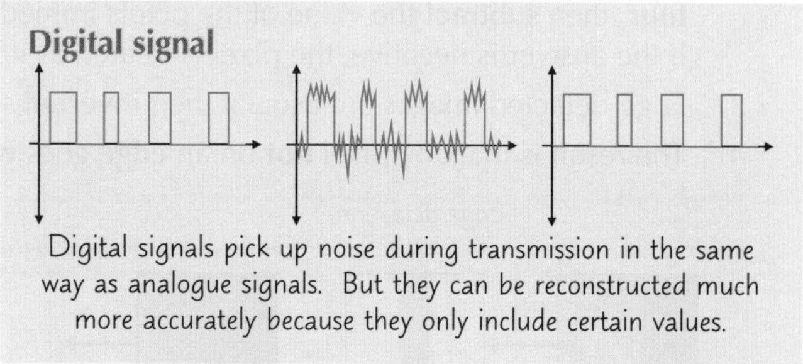

Digital signal
Digital signals pick up noise during transmission in the same way as analogue signals. But they can be reconstructed much more accurately because they only include certain values.

Analogue Signals can be Digitised

1) It's possible to turn an **analogue signal** into a **digital signal** — this is called **digitising** the signal.
2) To digitise a signal, you take the **value** of the signal at **regular time intervals**, then find the **nearest digital value**.
3) Each **digital value** is represented by a **binary number**, so you can **convert** the **analogue** values to **binary** numbers.
4) The **digital signal** you end up with won't be **exactly** the same as the **analogue signal**, but it's usually quite **close**.

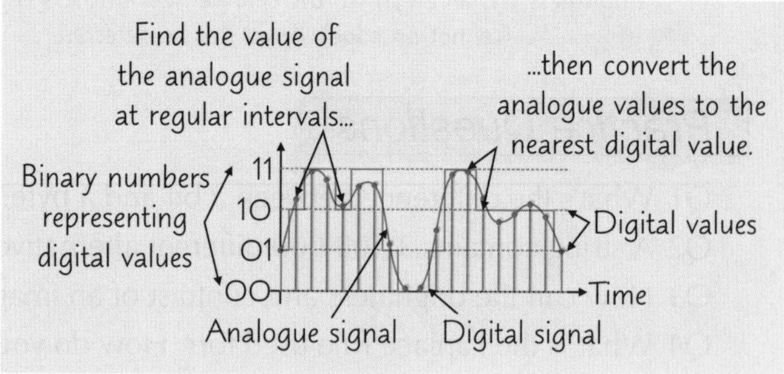

The Quality of a Digitised Signal Depends on its Resolution

1) How well a **digitised** signal matches the original depends on **two** factors — the **difference** between the possible **digital values** (**resolution**) and the **time** from one **sample** to the next (**sampling rate**, see p.26).
2) If a signal is digitised using only a **few**, **widely spaced** digital values, it's likely that a lot of the analogue values sampled will be **far** from the **nearest digital value**. But, if a **large** number of **closely spaced** digital values are used, most of the analogue values will be **very close** to a digital value, so will only change **slightly**.
3) This means that the **higher the resolution** (i.e. the **more possible digital values** there are), the **more closely** the digitised signal will **match** the original.
4) **Resolution** is determined by the **number of bits** in the **binary numbers** representing the digital values — the **greater** the number of **bits**, the **greater** the **resolution**.
5) When **music** is digitised to make **CDs**, a resolution of **16 bits** is used. This gives a total of **65 536 digital values** and means the recorded music is **very similar** to the **original**.

6) **Low resolution** digital signals are often used in **telephone lines**, and other systems where top-quality audio isn't essential. Telephone conversations have to be **audible**, but you **don't need** an **accurate reproduction** of the callers' voices — even if this does mean the music sounds **distorted** when you're put on hold. Using a lower resolution and sampling rate means a **lower rate of transmission** (p.27) can be used to send information.

Digital and Analogue Signals

Digital Signals Have Several Advantages Over Analogue Signals

1) Digital signals can often be **sent**, **received** and **reproduced** more easily than analogue signals because they can only take a limited number of values.
2) Digital files can be **compressed** to reduce their size, and **manipulated** easily for artistic effect.
3) **Noise** is more of a problem for analogue signals than digital signals (see previous page).
4) A digital signal can be used to represent **different** kinds of **information** in the **same way** — for example, **images** and **sounds** can both be represented as a string of bits.
5) **Computers** can be used to **easily process** digital signals, since computers are **digital devices** too.

But they have some Disadvantages too

1) Digital signals can **never** reproduce analogue signals **exactly** — some **information** will always be **lost**.
2) Because digital signals can be copied more easily, digital information like films and music can be **reproduced illegally unlimited times**.
3) **Confidential information**, such as **personal data** and **photographs**, may be **stolen** and **copied** without the owners' knowledge or consent more easily, for example by **hackers**, **infected networks** or **malicious websites**.

The UK Government wants to switch all radio broadcasts over to **digital (DAB) signals** as these can (in theory) have better audio quality and more stations can fit in less space. But **analogue** radio devices remain **very popular** among the public, and the **bit rate** used for DAB radio broadcasts is often **low**, producing a **lower quality sound** than FM radio.

Signals are Made Up of Lots of Different Frequencies

1) The wave on page 14 is the **simplest** kind of **signal** because it contains just **one frequency**. In practice, most **signals** are made up of **several** waves, all with **different frequencies**, added together.
2) When these waves are added together, the **amplitude** of the final signal is the **sum** of the **amplitudes** of the individual waves at each point in time.
3) For example, if you play a **musical note**, the sound you hear contains the **frequency** (pitch) of the **main note** and a load of **other frequencies**. It's these '**other frequencies**' that make instruments **sound different**, even though they're playing the **same note**.
4) The **fundamental frequency** is the **lowest frequency** wave that makes up a sound wave. You can spot it by finding the **shortest repeating part** of the sound wave and calculating the inverse of its period.

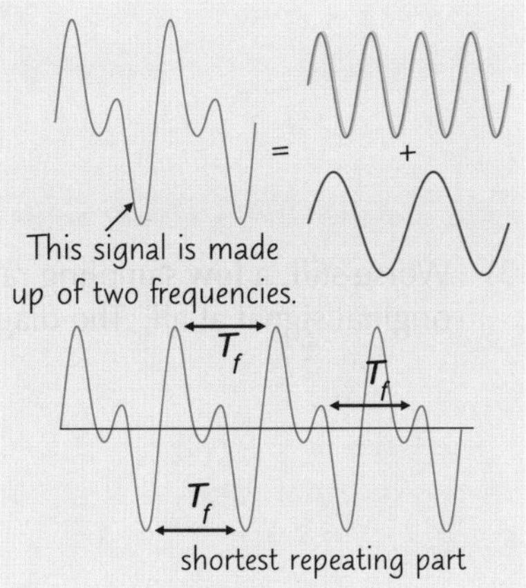

Practice Questions

Q1 Explain how a digital signal is different from an analogue one.

Q2 What is meant by resolution in the context of digitising analogue signals?

Q3 Give three advantages of digital signals over analogue signals.

Exam Question

Q1 The diagram shows the waveform of a musical note played on an instrument.

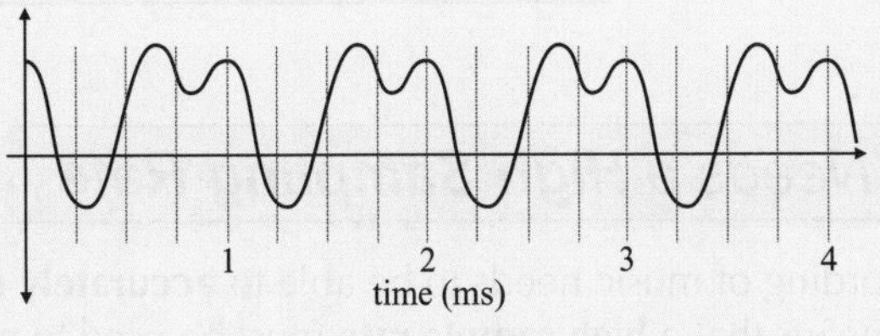

a) Calculate the fundamental frequency of the note. [1 mark]

b) The wave is sampled every 0.001 s.
The first sample occurs at 0.0 ms.
Sketch the waveform of the reconstructed signal. [2 marks]

How do finger puppets communicate? With digital signals...

Digital signals are everywhere these days — CDs, MP3s, DVDs, TV, DAB radio — there's just no escape. Analogue signals are still around, though — lots of radio stations broadcast FM or AM analogue signals (for now at least...). Some people prefer analogue signals for listening to music and use vinyl (ask your dad) instead of MP3s or CDs.

Sampling and Transmitting Signals

Noise Limits the *Number of Bits* used for *Sampling*

1) You've just seen that the **higher the resolution**, the **better** a digitised signal **matches** the original.
2) But, if the original signal contains **noise** (as most real signals do), then a really **fine resolution** will reproduce all the little wiggles caused by the **noise** — **not useful**.
3) In practice, the **resolution** is **limited** by the **ratio** of the total **variation** in the **signal** to the **variation** caused by **noise**:

Lesley made sure noise didn't affect the number of sweets sampled.

$$\textbf{Maximum number of bits} = \log_2\left(\frac{\textbf{total variation}}{\textbf{noise variation}}\right) \text{ or } b = \log_2\left(\frac{V_{total}}{V_{noise}}\right)$$

Here the variation is measured in volts, but the ratio has no units because they cancel.

Minimum Sampling Rate is *Twice* the *Maximum Frequency*

1) When you **digitise** a signal, you **record the value** of (**sample**) the original signal at **regular intervals**. The **rate** at which you **sample** the signal is called the **sampling rate** — imaginative name, I know.
2) The **sampling rate** has to be **high** enough to record all the **high frequency** detail of the signal. The diagram below shows how **detail** can be **lost** if the sampling rate is too **low**.

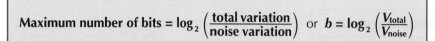

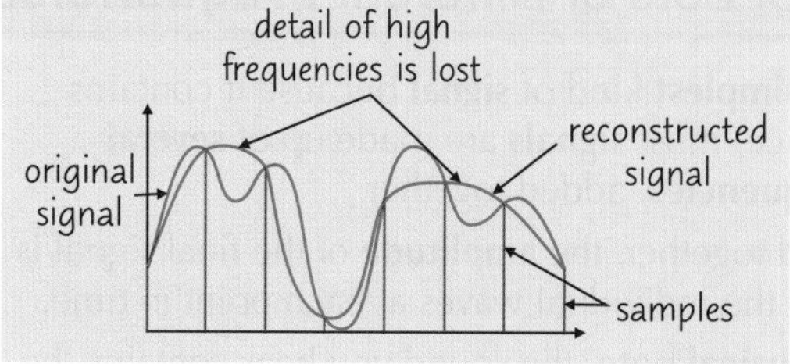

3) Worse still, a **low** sampling rate can **create** low frequency signals — called **aliases** — that **weren't** in the original signal at all. The diagram **below** shows how **aliases** can be **created** by a **low sampling rate**.

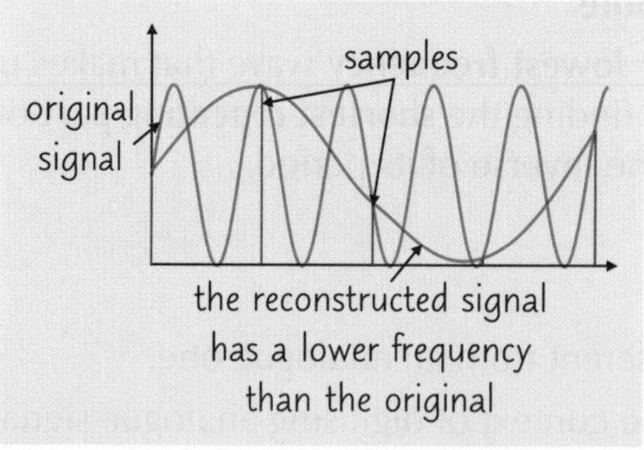

4) To avoid these problems, the **sampling rate** must be at least **twice** the **highest frequency** in the original signal.

Minimum rate of sampling > 2 × maximum frequency of signal

Music Needs a *High Sampling Rate*

1) A recording of music needs to be able to **accurately reproduce** the **original sounds**. This means that a **high sample rate** must be used to make sure **high frequency details** aren't **lost**, and to avoid the creation of **aliases** in the recording.
2) **CD** and **MP3-quality** audio uses a sampling rate of **44 100 Hz** . The maximum frequency sound that can be recorded at this sampling rate is about **20 000 Hz**, which is roughly the highest-frequency sound audible to the human ear.
3) The audio on **video DVDs** and in **digital TV broadcasts** uses a slightly higher sampling rate of **48 000 Hz**, while **Blu-ray Discs**™ can use a sampling rate of up to **192 000 Hz**.

Sampling and Transmitting Signals

Rate of Transmission = Samples per Second × Bits per Sample

By now you should know **how** signals are **transmitted** — what's also important is the **rate** at which they're transmitted. The **rate of transmission** of a digital signal depends on **two** factors:

1) The number of **samples per second** — this must be at least **twice** the **highest frequency** in the signal to ensure that all the frequencies within its spectrum are transmitted accurately.
2) The number of **bits per sample** — this must be **high enough** that the transmitted signal **closely** matches the original, but not so high that it is negatively affected by **noise**.

Rate of transmission of a digital information (bits per second) = samples per second × bits per sample

Time Taken to Transmit a Signal = Bits ÷ Rate of Transmission

To find the **time** it will take to **transmit** a signal, you need to know the **number of bits** that need to be transmitted, and the **rate of transmission** (in bits per second):

Time taken to transmit a signal = number of bits to transmit ÷ rate of transmission

The speed of your Internet connection is usually measured in **bits**, or more likely megabits (Mb), **per second**. Note the lower case b — M**b** means mega**bits**, whereas M**B** means mega**bytes**.

Don't get them confused — if you've got an Internet upload connection of 2 megabits per second and want to upload a 2 megabyte image to a social network, it won't take 1 second — it will take at least 8 seconds.

To **speed up** the process, and **use less storage space**, you could **compress** your image to **reduce** the file size.

Practice Questions

Q1 Why is there a maximum number of bits used for sampling?

Q2 Describe two problems that can be caused by an insufficient sampling rate.

Q3 The minimum rate of sampling for a signal is 72 kHz. What is the maximum frequency of the signal?

Q4 Why is music often sampled a rate of 40-50 kHz?

Exam Questions

Q1 A digital signal has a total variation of 160 mV and a noise variation of 10 mV.
Find the maximum number of bits that should be used when sampling this signal. [2 marks]

Q2 The telephone system samples your voice 8000 times a second and converts this into an eight bit digital signal.

a) Find the rate of transmission for bits in this telephone system. [1 mark]

b) Calculate how many bytes are sent each second. [1 mark]

Q3 An Internet radio station streams a single channel of digital audio at a rate of 128 kbit s^{-1}.

a) The audio the station broadcasts contains 16 bits per sample. Calculate the sampling rate. [1 mark]

b) A listener wants to stream the radio station using her mobile phone.
She tests her mobile data connection and finds that she can download a 2.0 MB file in 110 seconds.
State whether her connection is sufficient to stream the radio station. [3 marks]

Music needs a high sampling rate — just don't tell the copyright lawyers...

Aaaand that's the end of that section. I don't know about you, but I've enjoyed this little foray into the physics behind tech that most of us use every day. Once you've got every last bit learned, you can feel OK about taking a byte out of your revision time to stream a celebratory self array of binary numbers to your favourite social network...

Charge, Current and Potential Difference

This section isn't about the sixth sense, common sense or extrasensory perception. It's about proper, sensible physics...

*Many **Sensors** are **Powered** using **Electricity***

Make sure you learn all the circuit symbols that come up in this section, and know how to design and use circuits including them.

Your body is pretty amazing at sensing things, within limits.
E.g. skin is a good temperature sensor — you know about it when you spill hot tea on your lap — but you won't know that the temperature of the tea is 62.3 °C.

1) **Electronic sensors** are designed to sense things we can't (or are too lazy to) sense. Any change in whatever the sensor's detecting will change the current in the connected circuit. The **current** is processed to give you a reading.
2) There are loads of different types of sensor out there. From everyday things like temperature sensors that use **thermistors** (p.31), to **electron microscopes** which can be used to 'see' individual atoms (see p.49). Excited yet? I know I am...

Current** — the **Flow** of **Charged Particles

1) **Current** is measured as the **rate of flow** of **charged particles** (usually electrons). You can calculate current using the equation:

$$I = \frac{\Delta Q}{\Delta t}$$

Where I is the current in amperes (A), ΔQ is the charge in coulombs (C) that flows during Δt, and Δt is the time taken in seconds (s).

If it helps, think of the **current** in a **wire** like the flow rate of **water** in a **pipe**. Just as the flow rate is a measure of how much water goes through the pipe in a given time interval, the current is a measure of the number of charged particles that move past a point in a wire in a given time.

2) The **coulomb** is the unit of charge. One coulomb (C) is defined as the amount of charge that passes a point in 1 second when the current is 1 ampere.
3) You can measure the current flowing through part of a circuit using an **ammeter**. This is the circuit symbol for an ammeter:

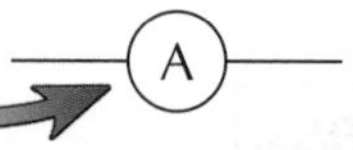

Attach an ammeter in series with the component you're investigating.

4) **Conventional current** flows from positive to negative terminal of a power supply. This direction was picked before scientists discovered current is usually caused by the flow of electrons. Electrons are negatively charged and flow from negative to positive terminals — so conventional current is in the **opposite direction** to electron flow.

Potential Difference** is the **Energy** per **Unit Charge

Potential difference is sometimes called voltage.

1) To make electric charge flow through a conductor, you need to do **work** on it.
2) **Potential difference** (p.d.), ***V***, is defined as the **energy converted per unit charge moved**:

$$V = \frac{W}{Q}$$

W is the energy in joules. It's the work you do moving the charge.

The **potential difference** across a component is **1 volt** (V) when you convert **1 joule** of energy moving **1 coulomb** of charge through the component. This **defines** the volt.

$$1\ \text{V} = 1\ \text{JC}^{-1}$$

Back to the 'water analogy' again. The p.d. is like the pressure that's forcing water along the pipe.

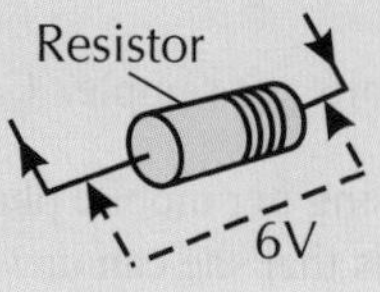

Here you do 6 J of work moving each coulomb of charge through the resistor, so the p.d. across it is 6 V. The energy gets converted to heat.

3) You can measure the potential difference across a component using a **voltmeter**. This is the circuit symbol for a voltmeter:

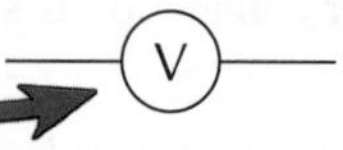

4) The potential difference across components in parallel is **the same**, so the **voltmeter** should be connected in **parallel** with the component you're investigating.

Charge, Current and Potential Difference

Power is the *Rate* of *Transfer* of *Energy*

Power (*P*) is **defined** as the **rate** of **transfer** of **energy** (the rate of work done). It's measured in **watts** (**W**), where **1 watt** is equivalent to **1 joule per second**.

in symbols: $P = \frac{W}{t}$

There's a really simple formula for **power** in **electrical circuits**: $P = IV$

This makes sense, since:

1) **Potential difference** (*V*) is defined as the **energy transferred** per **coulomb**.
2) **Current** (*I*) is defined as the **number** of **coulombs** transferred per **second**.
3) So **p.d.** × **current** is **energy transferred per second**, i.e. **power**.

By rearranging $P = IV$ and substituting in the potential equations for difference and current, you can see that: $V = \frac{P}{I} = \frac{W}{Q}$

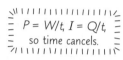

$P = W/t$, $I = Q/t$, so time cancels.

Energy is Easy to *Calculate* if you Know the *Power*

Sometimes it's the **total energy** transferred **(the total work done)** that you're interested in. In this case you simply need to **multiply** the **power** by the **time**.

$W = Pt$, so $W = VIt$

Example: A prancing electro-monkey is powered by a 6.0 V battery and draws a current of 0.80 A. How much energy would the electro-monkey transfer if switched on and left to prance for exactly 2 minutes?

$V = 6.0$ V, $I = 0.80$ A, $t = 120$ seconds. So, $W = VIt = 6.0 \times 0.80 \times 120 = 576 =$ **580 J (to 2 s.f.)**

Practice Questions

Q1 Describe in words how current and charge are related.

Q2 Define a) the coulomb and b) potential difference.

Q3 How does conventional current relate to the flow of electrons in a typical circuit?

Q4 Power is measured in watts. What is 1 watt equivalent to?

Q5 Calculate the current in a 12 W light bulb when it is connected to a 230 V electrical supply.

Exam Questions

Q1 A current of 0.18 A flows through a motor for 6.0 seconds. The motor does 75 J of work in this time.

a) Calculate the power of the motor. [1 mark]

b) Calculate the potential difference across the motor. [1 mark]

Q2 A kettle runs off the mains supply (230 V). Only 88% of the electrical energy that is input is transferred usefully to the water. Calculate how much electric charge will pass through the kettle if it transfers 308 J of energy to the water it contains. [2 marks]

[THIS JOKE HAS BEEN CENSORED]... it was a good one as well...

Talking of jokes, I saw this bottle of wine the other day called 'raisin d'être' — 'raison d'être' meaning 'reason for living', but spelled slightly differently to make 'raisin', meaning 'grape'. Ho ho. Chuckled all the way home.

Resistance and Conductance

Resistance is what causes components to heat up. It's how your toaster works, and why computers need cooling fans...

Everything has *Resistance*

1) If you put a **potential difference** (p.d.) across an **electrical component**, a **current** will flow.
2) **How much** current you get for a particular **p.d.** depends on the **resistance** of the component.
3) You can think of a component's **resistance** as a **measure** of how **difficult** it is to get a **current** to **flow** through it.
4) **Resistance** is measured in **ohms** (Ω). A component has a resistance of 1 Ω if a potential difference of 1 V makes a current of 1 A flow through it.

Mathematically, **resistance** is: $R = \frac{V}{I}$
This equation **defines** resistance.

Learn the equations for resistance and conductance — you won't be given them in the exam.

You also need to know the formula for the **inverse** of resistance — **conductance, *G*.** $G = \frac{I}{V}$

This is a measure of how good an electrical conductor a component is. It's measured in Ω^{-1} or siemens, S.

5) The resistance equation gives you a whole new way of calculating electrical power if you substitute it into $P = IV$. $V = IR$, so $P = IV = I^2R$
6) This power is the rate at which a component converts electrical energy into other types of energy, e.g. heat. This is known as **power dissipation**. This can be useful, e.g. the dissipation of power as light from a bulb. In other situations, power dissipation causes problems we need to work round. E.g. computers have cooling fans to get rid of some of the heat that builds up in their circuits, and mains electricity is transmitted at a high voltage (so low current) to minimise the power dissipated during transmission.

I-V Graphs Show How *Resistance Varies*

1) The term '***I-V* characteristic**' refers to a **graph** which shows how the **current** (*I*) flowing through a **component changes** as the **potential difference** (*V*) across it is increased.
2) The **shallower** the **gradient** of a characteristic ***I-V*** graph, the **greater** the **resistance** of the component.
3) A **curved line** shows that the resistance of the component **changes** with the potential difference across it.

You can investigate the *I-V* characteristic of a component using a **test circuit** like this one:

1) Use the **variable resistor** to alter the **potential difference** across the component and the **current** flowing through it, and record *V* and *I*.
2) **Repeat** your measurements and take **averages** to reduce the effect of random errors (see p.12) on your results.
3) **Plot a graph** of current against potential difference from your results. This graph is the ***I-V* characteristic** of the component and you can use it to see how the **resistance** changes.

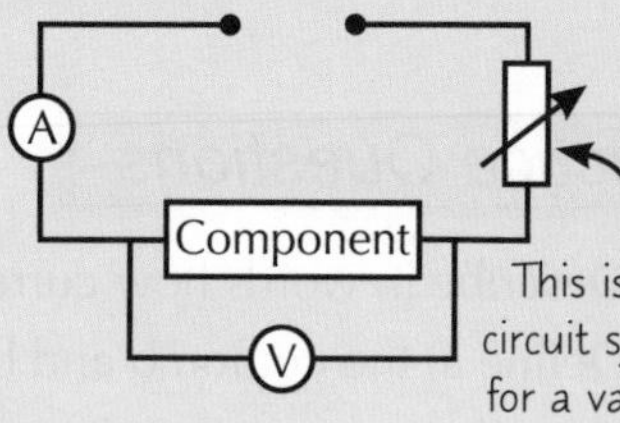

If you have access to a computer, you could enter your data into a spreadsheet and use this to plot the graph.

For an *Ohmic Conductor, R* is a *Constant*

Metal wires and resistors are ohmic conductors

Conductors that **obey** Ohm's law (mostly metals) are called **ohmic conductors**. Ohm's law states that:

Provided external factors such as **temperature** are **constant**, the **current** through an ohmic conductor is **directly proportional** to the **potential difference** across it (that's $V = IR$).

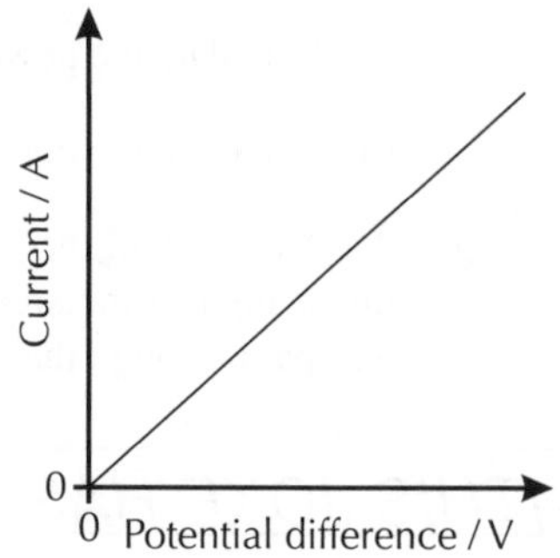

1) As you can see from the graph, **doubling** the **p.d. doubles** the **current**.
2) The gradient is **constant**, which means that **resistance** is **constant**.
3) Remember, Ohm's law is **only** true for **ohmic conductors** where external factors like **temperature** are **constant**.
4) **Non-ohmic conductors** don't have this relation between current and p.d. There are **examples** of non-ohmic conductors on the next page.

Resistance and Conductance

The *I-V* Characteristic for a Filament Lamp is Curved

Filament lamp circuit symbol:

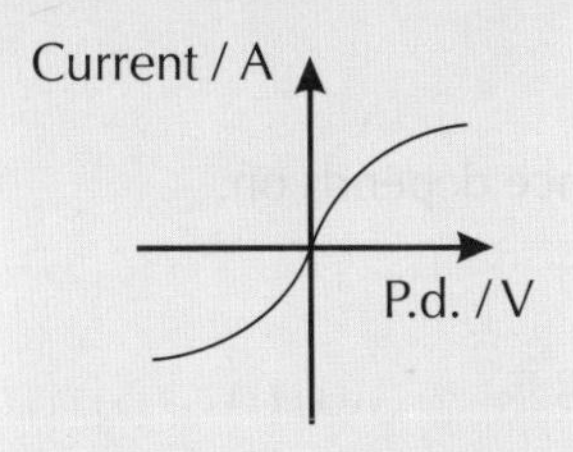

1) The characteristic graph for a **filament lamp** is a **curve**, which starts **steep** but gets **shallower** as the **potential difference rises.**
2) The **filament** in a lamp is just a **coiled up** length of **metal wire**, so you might think it should have the **same characteristic graph** as a **metallic conductor**.
3) However, **current** flowing through the lamp **increases** its **temperature**, so its **resistance increases** (see below).

The Resistance of a Thermistor Depends on Temperature

Thermistor circuit symbol:

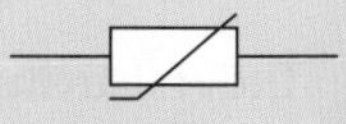

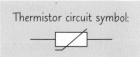

A **thermistor** is a **resistor** with a **resistance** that depends on its **temperature**, so you can use them as **temperature sensors**.

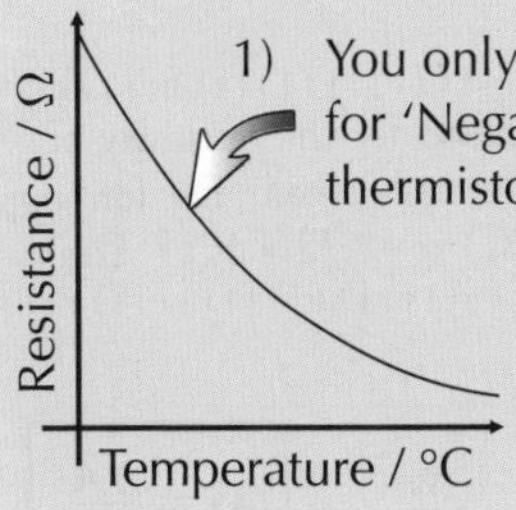

1) You only need to know about **NTC thermistors** — NTC stands for 'Negative Temperature Coefficient'. The resistance of an NTC thermistor **decreases** with **temperature** (so its conductance increases).
2) Increasing the **current** through the thermistor increases its **temperature**. The **increasing gradient** of this graph tells you that the **resistance is decreasing** as the thermistor heats up.

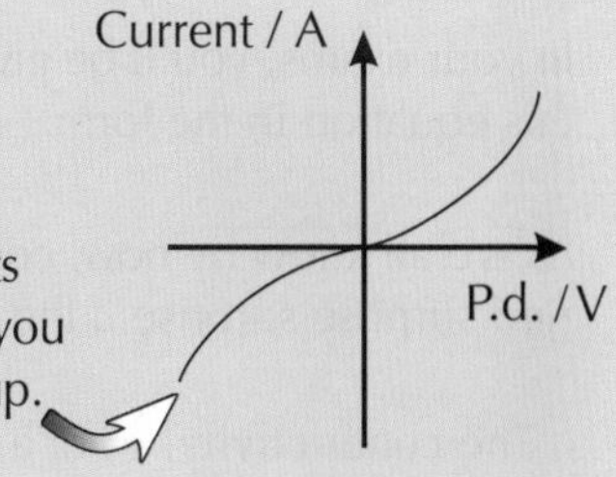

An **LDR** (**light dependent resistor**), is similar to a thermistor, but is sensitive to **light**, not heat — the more light falls on it, the lower its resistance.

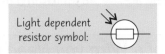

Light dependent resistor symbol:

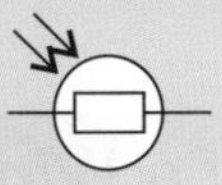

Filament lamps, thermistors, LDRs and diodes are all examples of non-ohmic conductors. You can tell by looking at their *I-V* graphs.

Diodes Only Let Current Flow in One Direction

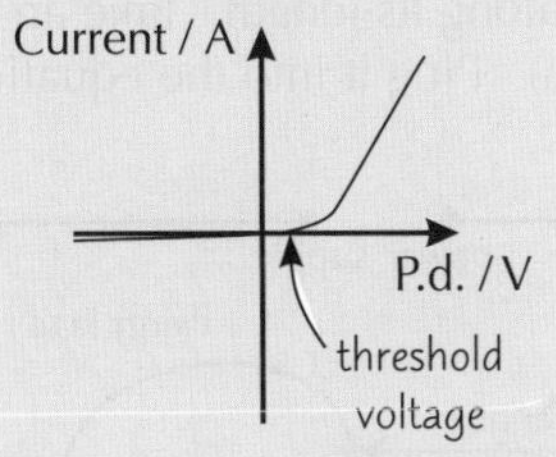

Diodes (including light emitting diodes (LEDs)) are designed to let **current flow** in **one direction** only. You don't need to be able to explain how they work, just what they do.

1) **Forward bias** is the **direction** in which the **current** is **allowed to flow.**
2) **Most** diodes require a **threshold voltage** of about **0.6 V** in the **forward direction** before they will conduct.
3) In **reverse bias**, the **resistance** of the diode is **very high** and the current that flows is **very tiny**.

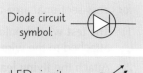

Diode circuit symbol:

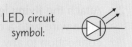

LED circuit symbol:

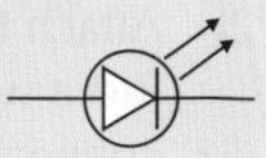

Practice Questions

Q1 State the formulas for resistance and conductance.

Q2 Sketch the test circuit used to investigate the *I-V* characteristic of a component, and explain how it is used.

Q3 State Ohm's law. Give an example of an ohmic conductor.

Q4 Draw an *I-V* characteristic graph for a diode. Label the areas of forward bias and reverse bias.

Exam Question

Q1 a) A current of 2.8 A is passed through a wire from a 1.5 V power supply. Find the resistance of the wire. [1 mark]

b) When the same power supply is connected to a different wire, the current is 0.15 A. Calculate the conductance of the wire. [1 mark]

c) Explain why the wires become warm after a period of operation. [2 marks]

You light up my world like an LED — with One-Directional current...

The examiners like testing this kind of stuff as if you've really done the experiment, so your results aren't perfect and you have fun errors to deal with. If errors aren't your thing, have a quick flick to page 12 to calm your nerves.

Electrical Properties of Solids

From a remote-controlled car to a supercomputer... if what you're building involves electricity, you're going to want to know about resistivity and conductivity...

Three Things Determine Resistance

If you think about a nice, **simple electrical component**, like a **length of wire**, its **resistance** depends on:

1) **Length (L)**. The **longer** the wire, the **more difficult** it is to make a **current flow**.
2) **Area (A)**. The **wider** the wire, the **easier** it will be for the electrons to pass along it.
3) **Resistivity (ρ)**. This **depends** on the **material** the wire's made from, as the **structure** of the material may make it easy or difficult for charge to flow. In general, resistivity depends on **external factors** as well, like **temperature**.

ρ is the Greek letter rho, the symbol for resistivity.

The **resistivity** of a material is defined as the **resistance of a 1 m length** with a **1 m² cross-sectional area** — it's given by $\rho = \frac{RA}{L}$. Resistivity is measured in **ohm metres** (Ωm).

In your exams, you'll be given this equation in the form:

$$R = \frac{\rho L}{A}$$

where R = resistance in Ω, A = cross-sectional area in m², and L = length in m

Typical values for the resistivity of conductors are really small. E.g. for copper (at 25 °C) $\rho = 1.72 \times 10^{-8}$ Ωm.

As we all know by now, conductance is the inverse of resistance (p.30). And surprise surprise... the inverse of resistivity is **conductivity**, σ.

The **conductivity**, σ, of a material is defined as the **conductance** of a **1 m length** with a **1 m² cross-sectional area** — it's given by $\sigma = \frac{GL}{A}$. It's measured in **siemens per metre** (S m⁻¹).

$$G = \frac{\sigma A}{L}$$

To Find the Resistivity of a Wire you Need to Find its Resistance

You'll need to **measure** the test wire's cross-sectional area before you start. Assume that the wire is **cylindrical**, and so its cross-section is **circular**. Then you can find the cross-sectional area using: **area of a circle = πr^2**

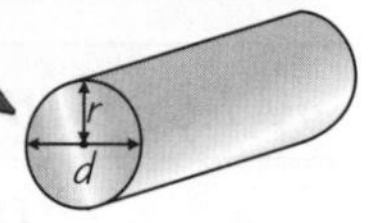

Using a **micrometer**, measure the **diameter** of the wire in at least **three** different points along its length. Take an **average** value of the diameter and divide by **two** to get the **radius** (make sure this is in m). Plug it into the equation for cross-sectional area and... **ta da**. Now you can get your teeth into the electricity bit...

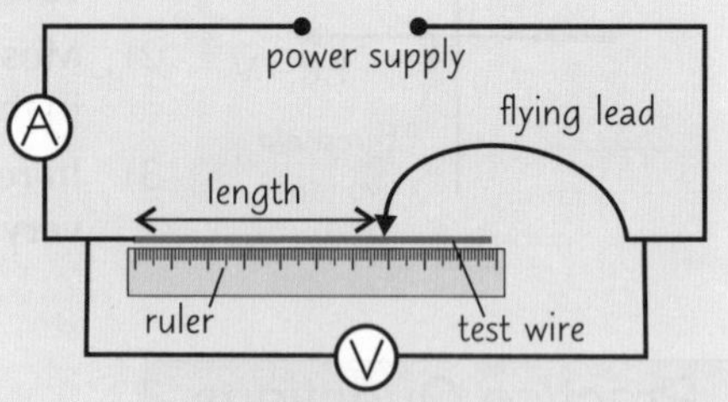

1) The **test wire** should be **clamped** to a ruler with the circuit attached to the wire where the ruler reads zero.
2) Attach the **flying lead** to the test wire — the lead is just a wire with a crocodile clip at the end to allow connection to any point along the test wire.
3) Record the **length** of the test wire **connected** in the circuit, the **voltmeter reading** and the **ammeter reading**.
4) Use your readings to calculate the **resistance** of the length of wire, using: $R = \frac{V}{I}$
5) Repeat this measurement and calculate an average resistance for the length.
6) Repeat for several **different** lengths, for example between 0.10 and 1.00 m.
7) Plot your results on a graph of R against L, and draw a **line of best fit**.

The **gradient** of the line of best fit is equal to $\frac{R}{L} = \frac{\rho}{A}$. So **multiply** the **gradient** of the line of best fit by the **cross-sectional area** of the wire to find the resistivity of the wire material.

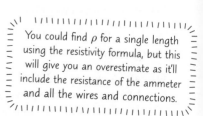

You could find ρ for a single length using the resistivity formula, but this will give you an overestimate as it'll include the resistance of the ammeter and all the wires and connections.

8) The other components of the circuit also have a resistance, but the gradient of the line of best fit isn't affected by the resistance within the rest of the circuit.
9) The **resistivity** of a material depends on its **temperature**, so you can only find the resistivity of a material **at a certain temperature**. Current flowing in the test wire can cause its temperature to increase, so you need to try to keep the temperature of the test wire **constant**, e.g. by only having small currents flow through the wire.
10) To find the conductivity of a wire instead, do the same experiment. As $\sigma = 1/\rho$, you can use your final result to calculate the metal's conductivity if that's what you need.

Electrical Properties of Solids

Different Materials have *Different Numbers of* Charge Carriers

How conductive a material is depends on its **number density of mobile charge carriers** — the number of free electrons (or ions that are free to move) there are per cubic metre of the material. The more **mobile charge carriers** a material has per unit volume, the **better** a **conductor** it will be.

Conductance and resistance graphs are often called conductivity and resistivity graphs.

Metals

In a **metal**, the **charge carriers** are **free electrons** (see p.48). Metals are **good conductors** because they have absolutely shedloads of them — the **number density of mobile charge carriers** is **high**.

If you **increase** the **temperature** of a metal, the **number** of mobile charge carriers **stays about the same**. As the electrons move, they scatter from the metallic lattice. As the temperature increases, the lattice **vibrates** more, increasing the electron scattering, so the electrons are slightly less free to move. This means that as the **temperature increases**, the **conductivity** of a metal will slightly **decrease**.

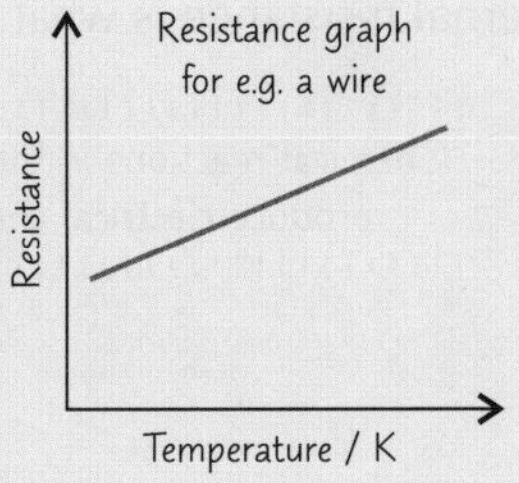

Semiconductors

Just as in metals, the mobile charge carriers in **semiconductors** are free electrons. Semiconductors have a much **lower** charge carrier number density (fewer free electrons) than metals, so they have a **lower conductivity**.

As you **increase** the **temperature** of a semiconductor, more electrons are freed to conduct. This means that as the temperature **increases**, the **conductivity** of a semiconductor **rapidly increases**.

Just as in metals, the semiconductor atom lattice will also vibrate more, scattering the free electrons as they move — but its effect is much smaller than the effect of the huge increase in charge carriers.

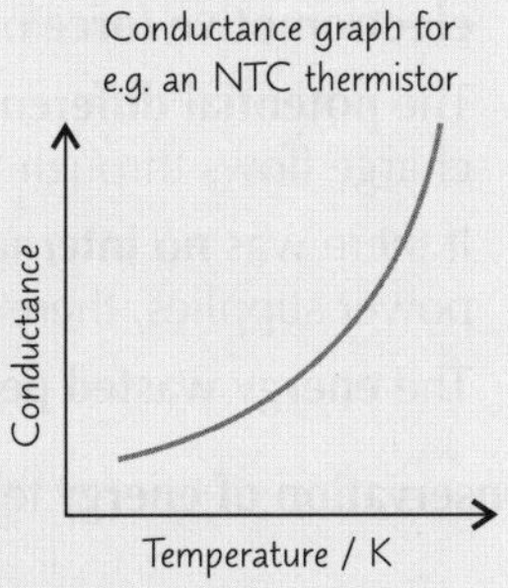

Thermistors are made up of semiconductors whose conductivity changes with **temperature**, as described above. **Light dependent resistors** (LDRs) are made up of semiconductors whose conductivity is mostly controlled by **light** rather than heat — their conductivity **increases** with increasing light levels.

Insulators

A **perfect insulator** wouldn't have **any mobile charge carriers**, so it wouldn't be able to conduct at all. (What can I say... it's short and sweet...)

Practice Questions

Q1 What three factors does the resistance of a length of wire depend on?

Q2 Write down the units of resistivity and conductivity.

Q3 Describe how a metal's conductance varies with temperature.

Q4 Why are semiconductors poorer conductors than metals at lower temperatures?

Q5 Explain why insulators do not conduct electricity.

Exam Question

Q1 This question is about an experiment to measure the resistivity of copper.

a) Describe the equipment and method you would use to measure the resistivity of copper using a copper wire. You should include a labelled circuit diagram as part of your answer. [6 marks]

b) Sketch graphs to show how conductance and resistance vary with temperature for a copper wire. Describe and explain why these graphs differ from those for a NTC thermistor. [5 marks]

Insulator Airlines — the no-charge carriers...

That resistivity experiment's a popular one to come up in exams — so make sure you learn it. Try to think about where errors are creeping into your measurements too, and how you might be able to reduce them... see p.9 for ideas...

E.m.f. and Internal Resistance

There's resistance everywhere — inside batteries, in all the wires (although it's very small) and in the components themselves. I'm assuming the resistance of the wires is zero on the next two pages, but you can't always do this.

*Batteries have **Resistance***

Resistor circuit symbol:

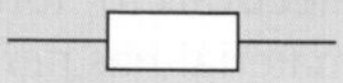

Resistance comes from **electrons colliding** with **atoms** and **losing energy** to other forms.

In a **battery**, **chemical energy** is used to make **electrons move**. As they move, they collide with atoms inside the battery — so batteries **must** have resistance. This is called **internal resistance**.

Internal resistance is what makes **batteries** and **cells warm up** when they're used.

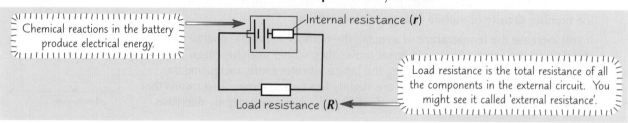

Chemical reactions in the battery produce electrical energy.

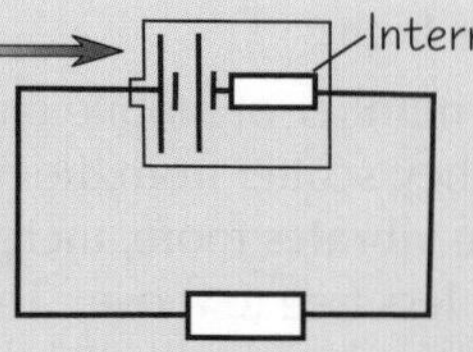

Load resistance is the total resistance of all the components in the external circuit. You might see it called 'external resistance'.

1) The amount of **electrical energy** the battery produces for each **coulomb** of charge is called its **electromotive force** or **e.m.f.** (ε). Be careful — e.m.f. **isn't** actually a force. It's measured in **volts**.
2) The **potential difference** across the **load resistance** (***R***) is the **energy transferred** when **one coulomb** of charge flows through the **load resistance**. This potential difference is called the **terminal p.d.** (***V***).
3) If there was **no internal resistance**, the **terminal p.d**. would be the **same** as the **e.m.f.** However, in **real** power supplies, there's **always some energy lost** (as heat energy) overcoming the internal resistance.
4) The **energy wasted per coulomb** overcoming the internal resistance is called the **lost volts** (***v***).

Conservation of energy tells us:

energy per coulomb supplied by the source = **energy per coulomb transferred in load resistance** + **energy per coulomb wasted in internal resistance**

*There are Loads of **Calculations** with **E.m.f.** and **Internal Resistance***

Examiners can ask you to do **calculations** with **e.m.f.** and **internal resistance** in loads of **different** ways. You've got to be ready for whatever they throw at you.

$$\varepsilon = V + v \qquad \varepsilon = I(R + r)$$
$$V = \varepsilon - v \qquad V = \varepsilon - Ir$$

Learn these equations for the exam. Only this one will be on your formula sheet.

These are all basically the **same equation**, just written differently. If you're given enough information you can calculate the e.m.f. (ε), terminal p.d. (***V***), lost volts (***v***), current (***I***), load resistance (***R***) or internal resistance (***r***). Which equation you should use depends on what information you've got, and what you need to calculate.

*You Can Work Out the **E.m.f.** of **Multiple** Cells in **Series** or **Parallel***

For cells **in series** in a circuit, you can calculate the **total e.m.f.** of the cells by **adding** their individual e.m.f.s.

$$\varepsilon_{total} = \varepsilon_1 + \varepsilon_2 + \varepsilon_3 + ...$$

This makes sense if you think about it, because each charge goes through each of the cells and so gains e.m.f. (electrical energy) from each one.

This requires all your cells to be connected in the **same direction** — if one is connected in the opposite direction, you should **subtract** its e.m.f. rather than adding it.

See p.36 for all the rules for parallel and series circuits.

For identical cells **in parallel** in a circuit, the **total e.m.f.** of the combination of cells is the **same size** as the e.m.f. of each of the individual cells.

$$\varepsilon_{total} = \varepsilon_1 = \varepsilon_2 = \varepsilon_3 + ...$$

This is because the current will split equally between identical cells. The charge only gains e.m.f. from the cells it travels through — so the overall e.m.f. in the circuit doesn't increase.

E.m.f. and Internal Resistance

Investigate **Internal Resistance** and **E.m.f.** With This **Circuit**

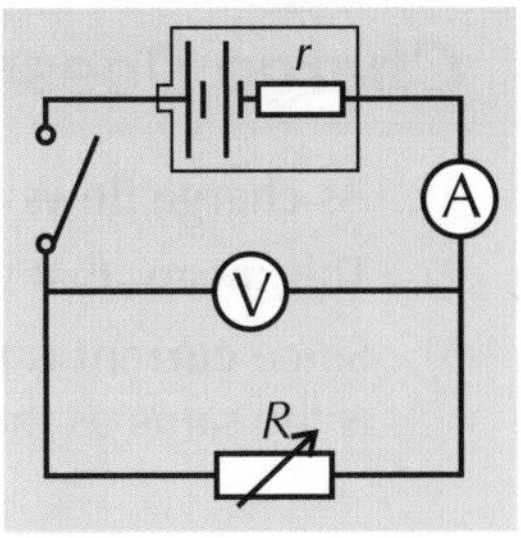

1) **Vary** the **current** in the circuit by changing the value of the **load resistance** (***R***) using the variable resistor. **Measure** the **p.d.** (*V*) for several different values of **current** (***I***). Include a **switch** in your circuit to **turn off** the current whenever possible to **reduce** the effect of **heating** in the wires on the **resistance** of the circuit.
2) Record your data for *V* and *I* in a table, and **plot the results** in a graph of *V* against *I*.

To find the **e.m.f.** and **internal resistance** of the cell, start with the equation: $V = \varepsilon - Ir$

1) Rearrange to give $V = -rI + \varepsilon$
2) Since ε and r are constants, that's just the equation of a **straight line**:

Equation of a straight line: gradient $y = mx + c$ y-intercept

3) So the intercept on the vertical axis is ε.
4) And the gradient is $-r$.

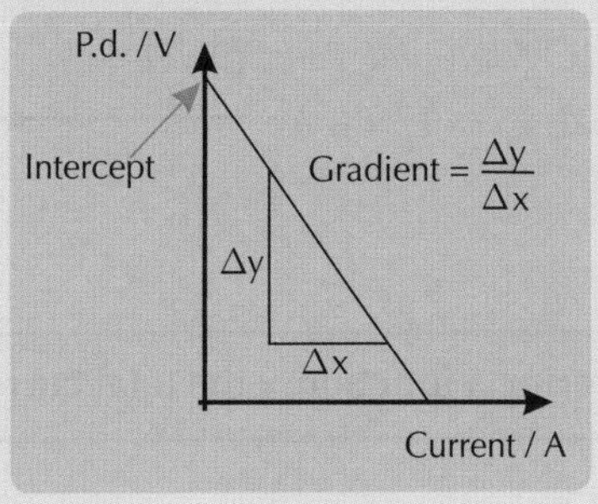

Think about how you'd reduce errors in this experiment. E.g. make sure the circuit doesn't change temperature so the resistance of the components doesn't change.

3) Choosing values for the **load resistance** is a **balancing act** — a **low load resistance** will give a **large current**, which will **reduce** the **percentage uncertainty** (see page 8) in the ammeter reading of the current. But **large currents** will cause significant **heating in the wires**, which will invalidate your results. So you need to **compromise**.
4) For this experiment (as for any experiment using voltmeters and ammeters), you can assume that the **voltmeter** has a very **high resistance**, and the resistance of the **ammeter** is very **low**.
5) Voltmeters have a **very high internal resistance**, so the **current** through them is so **low** you can usually assume it is **negligible** (zero). This means including the voltmeter in the circuit doesn't affect the **current** through the **variable resistor**.
6) The **ammeter** has a resistance that's so low it's negligible, and so the voltage across it is also negligible. This means including the ammeter in the circuit doesn't affect the **potential difference** across the **variable resistor**.
7) An **easier** way to **measure** the **e.m.f.** of a **power source** is by connecting a **voltmeter** across its **terminals**. As above, the **current** through the voltmeter is assumed to be **negligible** and so any **difference** between your measurements and the **e.m.f.** will be so small that the difference isn't usually significant.

Practice Questions

Q1 What is the effect of internal resistance on the potential difference supplied by a battery?

Q2 What is e.m.f.?

Q3 Write the equation to calculate the terminal p.d. of a power supply from e.m.f., current and internal resistance.

Q4 Describe an experiment you could carry out to determine the internal resistance of a battery.

Exam Questions

Q1 A battery with an internal resistance of 0.80 Ω and an e.m.f. of 24 V powers a dentist's drill with resistance 4.0 Ω.

a) Calculate the current in the circuit when the drill is connected to the power supply. [2 marks]

b) Calculate the potential difference wasted overcoming the internal resistance. [1 mark]

Q2 A bulb of resistance R is powered by two cells connected in series each with internal resistance r and e.m.f. ε. Which expression represents the current flowing through each cell? [1 mark]

A $\frac{\varepsilon}{R+r}$ B $\frac{\varepsilon}{2(R+2r)}$ C $\frac{2\varepsilon}{R+2r}$ D $\frac{\varepsilon}{R+2r}$

Overcome your internal resistance for revision...

Make sure you know all your e.m.f. and internal resistance equations, they're an exam fave. A good way to get them learnt is to keep trying to get from one equation to another... pretty dull, but it definitely helps.

Conservation of Energy & Charge in Circuits

There are some things in Physics that are so fundamental that you just have to accept them. Like the fact that there's loads of Maths in it. And that energy is conserved. And that Physicists get more homework than everyone else.

Charge Doesn't 'Leak Away' Anywhere — it's **Conserved**

1) As **charge flows** through a circuit, it **doesn't** get **used up** or **lost**.
2) This means that whatever **charge flows into** a junction will **flow out** again.
3) Since **current** is **rate of flow of charge**, it follows that whatever **current flows into** a junction is the same as the current **flowing out** of it.

Example: *CHARGE FLOWING IN 1 SECOND*

$Q_1 = 6\text{ C} \Rightarrow I_1 = 6\text{ A}$ → $Q_2 = 2\text{ C} \Rightarrow I_2 = 2\text{ A}$ and $Q_3 = 4\text{ C} \Rightarrow I_3 = 4\text{ A}$

$I_1 = I_2 + I_3$

Kirchhoff's first law says:

> The total **current entering a junction** = the total **current leaving it.**

Energy conservation is vital.

Energy *is* **Conserved** *too*

1) **Energy is conserved**. You already know that. In **electrical circuits**, **energy** is **transferred round** the circuit. Energy **transferred to** a charge is **e.m.f.**, and energy **transferred from** a charge is **potential difference**.
2) In a **closed loop**, these two quantities must be **equal** if energy is conserved (which it is).

Kirchhoff's second law says:

> The **total e.m.f.** around a **series circuit** = the **sum** of the **p.d.s** across each component.

(or $\varepsilon = \Sigma IR$ in symbols)

Exam Questions might get you to **Combine Resistors** *in* **Series** *and* **Parallel**

A **typical exam question** could give you a **circuit** with bits of information missing, leaving you to fill in the gaps. Not the most fun... but on the plus side you get to ignore any internal resistance stuff (unless the question tells you otherwise)... hurrah. You need to remember the **following rules**:

Series Circuits:

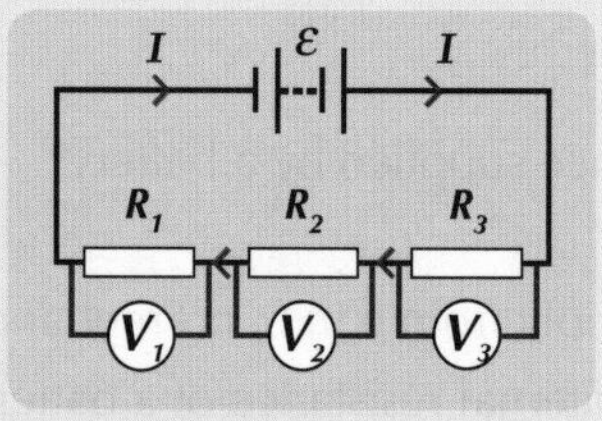

1) **same current** at **all points** of the circuit (since there are no junctions)
2) **e.m.f. split** between **components** (by Kirchhoff's 2nd law), so: $\varepsilon = V_1 + V_2 + V_3$
3) $V = IR$, so if I is constant: $IR_{total} = IR_1 + IR_2 + IR_3$
4) cancelling the Is gives:

$$R_{total} = R_1 + R_2 + R_3$$

5) As $R = \frac{1}{G}$, you can write this in terms of conductance: $\frac{1}{G_{total}} = \frac{1}{G_1} + \frac{1}{G_2} + \frac{1}{G_3}$

Parallel Circuits:

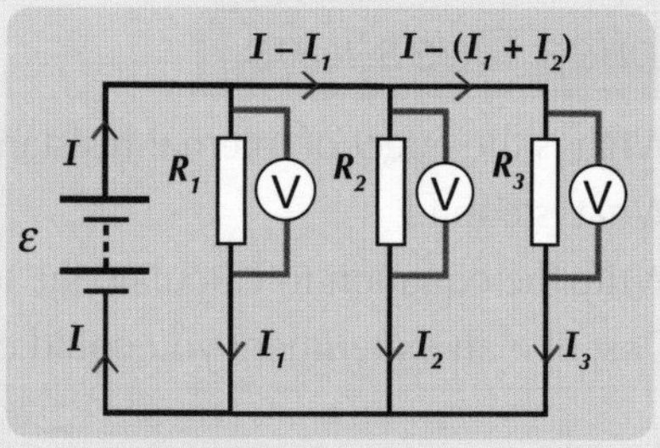

1) **current** is **split** at each **junction**, so: $I = I_1 + I_2 + I_3$
2) **same p.d.** across **all components** (three separate loops — within each loop the e.m.f. equals sum of individual p.d.s)
3) so, $V/R_{total} = V/R_1 + V/R_2 + V/R_3$
4) cancelling the Vs gives:

$$\frac{1}{R_{total}} = \frac{1}{R_1} + \frac{1}{R_2} + \frac{1}{R_3}$$

5) As $R = \frac{1}{G}$, you can write this in terms of conductance:

$$G_{total} = G_1 + G_2 + G_3$$

$\varepsilon = V$ in this case, as we're ignoring internal resistance.

Conservation of Energy & Charge in Circuits

Worked Exam Question

Example:

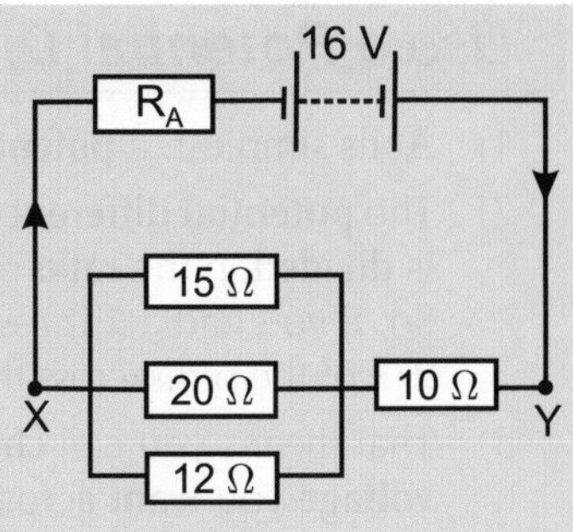

A battery of e.m.f. 16 V and negligible internal resistance is connected in a circuit as shown on the right.

a) Show that the group of resistors between X and Y could be replaced by a single resistor of resistance 15 Ω.

You can find the combined resistance of the 15 Ω, 20 Ω and 12 Ω resistors using:
$1/R = 1/R_1 + 1/R_2 + 1/R_3 = 1/15 + 1/20 + 1/12 = 1/5 \quad \Rightarrow R = 5\ \Omega$
So overall resistance between X and Y can be found by $R = R_1 + R_2 = 5 + 10 =$ **15 Ω**

b) If $R_A = 20\ \Omega$:
i) calculate the potential difference across R_A,

Careful — there are a few steps here. You need the p.d. across R_A, but you don't know the current through it. So start there: total resistance in circuit = 20 + 15 = 35 Ω,
so current through R_A can be found using $I = V_{total}/R_{total}$: $I = 16/35$ A
then you can use $V = IR_A$ to find the p.d. across R_A: $V = 16/35 \times 20 =$ **9 V (to 1 s.f.)**

ii) calculate the current in the 15 Ω resistor.

You know the current flowing into the group of three resistors and out of it, but not through the individual branches. But you know that their combined resistance is 5 Ω (from part a) so you can work out the p.d. across the group:
$V = IR = 16/35 \times 5 = 16/7$ V
The p.d. across the whole group is the same as the p.d. across each individual resistor, so you can use this to find the current through the 15 Ω resistor:
$I = V/R = (16/7) / 15 =$ **0.15 A (to 2 s.f.)**

Practice Questions

Q1 Write Kirchhoff's first and second laws.

Q2 State the formulas used to combine resistors in series and in parallel.

Q3 Find the current through and potential difference across each of two resistors, each with a conductance of 0.2 S, when they are placed in a circuit containing a 5 V battery, and are wired: a) in series, b) in parallel.

Exam Question

Q1 For the circuit on the right:

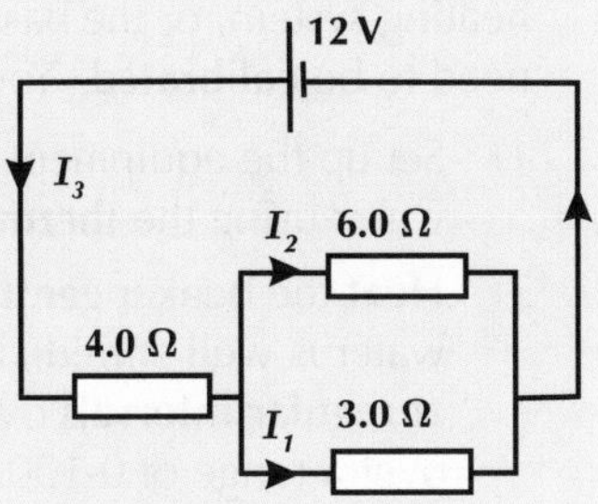

a) Calculate the total effective resistance of the three resistors in this combination. [2 marks]

b) Calculate the main current, I_3. [1 mark]

c) Calculate the potential difference across the 4.0 Ω resistor. [1 mark]

d) Calculate the potential difference across the parallel pair of resistors. [1 mark]

e) Using your answer from part d), calculate the currents I_1 and I_2. [2 marks]

This is a very purple page — needs a bit of yellow I think...

V = IR is the formula you'll use most often in these questions. Make sure you know whether you're using it on the overall circuit, or just one specific component. It's amazingly easy to get muddled up — you've been warned.

The Potential Divider

Potential dividers are used in light sensors (photoconductive sensors), displacement sensors, heat sensors and so much more. They can even let you crank up the volume when you're listening to a spot of Kylie on your stereo...

Use a **Potential Divider** to Get a **Fraction** of an **Input Voltage**

1) At its simplest, a **potential divider** is a circuit with a **voltage source** and a couple of **resistors** in series.
2) The **potential difference** of the voltage source (e.g. a power supply) is **divided** in the **ratio** of the **resistances**. As an equation: $\frac{V_1}{V_2} = \frac{R_1}{R_2}$
   So, if you had a **2 Ω** resistor and a **3 Ω** resistor, you'd get **2/5** of the p.d. across the **2 Ω** resistor and **3/5** across the **3 Ω**.
3) That means you can **choose** the **resistances** to get the **voltage** you **want** across one of them.

This rearranges to give $V_1/R_1 = V_2/R_2$. As $I = V/R$ this just means the current is the same through both resistors, which you know from page 36.

In the circuit shown, R_2 has $\frac{R_2}{R_1 + R_2}$ of the total resistance. So:

$$V_{out} = \frac{R_2}{R_1 + R_2} V_{in}$$

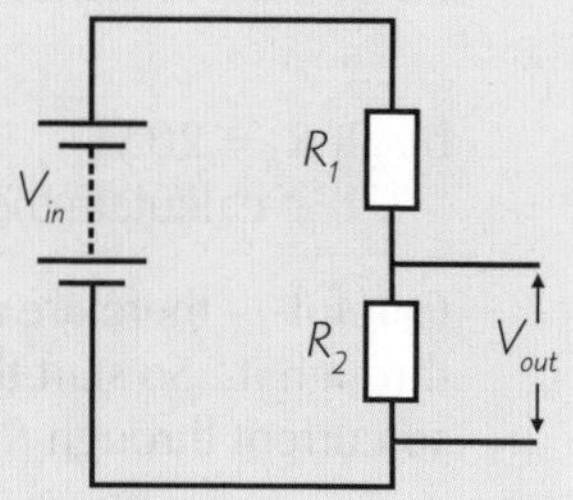

E.g. if V_{in} = 9 V and you want V_{out} to be 6 V, then you need: $\frac{R_2}{R_1 + R_2} = \frac{6}{9}$, which gives $R_2 = 2R_1$. So you could have, say, ***R*₁ = 100 Ω, *R*₂ = 200 Ω**

4) This circuit can be used for **calibrating voltmeters**, which have a **very high resistance**.
5) If you put something with a **relatively low resistance** across R_2 though, you start to run into **problems**. You've **effectively** got **two resistors** in **parallel**, which will **always** have a **total** resistance **less** than R_2. That means that V_{out} will be **less** than you've calculated, and will depend on what's connected across R_2. Hrrumph.

Add an **LDR** or **Thermistor** for a **Light** or **Temperature Sensor**

1) Potential dividers can be made into sensors by including components whose resistance changes with external factors, for example light dependent resistors and thermistors (p.31). This means **V_{out} varies** with light or heat, so you can make a potential divider that works as a light or heat **sensor**.
2) The **circuit** needs to be **calibrated** so you know how the voltage across the component and V_{out} varies as external conditions change. E.g. knowing the voltage across a thermistor at a given temperature.
3) You can use an experiment like the one below to plot a calibration curve of voltage against an external factor:

Example: Calibration of an electronic thermometer.

Here's a potential divider using an **NTC thermistor**.

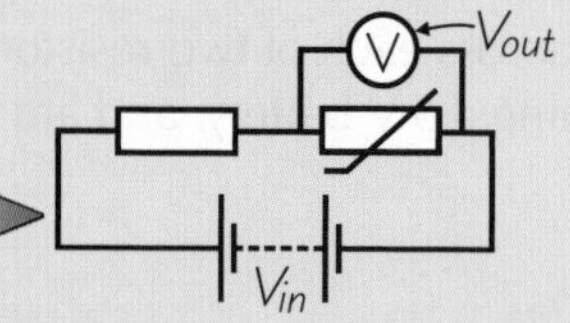

Think about safety before you start — keep the rest of the circuit as far away from the bunsen burner and the water bath as possible.

This kind of circuit could form part of the circuit for a **thermostat** in a central heating system, or the basis of an **electronic thermometer**. First, the circuit would need to be **calibrated**. You can do this using the equipment shown on the right:

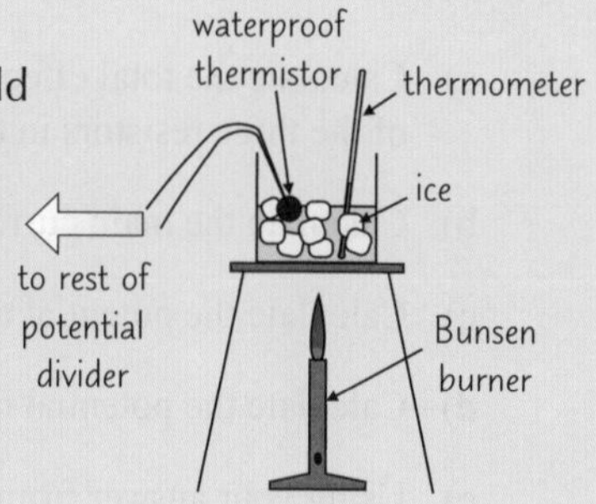

1) Set up the equipment as shown, then measure the **temperature** of the water using the **thermometer**, and record the **voltage** across the resistor.
2) **Heat** the beaker **gently** using the Bunsen burner (make sure the water is well-stirred), and record the temperature and the voltage at **regular intervals** over a **suitable range** (e.g. at 5 °C intervals over a range of 0-100 °C).
3) Plot a **graph** of temperature against voltage from your results. This graph is the thermistor's **calibration curve**. You can use it to find the temperature of the thermistor from the voltage across it, without needing the thermometer — the thermistor and the calibration curve together are effectively **another thermometer**.

Pick your fixed resistor carefully — if its resistance is too high, V_{out} won't vary enough with temperature, and if it's too low, V_{out} might vary over a bigger range than your voltmeter can handle.

The Potential Divider

A Potentiometer Uses a Variable Resistor to Give a Variable Voltage

1) A **potentiometer** has a **variable resistor** replacing R_1 and R_2 of the potential divider, but it uses the **same idea** (it's even sometimes **called** a potential divider just to confuse things).
2) You move a **slider** or turn a knob to **adjust** the **relative sizes** of R_1 and R_2. That way you can vary V_{out} from 0 V up to the input voltage, V_{in}.
3) This is dead handy when you want to be able to **change** a **voltage continuously**, like in the **volume control** of a stereo.

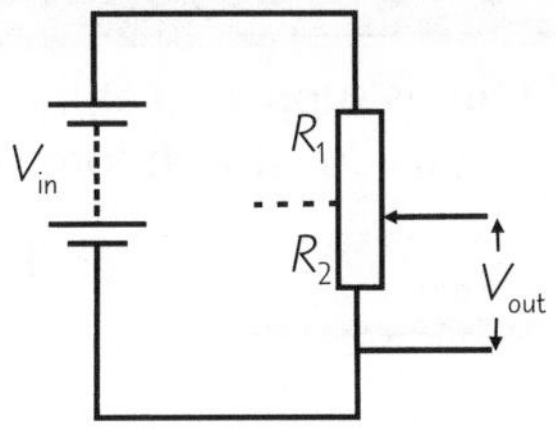

Here, V_{in} is replaced by the input signal (e.g. from a CD player) and V_{out} is the output to the amplifier and loudspeaker.

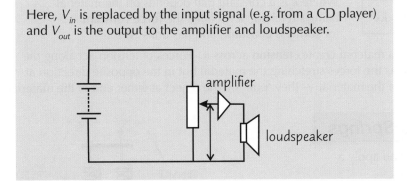

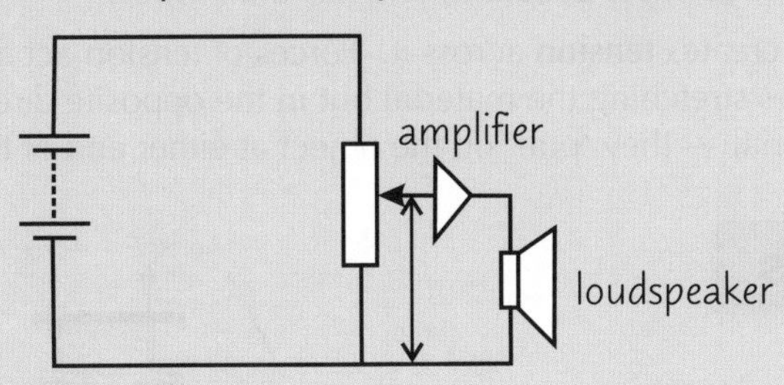

I've often wished bagpipes had a volume control. Or just an off switch.

Practice Questions

Q1 Write down the equation linking output p.d., input p.d., and component resistance for a potential divider circuit.

Q2 Draw the circuit diagram for a potential divider that works as a light sensor, where the output p.d. increases when the light level increases.

Q3 Explain how you could calibrate a circuit containing a thermistor.

Q4 What is a potentiometer?

Exam Questions

Q1 Two resistors, A and B, are connected in series as shown in the circuit diagram. Resistor A has a resistance of 35 Ω and resistor B has a resistance of 45 Ω.

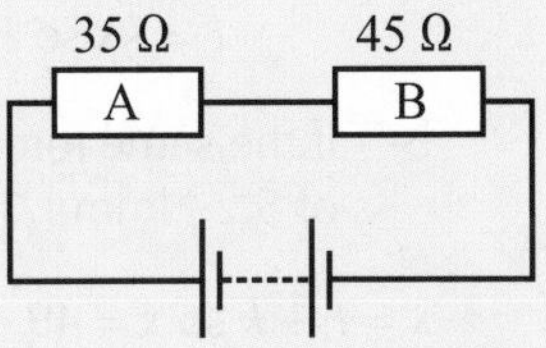

a) Given that the potential difference across resistor B is 6.75 V, calculate the potential difference across resistor A. [1 mark]

b) Calculate the input p.d. supplied by the battery. [1 mark]

c) Resistor A is removed, and replaced with a 75 Ω resistor. Calculate the new potential difference across resistor B. [1 mark]

Q2 Look at the circuit on the right.

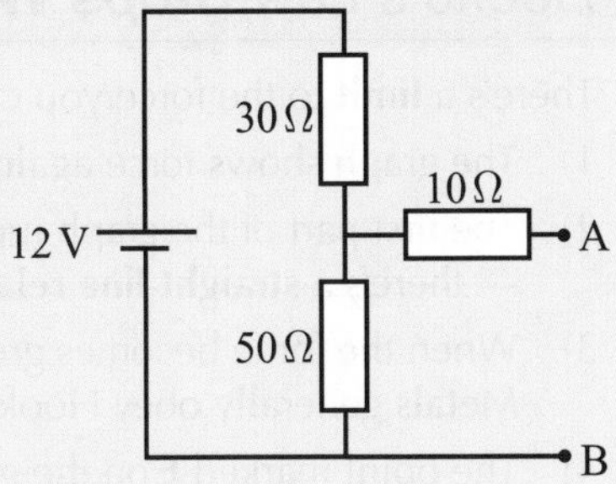

a) Calculate the p.d. between A and B as shown by a high resistance voltmeter placed between the two points. [1 mark]

b) A 40 Ω resistor is now placed between points A and B. Calculate the p.d. across AB and the current flowing through the 40 Ω resistor. [4 marks]

OI...YOU... [bang bang bang]... turn that potentiometer down...

Potentiometers come up a lot in experiments to do with electricity, so like them or not, you'd better get used to them. I can't stand the things myself, but then lab and me don't mix — it's all far too technical I'm afraid.

Hooke's Law

Hooke's law applies to all materials, but only up to a point...

Hooke's Law Says that Extension is Proportional to Force

If a **metal wire** is supported at the top and then a weight attached to the bottom, it **stretches**. The weight pulls down with force ***F***, producing an equal and opposite force at the support.

The material will only deform (stretch, bend, twist etc.) if there's a pair of opposite forces acting on it.

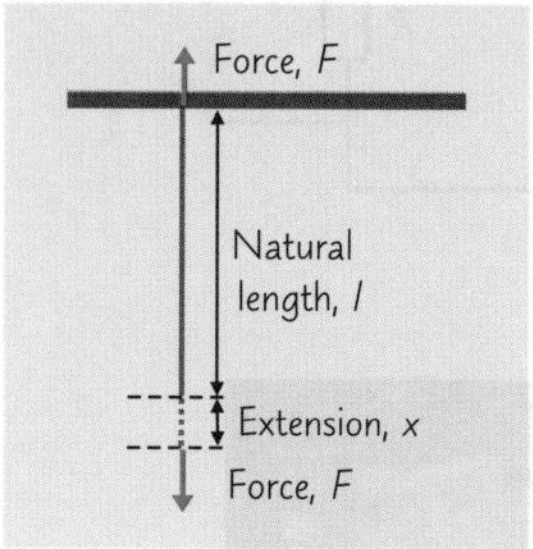

1) **Robert Hooke** discovered in the 17th century that the extension of a stretched wire, ***x***, is **proportional** to the load or force, ***F***. This relationship is now called **Hooke's law**.
2) Hooke's law can be written:

$$F = kx$$

Where ***k*** is a constant that depends on the material being stretched. ***k*** is called the **force constant** (or **stiffness constant**) and has units Nm^{-1}.

3) Stretching a material creates **tension** across it. Forces of tension act along the same line as the forces stretching the material but in the opposite direction at each end of the material — they 'pull' on the object at either end of the material.

Hooke's Law Also Applies to Springs

A metal spring also changes length when you apply a **pair of opposite forces**.

1) The **extension** of a spring is **proportional** to the **force** applied — so Hooke's law applies. If the forces are **compressive**, the spring is **squashed** and the extension is negative.
2) For springs, ***k*** in the formula ***F = kx*** can also be called the **spring stiffness** or **spring constant**.

Hooke's law works just as well for **compressive** forces as **tensile** forces. For a spring, ***k*** has the **same value** whether the forces are tensile or compressive (that's not true for all materials).

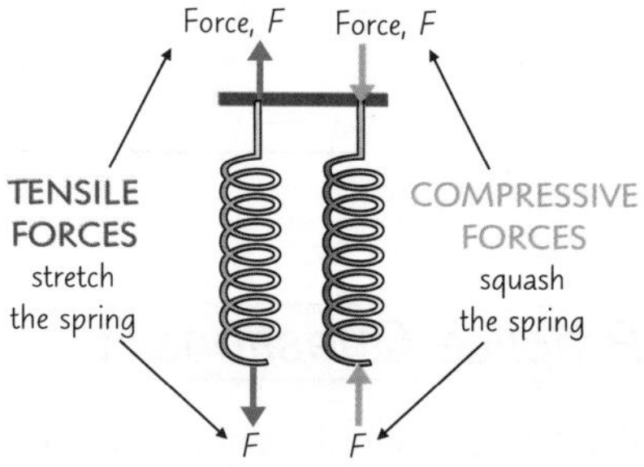

Tensile forces create tension in a stretched spring. Compressive forces create compression in a squashed spring. Tensile or compressive forces in the spring act in the opposite direction to the tensile or compressive forces stretching or squashing it.

3) **Hooke's Law** doesn't just apply to metal **springs** and **wires** — all **other materials** obey it up to a point.

Example: a) A force is applied to a spring, causing the spring to be stretched by 5.0 mm. The stiffness constant of the spring is 9800 Nm^{-1}. Calculate the magnitude of the applied force.

$F = kx$ so $F = 9800 \times 0.005 =$ **49 N**

b) If the same force was applied to a spring with a stiffness constant of 5.2 Nmm^{-1}, how much would the spring extend by?

Convert the stiffness constant into more appropriate units first: $5.2 \text{ Nmm}^{-1} = 5200 \text{ Nm}^{-1}$

$x = F \div k$ so $x = 49 \div 5200 = 0.00942... = 0.0094$ m = **9.4 mm (to 2 s.f.)**

Hooke's Law Stops Working when the Load is Great Enough

There's a **limit** to the force you can apply for Hooke's law to stay true.

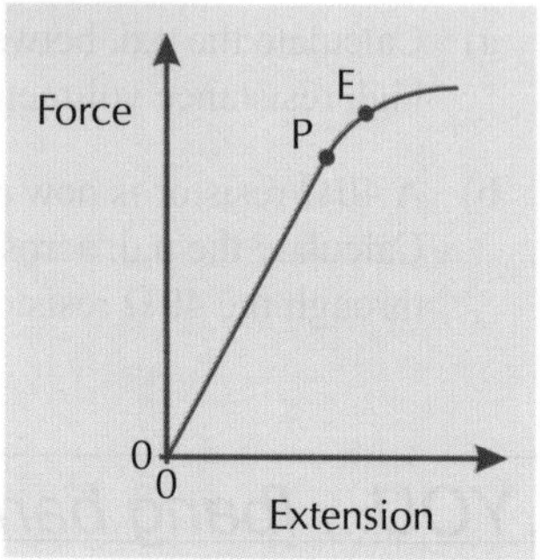

1) The graph shows force against extension for a **typical metal wire** or **spring**.
2) The first part of the graph (up to point P) shows Hooke's law being obeyed — there's a **straight-line relationship** between **force** and **extension**.
3) When the force becomes great enough, the graph starts to **curve**. **Metals** generally obey Hooke's law up to the **limit of proportionality**, **P**.
4) The point marked **E** on the graph is called the **elastic limit**. If you exceed the elastic limit, the material will be **permanently stretched**. When all the force is removed, the material will be **longer** than at the start.
5) Beyond the elastic limit, the material will **stretch further** for a given force.
6) Be careful — there are some materials, like **rubber**, that only obey Hooke's law for **really small** extensions.

Hooke's Law

A Stretch can be **Elastic** or **Plastic**

A material will show elastic deformation **up to** its **elastic limit**, and plastic deformation **beyond** it.
If a **deformation** is **elastic**, the material returns to its **original shape** once the forces are removed.

1) When the material is put under **tension**, the **atoms** of the material are **pulled apart** from one another.
2) Atoms can **move** slightly relative to their **equilibrium positions**, without changing position in the material.
3) Once the **load** is **removed**, the atoms **return** to their **equilibrium** distance apart.

An 'elastic material' is a material that deforms elastically, a 'plastic material' is one that deforms plastically.

If a deformation is **plastic**, the material is **permanently stretched**.

1) Some atoms in the material move position relative to one another.
2) When the load is removed, the **atoms don't return** to their original positions.

You can Investigate **Extension** by Stretching an Object

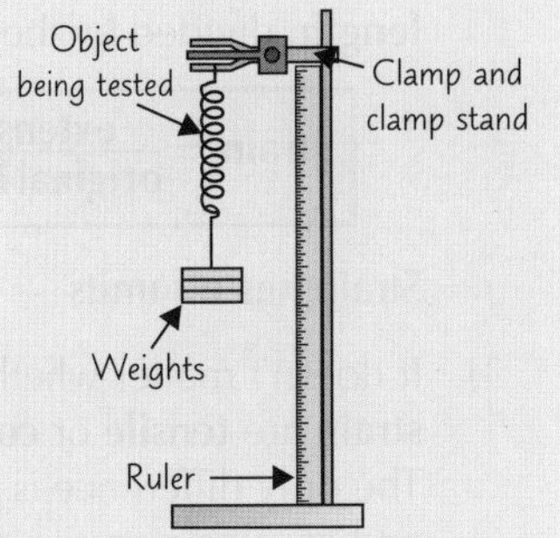

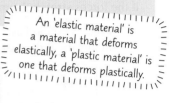

1) Set up the experiment shown in the diagram. Support the object being tested at the top (e.g. with a clamp) and measure its original length with a ruler.
2) Add masses one at a time to the bottom of the object.
3) After each weight is added, measure the new length of the object, then **calculate the extension**:

extension = new length – original length

4) Plot a graph of **force** (weight) against **extension** for your results. Where the line of best fit is **straight**, then the object obeys Hooke's law and the gradient = $\boldsymbol{k}$ (as $F = kx$). If you've loaded the object beyond its limit of proportionality, the graph will start to curve.
5) Make sure you carry out the experiment **safely**. You should be **standing up** so you can get out of the way quickly if the weights fall, and wearing **safety goggles** to protect your eyes in case the object snaps.

Practice Questions

Q1 State Hooke's law and explain what is meant by the elastic limit of a material.
Q2 Define tension and compression in terms of the forces acting on a spring.
Q3 From studying the force-extension graph for a material as it is loaded and unloaded, how can you tell:
a) if Hooke's law is being obeyed, b) if the elastic limit has been reached?
Q4 What is meant by elastic and plastic deformation of a material?
Q5 Describe how you could investigate the effect of force on extension for a length of wire.

Exam Questions

Q1 A metal guitar string stretches 4.0 mm when a 10 N force is applied.

a) Calculate the force constant for the string, and calculate how far the string will stretch when a 15 N force is applied. [2 marks]

b) The string is then stretched beyond its elastic limit, without snapping. Describe the effect this will have on the string. [1 mark]

Q2 A rubber band is 6.0 cm long. When it is loaded with 2.5 N, its length increases to 10.4 cm. Increasing the load to 5.0 N further increases the length to 16.2 cm. State whether the rubber band will obey Hooke's law when the force on it is 5.0 N. Explain your answer. [2 marks]

Sod's Law — if you don't learn it, it'll be in the exam...

Three things you didn't know about Robert Hooke — he was the first person to use the word 'cell' (as in biology, not prisons), he helped Christopher Wren with his designs for St. Paul's Cathedral and no-one's sure what he looked like. I'd like to think that if I did all that stuff, then someone would at least remember what I looked like — poor old Hooke.

Stress, Strain and Elastic Energy

How much a material stretches for a particular applied force depends on its dimensions.
If you want to compare one material to another, you need to use stress and strain instead.
A stress-strain graph is the same for any sample of a particular material — the size of the sample doesn't matter.

A Stress Causes a Strain

As you saw on page 40, a material subjected to a pair of **opposite forces** might **deform**, i.e. **change shape**. If the forces **stretch** the material, they're **tensile**. If the forces **squash** the material, they're **compressive**.

1) **Stress** is defined as the **tension** (the **force applied**) divided by the **cross-sectional area**:

$$\text{stress} = \frac{\text{tension}}{\text{cross-sectional area}}$$

The **units** of stress are **Nm^{-2}** or pascals, **Pa**.

2) **Strain** is defined as the **extension**, i.e. the **change in length**, divided by the **original length** of the material:

$$\text{strain} = \frac{\text{extension}}{\text{original length}}$$

Strain has **no units** — it's given as a **number** or **percentage**.

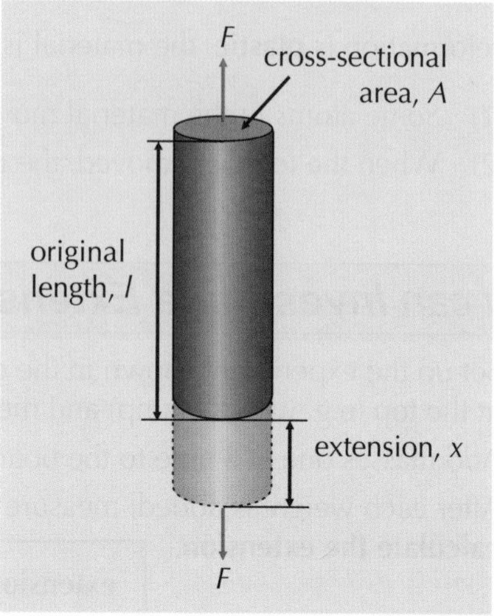

3) It doesn't matter whether the forces producing the **stress** and **strain** are **tensile** or **compressive** — the **same equations** apply. The only difference is that you tend to think of **tensile** forces as **positive**, and **compressive** forces as **negative**, and causing negative extension.

A Stress Big Enough to Break a Material is Called the Fracture Stress

As a greater and greater tensile **force** is applied to a material, the **stress** on it **increases**.

1) The effect of the **stress** is to start to **pull** the **atoms apart** from one another.
2) Eventually the stress becomes **so great** that atoms **separate completely**, and the **material fractures** (breaks). This is shown by point **B** on the graph. The stress at which this occurs is called the **fracture stress**.
3) The point marked **UTS** on the graph is called the **ultimate tensile strength**. This is the **maximum stress** that the material can withstand before breaking.
4) **Engineers** have to consider the **UTS** and **fracture stress** of materials when designing a **structure**.

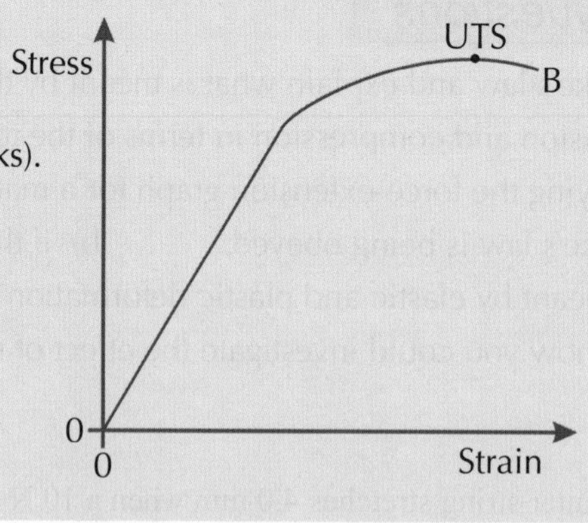

Elastic Strain Energy is the Energy Stored in a Stretched Material

When a material is **stretched** or **compressed**, **work** is done in **deforming** the material.

1) On a **graph of force against extension**, the **work done** is given by the **area under the graph**.
2) **Before the elastic limit, all** the **work done** in stretching or compressing the material is **stored** as **energy** in the material.
3) This stored energy is called **elastic strain energy**. There's more about how to calculate elastic strain energy on the next page.

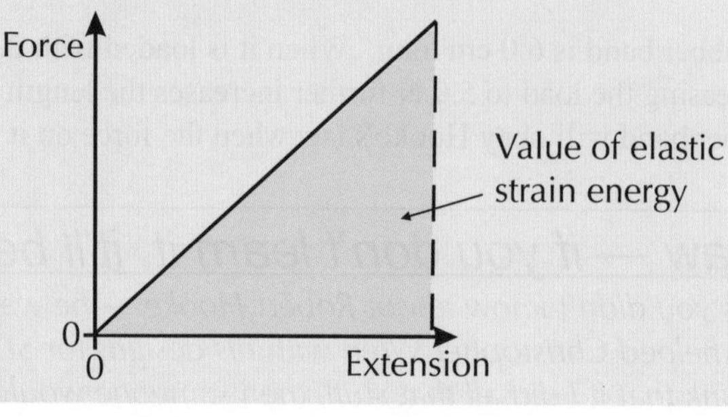

Stress, Strain and Elastic Energy

You can Calculate the *Energy Stored* in an *Elastic Material*

Provided a material obeys Hooke's law, the **strain energy** stored inside it can be **calculated** quite easily.

1) The **work done** on an elastic material in stretching it is **equal** to the **energy stored** in the material as **elastic strain energy**.
2) **Work done** equals **force × displacement**.
3) However, the **force** on the material **isn't constant**. It rises from zero up to force F. To calculate the **work done**, use the average force between zero and F, i.e. $\frac{1}{2}F$.

work done = $\frac{1}{2}Fx$

This is the triangular area under the force-extension graph — see previous page.

4) Then the **elastic strain energy**, E, is: $E = \frac{1}{2}Fx$
5) Because Hooke's law is being obeyed, $F = kx$, which means F can be replaced in the equation to give:

$$E = \frac{1}{2}kx^2$$

6) If the material is stretched beyond the **elastic limit**, some work is done separating atoms. This energy will **not be stored** as elastic strain energy, and so isn't released when the force is removed.

Practice Questions

Q1 Write a definition for the stress of a material being stretched by applying a load.

Q2 Explain what is meant by the strain on a material.

Q3 What is meant by the fracture stress of a material?

Q4 How can the work done in stretching a material be found from the force against extension graph of the material?

Q5 The work done is usually calculated as force multiplied by displacement. Explain why the work done in stretching a wire is $\frac{1}{2}Fx$.

Exam Questions

Q1 A steel wire is 2.00 m long. When a 300 N force is applied to the wire, it stretches 4.0 mm. The wire has a circular cross-section with a diameter of 1.0 mm.

a) Calculate the strain of the wire. [1 mark]

b) Calculate the stress on the wire. [2 marks]

Q2 A copper wire (which obeys Hooke's law) is stretched by 3.0 mm when a force of 50 N is applied.

a) Calculate the force constant for this wire in Nm^{-1}. [1 mark]

b) Calculate the value of the elastic strain energy in the stretched wire. [1 mark]

Q3 A pinball machine contains a spring which is used to fire a small, 12.0 g metal ball to start the game. The spring has a stiffness constant of 40.8 Nm^{-1}. It is compressed by 5.00 cm and then released to fire the ball.

Calculate the maximum possible speed of the ball. [3 marks]

UTS a laugh a minute, this stuff...

Bet you thought I was going to make a joke about this being stressful then, didn't you? There's a pile of equations to learn on these pages, as well a couple of graphs to drill into your brain, and they all might come up in the exam, so you need to learn the lot I'm afraid. Plus, it'll come in handy if you ever want to, I dunno, build a skyscraper or something.

The Young Modulus

Busy chap, Thomas Young. He did this work on tensile stress as something of a sideline. Light was his main thing. He proved that light behaved like a wave, explained how we see in colour and worked out what causes astigmatism.

The **Young Modulus** is Stress ÷ Strain

When you apply a **load** to stretch a material, it experiences a **stress** and a **strain**.

1) Up to a point called the **limit of proportionality** (see p.40), the stress and strain of a material are proportional to each other.
2) So below this limit, for a particular material, stress divided by strain is a constant. This constant is called the **Young modulus, *E***.

$$\textbf{Young modulus} = E = \frac{\textbf{stress}}{\textbf{strain}}$$

The Young Modulus is a measurement of stiffness (p.46).

3) The **units** of the Young modulus are the same as stress ($\mathbf{Nm^{-2}}$ or pascals), since strain has no units.
4) The Young modulus is used by **engineers** to make sure their materials can withstand sufficient forces.

To **Find** the Young Modulus, You Need a **Very Long Wire**

This is the experiment you're most likely to do in class:

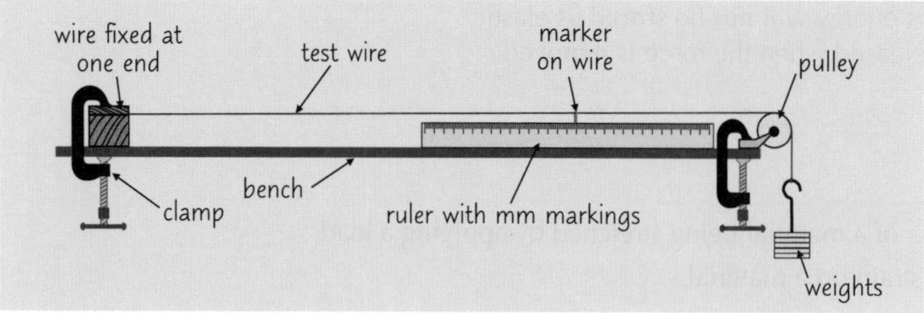

"Okay, found one. Now what?"

If you're doing this experiment, make sure you're standing up so you can get out of the way quickly if the weights fall. And wear safety goggles — if the wire snaps, it could get very messy...

1) The test wire should be thin, and as long as possible. The **longer and thinner** the wire, the more it **extends** for the same force. This reduces the **uncertainty** (p.12) in your measurements.
2) First you need to find the **cross-sectional area** of the wire. Use a **micrometer** to measure the **diameter** of the wire **three times** in different places along the wire, before taking an **average** of your results. By assuming that the cross-section is **circular**, you can use the formula for the area of a circle: → **area of a circle = πr^2**
3) **Clamp** the wire to the bench (as shown in the diagram above) so you can hang **weights** off one end of it. Start with the **smallest weight** necessary to **straighten** the wire. (**Don't** include this weight in your final calculations.)
4) Measure the **distance** between the **fixed end of the wire** and the **marker** — this is your unstretched length.
5) Then if you increase the weight, the **wire stretches** and the **marker moves**.
6) **Increase** the **weight** in steps (e.g. 1 N intervals), recording the marker reading each time — the **extension** is the **difference** between this reading and the **unstretched length**. Use a **mass meter** or a set of **digital scales** to accurately find the weight you add at each step.
7) You can use your results from this experiment to calculate the **stress** and **strain** on the wire and plot a stress-strain graph (see next page).

To reduce random errors you should use a thin marker on the wire, and always look from directly above the marker and ruler when measuring the extension.

As you unload the wire, re-measure the extension for each weight to make sure you haven't gone past the wire's elastic limit.

(The other standard way of measuring the Young modulus in the lab is using **Searle's apparatus**. This is a bit more accurate, but it's harder to do and the equipment's more complicated.)

You can also use this apparatus to find the **fracture stress** of a material. Do a preliminary experiment where you add weights to the wire to **roughly** find the force required to **break** the wire. **Repeat** the experiment with an **identical wire**, but this time add weights in small increments as the force applied approaches the force that previously broke the wire. This will help you find the breaking force (and fracture stress) more **accurately**. Then all you need to do is calculate the fracture stress from the breaking force.

The Young Modulus

Plot a **Stress-Strain Graph** of Your Results to Find **E**

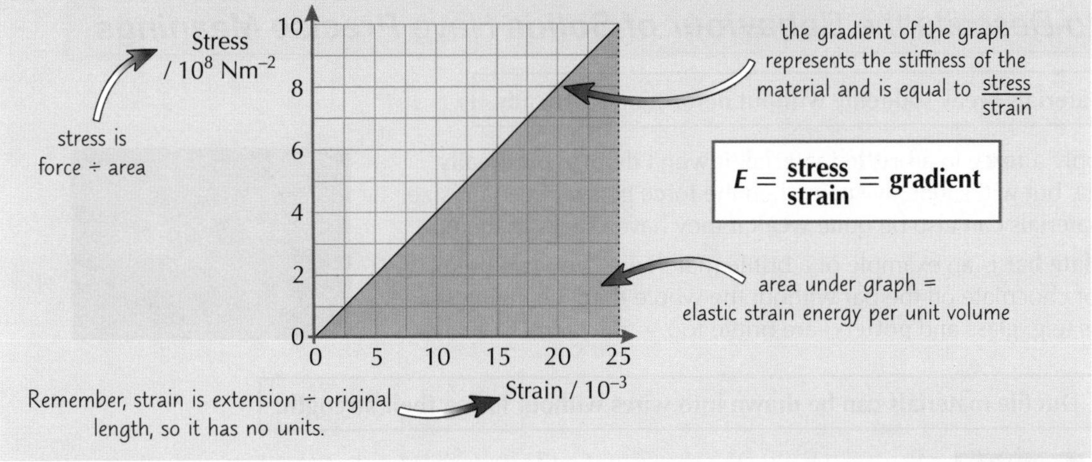
Stress / 10^8 Nm^{-2}
10
8
6
4
2
0
stress is force ÷ area
0 5 10 15 20 25
Strain / 10^{-3}
Remember, strain is extension ÷ original length, so it has no units.
the gradient of the graph represents the stiffness of the material and is equal to $\frac{\text{stress}}{\text{strain}}$
$E = \frac{\textbf{stress}}{\textbf{strain}} = \textbf{gradient}$
area under graph = elastic strain energy per unit volume

1) The **gradient** of the graph gives the Young modulus, E.
2) The **area under the graph** gives the **elastic strain energy** (or energy stored) **per unit volume** (i.e. the energy stored per 1 m^3 of wire).

Example: The stress-strain graph above is for a thin metal wire. Find the Young modulus of the wire from the graph.

***E* = stress ÷ strain = gradient**

The gradient of the graph = $\frac{\Delta\text{stress}}{\Delta\text{strain}} = \frac{10 \times 10^8}{25 \times 10^{-3}}$

$= \mathbf{4 \times 10^{10}\ Nm^{-2}}$

Practice Questions

Q1 Define the Young modulus for a material.

Q2 What are the units of the Young modulus?

Q3 Describe an experiment to find the Young modulus of a test wire. Explain why a thin test wire is used.

Q4 How could you adapt the experiment to find the fracture stress of a wire?

Q5 How would you calculate the stiffness of a material from a stress-strain graph for that material?

Exam Questions

Q1 The Young modulus for copper is 1.3×10^{11} Nm^{-2}.

a) The stress on a copper wire is 2.6×10^8 Nm^{-2}. Calculate the strain of the wire. [2 marks]

b) The load applied to the copper wire is 100 N. Calculate the average cross-sectional area of the wire. [1 mark]

Q2 A steel wire is stretched elastically. For a load of 80 N, the wire extends by 3.6 mm. The original length of the wire is 2.50 m and its average diameter is 0.6 mm. Calculate the value of the Young modulus for steel. [5 marks]

Q3 An aluminium wire is elastically stretched. The graph of stress against strain is plotted and shown on the right. Estimate the Young modulus for aluminium. [1 mark]

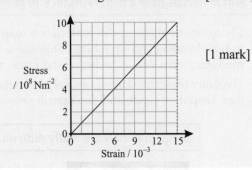

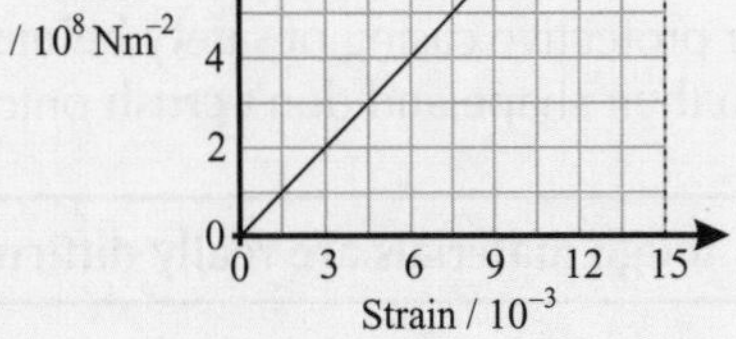
10
8
Stress / 10^8 Nm^{-2}
6
4
2
0
0 3 6 9 12 15
Strain / 10^{-3}

Learn that experiment — it's important...

Getting back to the good Dr Young... As if ground-breaking work in light, the physics of vision and materials science wasn't enough, he was also a well-respected physician, a linguist and an Egyptologist. He was one of the first to try to decipher the Rosetta stone (he didn't get it right, but nobody's perfect). Makes you feel kind of inferior, doesn't it?

Mechanical Properties of Solids

You wouldn't try doing surgery with scalpels made out of marshmallows, just as you wouldn't make a glass crash mat. It's important to know the mechanical properties of materials so you can select the best ones to suit your needs.

Terms to Describe the **Behaviour of Solids** Have **Precise Meanings**

Brittle materials break suddenly without deforming plastically.

If you apply a **force** to a **brittle material**, it won't **deform plastically** (see p.41), but will suddenly **snap** when the force gets to a certain size. Brittle materials can also be quite **weak** if they have **cracks** in them.

A **chocolate bar** is an example of a brittle material — you can break chunks of chocolate off the bar without the whole thing changing shape. **Ceramics** (e.g. **glass** and **pottery**) are brittle too — they tend to shatter.

Ductile materials can be drawn into wires without losing their strength.

You can change the **shape** of **ductile materials** by drawing them into **wires** or other shapes. The important thing is that they **keep their strength** when they're deformed like this.

Copper is ductile, and with its high electrical conductivity this means that it's ideal for **electric wires**. A **ductile material** has been used for the cables supporting the **ski lift** in the photo — it's been drawn into long wires, but kept its strength.

Strong materials can withstand high stresses without deforming or breaking.

Strength is a measure of how much a material can **resist** being **deformed** (bent, stretched, fractured etc.) by a force without breaking. This can be resisting a **pulling** force (tensile strength) or a **squeezing** force (compressive strength).

Steel beams used to create structures like **bridges** are very strong — they withstand the force caused by lots of vehicles going over them without bending or breaking.

Hard materials are very resistant to cutting, indentation and abrasion.

If you try to cut, dent or scratch a hard material, you'll probably have very little effect. Their structure means **hard materials** are **resistant** to **cutting**, **indentation** (becoming dented) and **abrasion** (scratching).

Cutting tools (e.g. chisels) need to be harder than the stuff they're cutting — they're often made from **hardened steel**. **Diamond** is just about the hardest material there is — it's often used to reinforce the tips of drill bits.

Stiff materials have a high resistance to bending and stretching.

Changing the shape of **stiff materials** is really difficult as they are **resistant** to both **bending** and **stretching**. Stiffness is measured by the **Young modulus** (see p.44) — the higher the value, the stiffer the material.

The outer protective casing of **safety helmets** and **safety boots** need to be very stiff so that they keep their shape and don't **crush** onto your body when something impacts on them.

Tough materials are really difficult to break.

Toughness is a measure of the **energy** a material can **absorb** before it breaks. Really **tough materials** can absorb a lot of energy so are very **difficult** to **break**.

Some **polymers**, including certain types of **polythene**, are very tough.

The hull of this **kayak** is made of a tough material so it won't break on rocks.

Mechanical Properties of Solids

Stress-Strain *Graphs for* ***Ductile*** *Materials* ***Curve***

It turns out that because different solids have different properties, their stress-strain graphs look different too. The diagram shows a **stress-strain graph** for a typical **ductile** material — e.g. a copper wire.

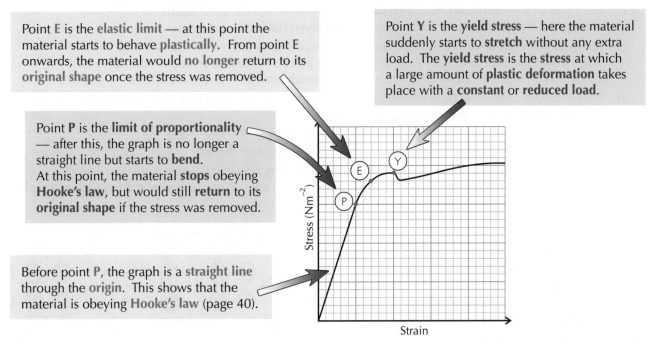

Point **E** is the **elastic limit** — at this point the material starts to behave **plastically**. From point E onwards, the material would **no longer** return to its **original shape** once the stress was removed.

Point **Y** is the **yield stress** — here the material suddenly starts to **stretch** without any extra load. The **yield stress** is the **stress** at which a large amount of **plastic deformation** takes place with a **constant** or **reduced load.**

Point **P** is the **limit of proportionality** — after this, the graph is no longer a straight line but starts to **bend.** At this point, the material **stops** obeying **Hooke's law**, but would still **return** to its **original shape** if the stress was removed.

Before point **P**, the graph is a **straight line** through the **origin**. This shows that the material is obeying **Hooke's law** (page 40).

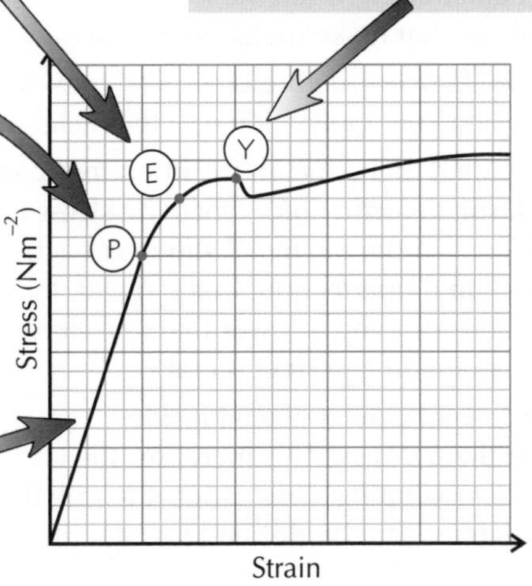

Brittle materials (e.g. glass, perspex, cast iron, chocolate chip cookies... mmmm... cookies) **don't** tend to behave plastically. They **fracture** before they reach the elastic limit.

Practice Questions

Q1 Write short definitions of the following terms: ductile, stiff, tough, strong.

Q2 Give examples of materials which are: brittle, strong, hard and ductile.

Q3 Why does a kayak need to be made out of tough material?

Q4 What properties of a material are tested by finding the fracture stress needed to break a material?

Q5 What is the difference between the limit of proportionality and the elastic limit?

Q6 Define the yield stress of a material.

Q7 Sketch a stress-strain graph of a typical ductile material.

Exam Questions

Q1 A material is being chosen to create support beams for a small bridge. Choose a suitable material for this purpose from the table and explain your choice.

Material	Strength (MPa)	Toughness (kJm^{-2})
A	4	10
B	30	3
C	2000	1
D	20	0.005

[3 marks]

Q2 Riding helmets are designed to protect a rider's head from injury should they fall off their horse. Describe three properties of a material that would be suitable for a riding helmet and explain why each of these properties is advantageous. [6 marks]

My brain must be stiff — it's resistant to being stretched...

Make sure you learn all of those definitions of material properties and an example of when each property is useful. It might just pick you up some easy marks in the exam. Then practice drawing the stress-strain graph for ductile materials.

Structures of Materials

The reason materials are flexible or tough is down to their structure.
When the going gets tough, the tough get going to page 46 to look up the definition of tough...

Metals — Positive Ions in a **'Sea'** of **Free Electrons**

1) The atoms in a metal usually form a **crystalline** lattice — where the metal atoms are arranged in a **regular repeating pattern**. (They can also be **polycrystalline** — see below).
2) The outer electrons of the metal atoms don't need much energy to be able to desert their atoms in this crystalline structure. They form a 'sea' of **free electrons**, leaving behind a lattice of ions. It's these free electrons that make metals such **good conductors** of heat and electricity.
3) The electrostatic attraction between the ion lattice and the free electrons forms metallic bonds. It's these **strong** bonds that make metals **stiff** materials.
4) The strongly bonded lattice structure of a metal makes it **tough**. The ions within the lattice can **move** when you apply a force to the metal — making it **ductile**.
5) When a **force** is applied to the metal, the **interatomic spacing** between the ions increases. This increase is **uniform** during **elastic deformation**. Once the **stress** is high enough to cause **plastic deformation**, the **planes** ('sheets' of metal ions) within the metal **slip** over each other.
   If there is a **dislocation** (imperfection) in the metal, the **stress** needed to cause slipping is **lower** than the stress needed to cause slipping in a **perfect metal**.
6) **Atoms** of a **second metal can be placed inside dislocations** to **pin them down**. This **increases** the **stress** needed to cause **slipping**. This process is called **alloying** and makes the metal **harder** and less **ductile**.

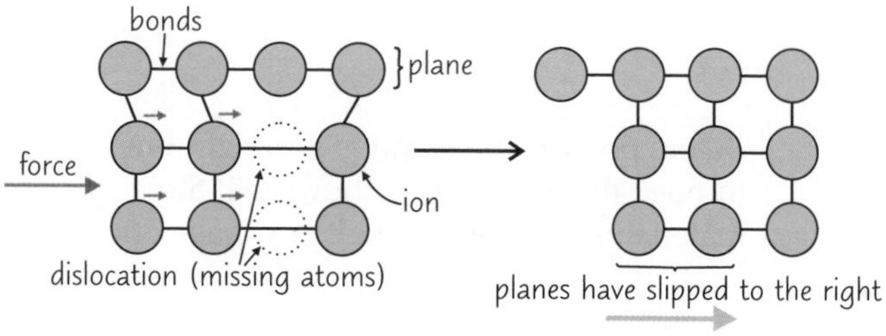

Ceramics — Giant **Rigid** Structures

1) Ceramics like **pottery**, **brick** and **glass** are made by melting certain materials, and then letting them cool.
2) The arrangement of atoms in a ceramic can be **crystalline** or **polycrystalline** — where there are many regions (or **grains**) of crystalline structure. The atoms in each grain line up in the same direction.
3) Some ceramics like **glass** are **amorphous** — there's no overall pattern; the atoms are arranged at **random**. The **quicker** a molten ceramic material is cooled, the more likely it is to be amorphous.

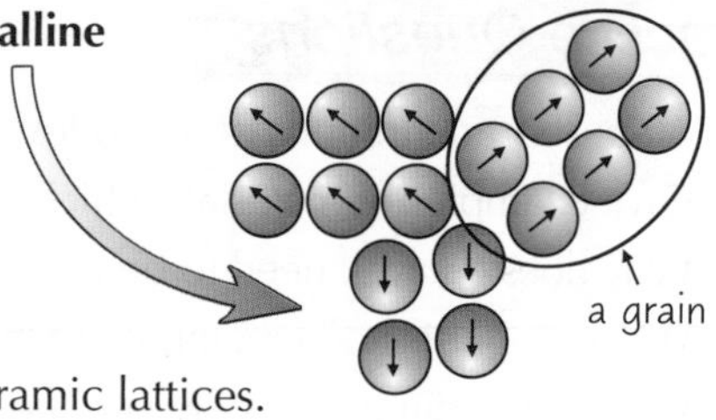

4) This **random** atomic bonding means that there are **no slip planes** in ceramic lattices. They also don't have **mobile dislocations** (dislocations which can **move**) — meaning that ceramic materials rarely deform **plastically** before they **fracture** (p.42).
5) However they're arranged, the atoms in a ceramic are either **ionically** or **covalently** bonded in a **giant rigid structure**. The **strong bonds** between the atoms make ceramics **stiff**, while the **rigid** structure means that ceramics are very **brittle** materials.
6) Ceramics being **brittle** means that **cracks spread** through them when they **fracture**. This is because the applied **force** acts on a **small area** (the **tip** of the crack) so the **stress** is high.

Polymers — Lots of **Monomers Joined Together**

1) A **polymer** is a molecular **chain**, made up of a **single repeating unit** called a **monomer**.
2) You get **natural** polymers like rubber, as well as a whole host of **man-made** ones like polythene.
3) The monomers in a polymer chain are **covalently** bonded together, and so are very hard to separate. This means even the thin polymer material used to make carrier bags is still pretty **strong**.
4) The **polymer chains** are often **entangled** (twisted and scrunched together), and can be **unravelled** by **rotating** about their bonds when you pull them. This is what makes polymer materials **flexible**.
   The more easily the monomers can **rotate**, the more the **chains** will **untangle** and the more **flexible** the polymer will be.
5) The strength and number of bonds **between** the chains also affect a polymer's flexibility. The stronger the cross-linking bonds, and the more cross-linking bonds you've got, the more **rigid** the material.

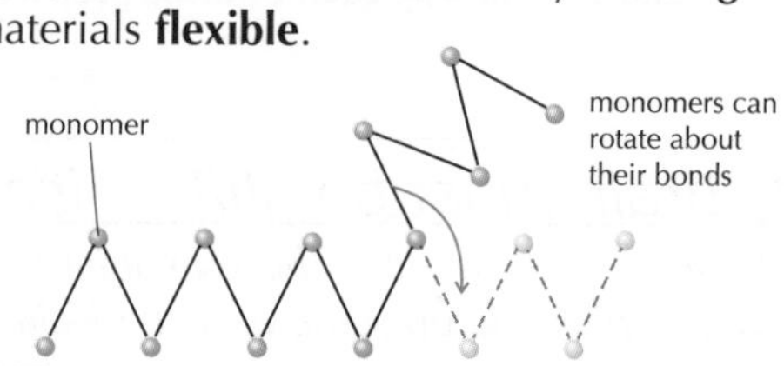

Structures of Materials

Rayleigh Estimated Atom Sizes with Oil Drops...

1) One of the first experiments used to calculate atomic size was **Rayleigh's oil drop experiment** in 1890.
2) Olive oil was released, one drop at a time, into a **tub of water** until it **just** covered the **entire surface**. Rayleigh assumed the oil would **spread** as much as it could, so this **thickness** would be the **size** of one **molecule of oil**.
3) By knowing the **surface area** of the tub and the **volume** of the oil dropped, the **thickness** of the oil film could be found. The **size of an atom** is roughly equal to the size of an **oil molecule** divided by the **number of atoms** in an oil molecule, so Rayleigh could use his measurements to find an **upper limit** for the size of the **individual atoms**.

...Now We Use Other Methods

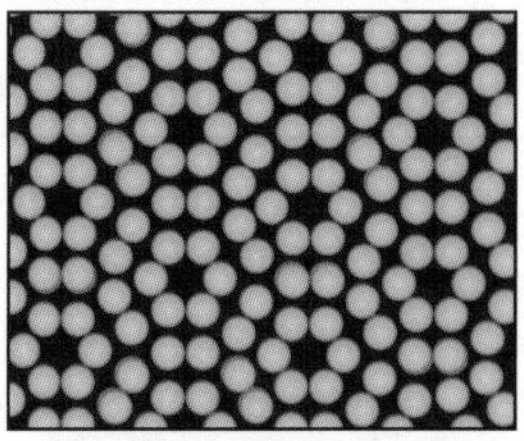
Scanning Tunnelling Microscopes can produce images of atoms.

1) There are loads of ways of measuring both the size of atoms and their spacing.
2) **X-ray crystallography** involves firing X-rays at a sample and using their **diffraction patterns** (see page 57) to investigate atomic spacing and structure.
3) **Scanning Tunnelling Microscopes** (**STM**) have a very fine tip which a voltage is applied to. **Electrons** from the sample surface **tunnel** (you don't need to know how this works) from the **surface** to the **tip** and cause a **current** to flow. The tip is moved across the surface of the sample, and the **height** of the tip is adjusted to keep the current **constant**, meaning that any small **bumps** or **dips** in the surface can be detected. An STM has such a **fine resolution** that **individual atoms** can be resolved and their **size** and **spacing** measured.
4) **Scanning Electron Microscopes** (**SEM**) and **Atomic Force Microscopes** (**AFM**) can also be used to measure atomic sizes. They don't let you 'see' a material's surface directly, but can be used to build up an **atom-by-atom** image of the surface on a **computer screen**. By knowing the **magnification** of the **image** on the computer screen and the size of the 'blobs' representing each atom, the sizes of the **atoms** can be calculated.
5) Modern techniques give the diameter of an atom as **0.1–0.5 nm**, depending on the atom being measured. This is much more **accurate** than the values Rayleigh **estimated** from his experiment.

Practice Questions

Q1 Describe the structure of metals.

Q2 Explain, in terms of its structure, what makes a metal stiff and what makes a metal tough.

Q3 Describe, in terms of interatomic spacing, what happens to the ions in a metal as it undergoes elastic deformation.

Q4 Describe the structure of ceramics and the directions of atoms in a polycrystalline ceramic.

Q5 Explain why there are no slip planes in ceramic materials.

Q6 Why do cracks spread through ceramics when a force is applied to them?

Exam Questions

Q1 Stress is applied to a sample of iron which contains dislocations.
The sample begins to plastically deform at a lower stress than expected.

a) Explain what is happening to the ions in the iron as it plastically deforms and comment on why plastic deformation occurred at a lower stress than expected. [2 marks]

b) Describe alloying and what effect it would have on the sample. [4 marks]

Q2 Select the statement that does **not** correctly describe polymers:

A Monomers are covalently bonded together to create a polymer.
B Polymer chains are tangled together.
C The more cross-linking bonds there are, the more flexible a polymer is.
D Polymers are unravelled when you pull on them, causing the monomers to rotate. [1 mark]

Q3 Describe how our knowledge of atomic size and spacing have changed over the past 150 years.
You should include a description of at least two methods of measuring atomic size in your answer. [6 marks]

And that's why shops don't make their bags out of clay...

It's true what they say — it's what's on the inside that counts... and it's no different for bricks. Make sure you get to grips with the structure of each class of materials so you can explain why materials have certain properties.

Superposition and Coherence

When two waves get together, it can be either really impressive or really disappointing.

Superposition Happens When Two or More Waves Pass Through Each Other

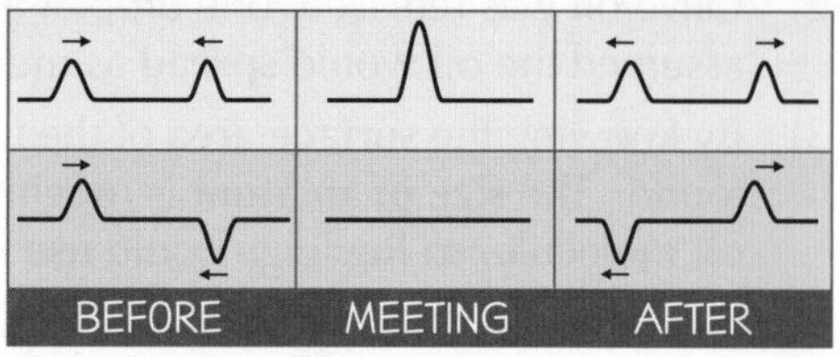

1) At the **instant** the waves **cross**, the **displacements** due to each wave **combine**. Then **each wave** goes on its merry way. You can **see** this if **two pulses** are sent **simultaneously** from each end of a rope.
2) The **principle of superposition** says that when two or more **waves cross**, the **resultant** displacement equals the **vector sum** of the **individual** displacements.

Interference can be Constructive or Destructive

1) A **crest** plus a **crest** gives a **big crest**. A **trough** plus a **trough** gives a **big trough**. These are both examples of **constructive interference**.
2) A **crest** plus a **trough** of **equal size** gives... **nothing**. The two displacements **cancel each other out** completely. This is called **total destructive interference**.
3) If the **crest** and the **trough** aren't the **same size**, then the destructive interference **isn't total**. For the interference to be **noticeable**, the two **amplitudes** should be **nearly equal**.

Graphically, you can superimpose waves by adding the individual displacements at each point along the x-axis, and then plotting them.

"Superposition" means "one thing on top of another thing". You can use the same idea in **reverse** — a complex wave can be **separated out** mathematically into several simple sine waves of various sizes.

You Can Use Phasors to Show Superposition

You can use little rotating arrows to represent the phase (see below) of each point on a wave. These arrows are called **phasors**. The phasor **rotates anticlockwise** through one whole turn as the wave completes a full cycle.

The length of the arrow shows the amplitude of the wave.

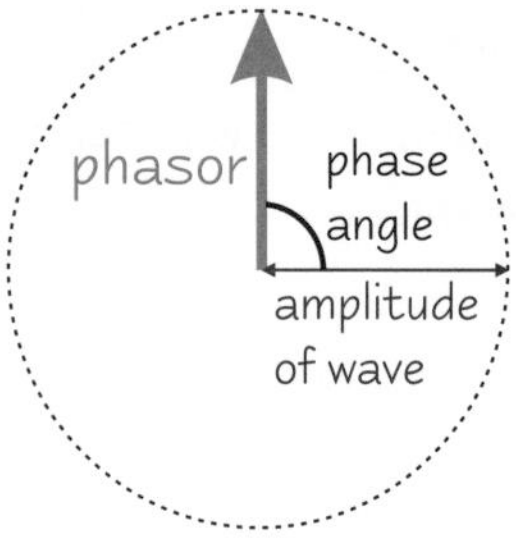

To superimpose waves using phasors, just add the arrows tip to tail:

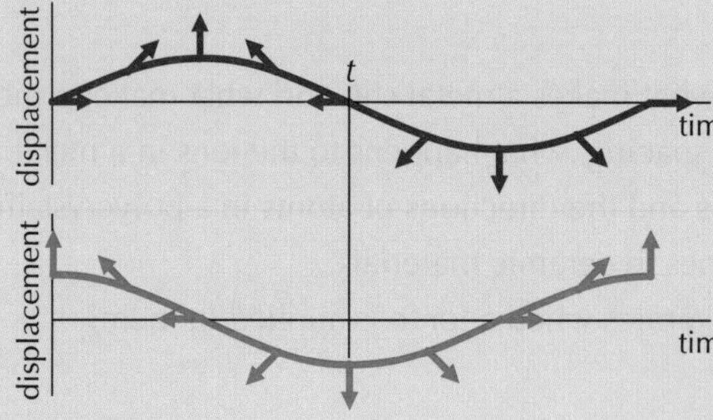

To find the resultant at time t, add the phasors tip to tail:

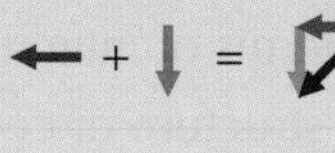

(So in this case, the resultant wave has a greater amplitude than the component waves and is 45° out of phase with both.)

In Phase Means In Step

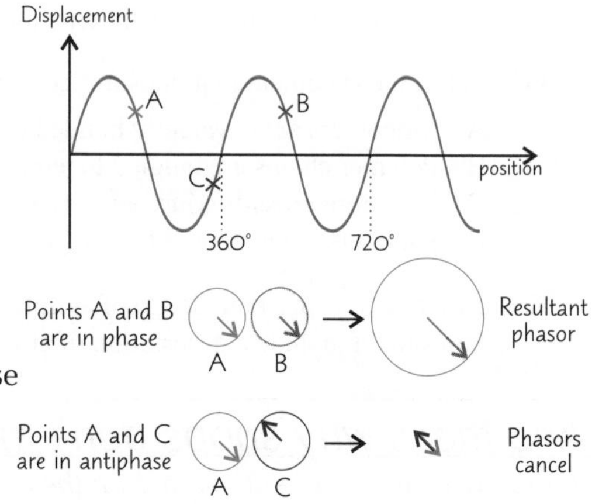

1) Two points on a wave are **in phase** if they are both at the **same point** in the **wave cycle**.
2) It's mathematically **handy** to show one **complete cycle** of a wave as an **angle of 360° (2π radians)**, the angle a phasor will travel through.
3) **Points** that have a **phase difference** of **zero** or a **multiple of 360°** are **in phase** — their phasors point in the **same direction**.
4) **Points** with a **phase difference** of **odd-number multiples** of **180° (π radians)** are **exactly out of phase**, called **antiphase**. Their phasors point in **opposite directions**. And there's not just phase and antiphase — points can have a **phase difference** of **any** angle.
5) You can also talk about two **different waves** being **in phase**. **In practice** this happens because **both** waves came from the **same oscillator**. In **other** situations there will nearly always be a **phase difference** between two waves.

Superposition and Coherence

To Get **Interference Patterns** the **Two Sources** Must Be **Coherent**

Interference **still happens** when you're observing waves of **different wavelength** and **frequency** — but it happens in a **jumble**. In order to get clear **interference patterns**, the two or more sources must be **coherent**.

Two sources are **coherent** if they have the **same wavelength** and **frequency** and a **fixed phase difference** between them.

In exam questions, the 'fixed phase difference' is almost certainly going to be zero. The two sources will be in phase.

Constructive or **Destructive** Interference Depends on the **Path Difference**

1) Whether you get **constructive** or **destructive** interference at a **point** depends on how **much further one wave** has travelled than the **other wave** to get to that point (assuming the sources are **coherent** and **in phase**).
2) The **amount** by which the path travelled by one wave is **longer** than the path travelled by the other wave is called the **path difference**.

Constructive Interference — at any point an **equal** distance from both sources (that are coherent and in phase), or where the path difference is a **whole number** of **wavelengths**.

path difference = $n\lambda$ (where n is an integer)

Total Destructive Interference — at any point where the path difference is an **odd** number of **half wavelengths**.

path difference = $\frac{(2n + 1)\lambda}{2} = (n + \frac{1}{2})\lambda$

You Can Observe Interference With Sound Waves

1) Connect two **speakers** to the same oscillator (so they're **coherent** and **in phase**) and place them in line with each other.
2) Slowly move a **microphone** in a **straight line** parallel to the line of the speakers.
3) Using a data logger and a computer, you can see where the sound is **loudest** and **quietest** — the locations of maximum **constructive** and **destructive** interference.

Practice Questions

Q1 What is the principle of superposition?

Q2 When does the interference between two waves produce a clear pattern?

Q3 If two points on a wave have a phase difference of 1440°, are they in phase?

Q4 Define coherence.

Q5 Describe briefly an experiment to show interference using sound waves.

Exam Question

Q1 Sound waves that are coherent and in phase, each with a wavelength of 0.6 m, are produced by two speakers.

a) State whether maximum constructive or destructive interference would occur at a distance away from the speaker where the path difference between the two sound waves was 10.2 m. [1 mark]

b) At a point of total destructive interference, the phasor describing one of the waves at that point is shown. Draw the phasor describing the second sound wave at that point and state whether its magnitude is bigger than, smaller than or the same as the first sound wave. [2 marks]

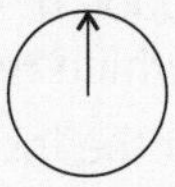

Learn this and you'll be in a super position to pass your exam...

...I'll get my coat.

There are a few really crucial concepts here: a) interference can be constructive or destructive, b) the sources must be coherent and in phase, c) constructive interference happens when the path difference is a whole number of wavelengths.

Standing Waves

Standing waves are waves that... er... stand still... well, not still exactly... I mean, well... they don't go anywhere... um...

*You get a Standing Wave When a **Progressive Wave** is **Reflected** at a **Boundary***

A standing wave is the **superposition** of **two progressive waves** with the **same wavelength**, moving in **opposite directions**.

1) Unlike progressive waves, **no energy** is transmitted by a standing wave.
2) You can demonstrate standing waves by setting up a **driving oscillator** at one end of a **stretched string** with the other end fixed. The wave generated by the oscillator is **reflected** back and forth.
3) For most frequencies the resultant **pattern** is a **jumble**. However, if the oscillator happens to produce an **exact number of waves** in the time it takes for a wave to get to the **end** and **back again**, then the **original** and **reflected** waves **reinforce** each other.
4) At these **"resonant frequencies"** you get a **standing wave** where the **pattern doesn't move** — it just sits there, bobbing up and down. Happy, at peace with the world...

A sitting wave.

*Standing Waves in **Strings** Form **Oscillating "Loops"** Separated by **Nodes***

1) Take a piece of string and **fix** it in place at **one end**.
2) Attach the other end to an **oscillator**.
3) Adjust the **frequency** of the oscillator, until a **standing wave** is formed.
4) This is when the wave is **reflected** back on itself and **interferes**, causing "loops" to form, with **antinodes** (positions of **maximum** amplitude) and **nodes** (positions of **zero** amplitude).
5) You can then use an **oscilloscope** (see next page) to calculate the **resonant frequency**.

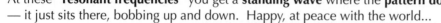

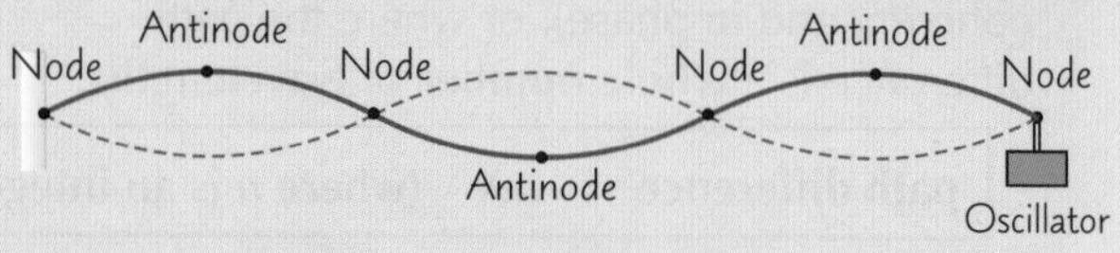

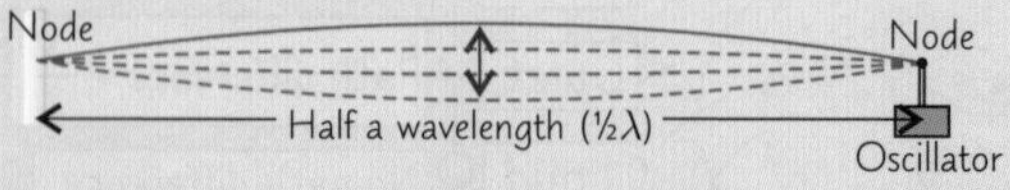

The standing wave above is vibrating at the **lowest possible** resonant frequency (the **fundamental frequency**). This is the **first harmonic**. It has **one "loop"** with a **node at each end**.

This is the **second harmonic** (or **first overtone**). It is **twice** the **fundamental frequency**. There are two "**loops**" with a **node** in the **middle** and **one at each end**.

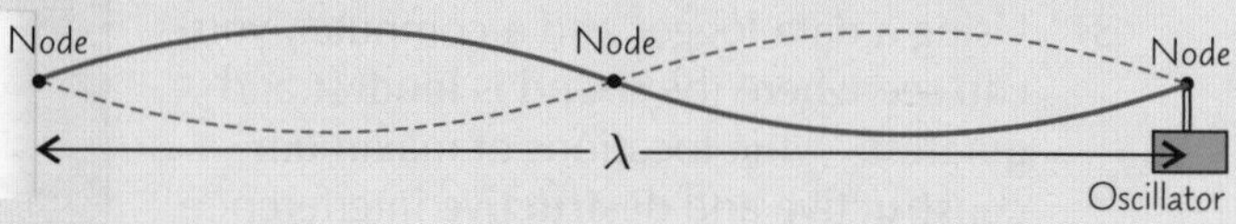

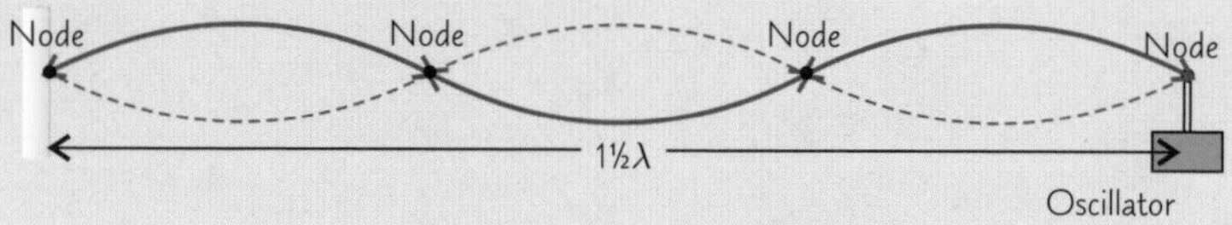

The **third harmonic** (or **second overtone**) is **three times** the fundamental frequency. **1½ wavelengths** fit on the string.

*The **Notes** Played by **Stringed** and **Wind Instruments** are Standing Waves*

Transverse standing waves form on the strings of **stringed instruments** like **violins** and **guitars**. Your finger or the bow sets the **string vibrating** at the point of contact. Waves are sent out in **both directions** and **reflected** back at both ends.

Longitudinal** Standing Waves Form in a **Wind Instrument** or Other Air **Column

1) If a source of sound is placed at the open end of a flute, piccolo, oboe or other column of air, there will be some **frequencies** for which **resonance** occurs and a standing wave is set up.
2) If the instrument has a **closed end**, a **node** will form there. You get the lowest resonant frequency when the length, *l*, of the pipe is a **quarter wavelength**.

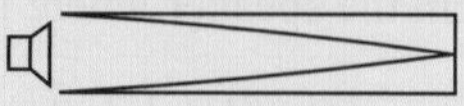

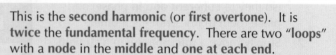

$$l = \frac{\lambda}{4}$$

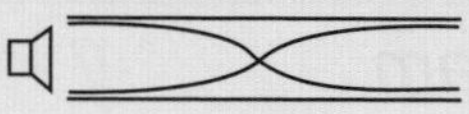

$$l = \frac{\lambda}{2}$$

3) **Antinodes** form at the **open ends** of pipes. If both ends are open, you get the lowest resonant frequency when the length, *l*, of the pipe is a **half wavelength**.

Remember, the sound waves in wind instruments are longitudinal — they don't actually look like these diagrams.

Standing Waves

You Can Calculate Frequency with an Oscilloscope

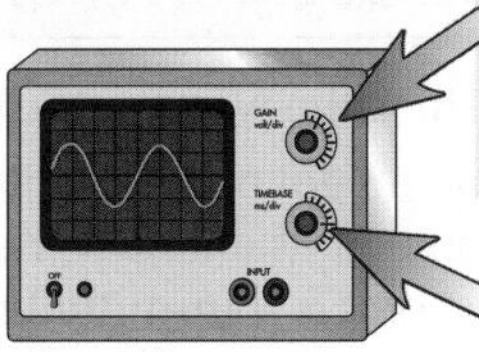

1) A cathode ray **oscilloscope** (CRO) measures **voltage**. It **displays** waves from an **oscillator** as a function of **voltage** over **time**.
2) The screen is split into squares called **divisions**.
3) The vertical axis shows the **voltage**, and the **gain dial** controls the voltage represented by each **division**.
4) The horizontal axis shows **time**, and the **timebase dial** controls the time represented by each division.
5) To calculate the **frequency** of the wave, first you must find the **period**, T. Do this by counting how many **horizontal squares** one **wavelength** covers.
6) **Multiply** this number by the **timebase** value you set on the oscilloscope. This gives the **period**.
7) Use $f = \frac{1}{T}$ to calculate the **frequency** of the wave being **generated** by the **oscillator**.

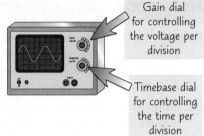

You can Use Standing Waves to Measure the Speed of Sound

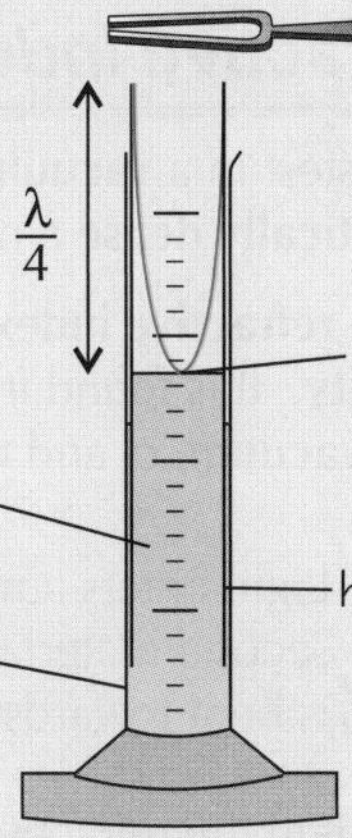

1) You can create a **resonance tube** by placing a **hollow tube** into a measuring cylinder of water.
2) Choose a tuning fork and note down the **frequency** of sound it produces (it'll be stamped on the side of it).
3) Gently tap the tuning fork and hold it just above the hollow tube. The sound waves produced by the fork travel down the tube and get reflected (and form a **node**) at the air/water surface.
4) Move the tube up and down until you find the **shortest distance** between the top of the tube and the water level that the sound from the fork **resonates** at. This will be when the sound appears **loudest**.
5) Measure the **distance** between the air/water surface and the **tuning fork** — just like with any closed pipe, this distance is a **quarter** of the **wavelength** of the standing sound wave.
6) Once you know the frequency and wavelength of the standing sound wave, you can work out the speed of sound (in air), v, using the equation $v = f\lambda$.
7) Then, **repeat** this experiment using tuning forks with **different frequencies**. You could also **move** the tuning fork higher above the cylinder until you find the next **harmonic** (equal to **three quarters** of the wavelength).

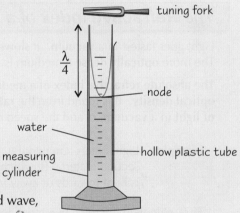

Practice Questions

Q1 How do standing waves form?

Q2 At four times the fundamental frequency, how many half wavelengths fit on a violin string?

Q3 Describe an experiment to find the speed of sound in air using standing waves.

Exam Question

Q1 a) A standing wave of three times the fundamental frequency is formed on a stretched string of length 1.2 m. Sketch a diagram showing the form and length of the wave. [2 marks]

b) Calculate the wavelength of the standing wave. [1 mark]

c) Explain how the amplitude varies along the string and how this compares to a progressive wave. [2 marks]

d) An oscilloscope is connected to the oscillator used to produce the standing wave. The seconds per division is set at 2 ms per division. One wavelength spans 4 squares on the oscilloscope display. Calculate the frequency of the wave. [2 marks]

CGP — putting the FUN back in FUNdamental frequency...

Resonance was a big problem for the Millennium Bridge in London. The resonant frequency of the bridge was roughly normal walking pace, so as soon as people started using it they set up a huge standing wave. An oversight, I feel...

Refraction and Refractive Index

The stuff on the next two pages explains why your legs look short in a swimming pool.

Refraction *Occurs When the* ***Medium*** *a Wave is Travelling in Changes*

Refraction (p.18) is the way a wave **changes direction** as it enters a **different medium**.

1) When a ray of light meets a boundary between one medium and another, some of its energy is **reflected** back into the first medium and the rest of it is **transmitted** through into the second medium.
2) If the light meets the boundary at an angle to the normal, the transmitted ray is bent or "**refracted**" as it travels at a **different speed** in each medium.
3) When the speed changes, the **frequency** stays **constant**, so the **wavelength** changes too ($v = f\lambda$).
4) If the ray bends **towards** the normal — it is **slowing** down. The ray is going from a **less** optically dense material to a **more** optically dense material. The wavelength **decreases**.
5) If the ray bends **away** from the normal — the wave is **speeding up**. It is going from a more optically **dense** material to a **less** optically dense material. The wavelength **increases**.

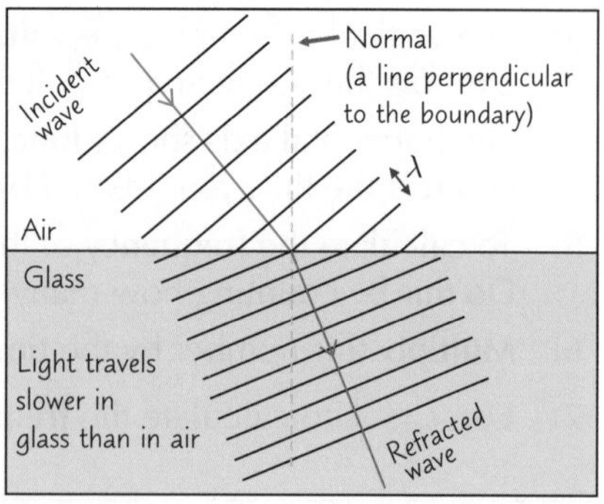

The ***Refractive Index*** *of a Material Measures* ***How Much*** *It Slows Down Light*

Light goes fastest in a **vacuum**. It **slows down** in other materials, because it **interacts** with the particles in them. The more **optically dense** a medium is, the more light slows down when it enters it.

The **absolute refractive index** of a medium, ***n***, is a measure of **optical density**. It is found from the **ratio** between the **speed of light** in a **vacuum**, ***c***, and the speed of light in that **medium**, c_{medium}.

$$n = \frac{c}{c_{medium}}$$

$c = 3.00 \times 10^8$ ms^{-1}

Example: Light enters a material A, where it travels at a speed of 1.9×10^8 ms^{-1}. It then enters a second material B, which has a refractive index of 2.1. Determine whether the light ray is bent towards or away from the normal when it travels from material A to material B.

First, calculate the refractive index for material A:

$$n = \frac{c}{c_{medium}} = \frac{3.00 \times 10^8}{1.9 \times 10^8} = 1.57...$$

As the refractive index of material A is lower than that of material B, A is less optically dense than B. This means the light wave will slow down when it travels from A to B and will bend towards the normal.

Snell's Law *uses* ***Angles*** *to Calculate the Refractive Index*

When a ray of light is refracted at a boundary between two materials:

1) The light is crossing a **boundary**, going from medium 1 with **refractive index** n_1 to medium 2 with refractive index n_2.
2) The **angle** the **incoming light** makes to the **normal** is called the **angle of incidence**, ***i***.
3) The **angle** the **refracted ray** makes with the **normal** is the **angle of refraction**, ***r***.
4) n_1, n_2, i and r are related by **Snell's law**:

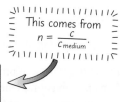

$$\frac{\sin i}{\sin r} = \frac{n_2}{n_1} \quad \text{or} \quad \frac{\sin i}{\sin r} = \frac{c_{1st\ medium}}{c_{2nd\ medium}}$$

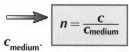

This comes from $n = \frac{c}{c_{medium}}$.

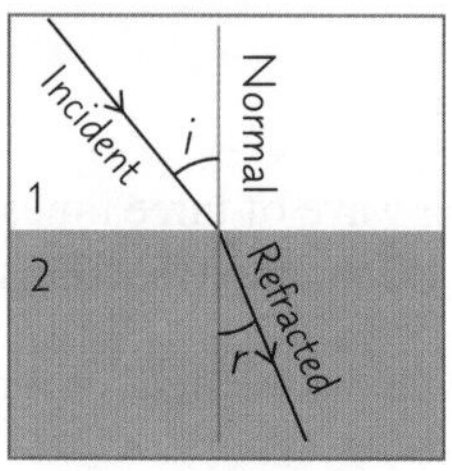

The equivalent angles between the wavefronts and the boundary line can sometimes also be labelled as *r* and *i*.

5) The **speed of light** in **air** is only a **tiny** bit smaller than *c*. This means you can assume the **refractive index** of air is **1** ($n_{air} \approx c \div c$). So for an **air-to-material** boundary, Snell's law becomes:

$$n = \frac{\sin i}{\sin r}$$

where *n* is the refractive index of the material

Refraction and Refractive Index

You Can Calculate the Refractive Index of a Transparent Block

1) Place a glass block on a piece of paper and draw around it.
2) Use a **ray box** to shine a beam of light into the glass block. Turn off any other lights so you can see the path of the light beam through the block clearly.
3) **Trace** the path of the **incoming** and **outgoing** beams of light either side of the block.
4) Remove the block and join up the two paths you've drawn with a **straight line**. The line will follow the path the light beam took through the glass block. You should be able to see from your drawing how the path of the ray **bent** when entering and leaving the block.
5) Measure the angles of **incidence** and **refraction** where the light enters the block.
6) Use **Snell's law** for an **air-to-material** boundary to calculate the refractive index of the block.

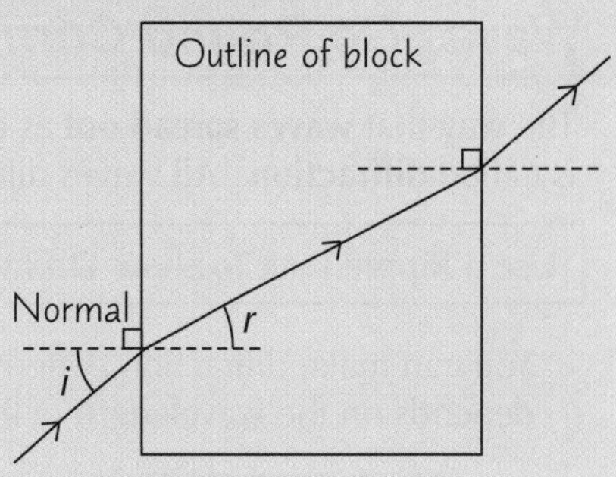

Example: Light is shone through a transparent block. The angle of incidence at the air/material boundary is 30° and the angle of refraction is 25°. Calculate the refractive index of the block.

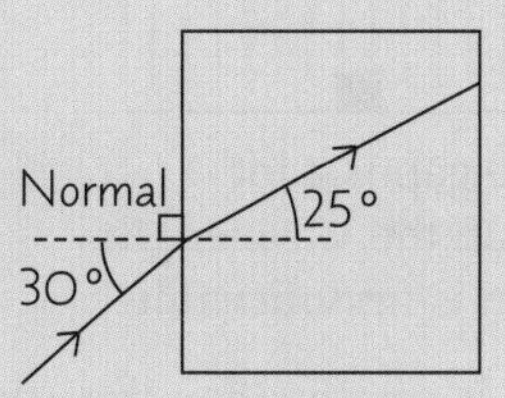

Using Snell's law for an air/material boundary:

$$n = \frac{\sin i}{\sin r} = \frac{\sin(30°)}{\sin(25°)} = 1.18... = \mathbf{1.2\ (to\ 2\ s.f.)}$$

Practice Questions

Q1 What is refraction?

Q2 Why does light go fastest in a vacuum and slow down in other media?

Q3 Give the equation for the absolute refractive index of a material.

Q4 Write down Snell's law for an air-to-material boundary.

Q5 Describe an experiment for calculating the refractive index of a transparent block.

Exam Questions

Q1 a) Light travels in diamond at 1.24×10^8 ms^{-1}. Calculate the refractive index of diamond. [1 mark]

b) Calculate the angle of refraction if light strikes a facet of a diamond ring at an angle of 50° (to 2 s.f.) to the normal of the air/diamond boundary. [2 marks]

Q2 Light travels from air, through a cube of material A (refractive index 1.4) and into a cube of material B.

a) As the light ray travels from air into the block of material A, it enters at an angle of 40° (to 2 s.f.) to the normal and creates an angle of refraction of 27° to the normal.
Calculate the speed of the light ray as it travels through material A. [2 marks]

b) Light travels at 1.7×10^8 ms^{-1} in material B. Calculate the refractive index of material B. [1 mark]

c) Calculate the angle of refraction as the light ray passes from material A to material B. [2 marks]

I don't care about expensive things — all I care about is wave speed...

Physics examiners are always saying how candidates do worst in the waves bit of the exam. You'd think they'd have something more important to worry about — poverty, war, their favourite band splitting up... but apparently not.

Diffraction

Astronomers trying to observe radio waves have to battle diffraction. They've been known to cheat and set up a network of telescopes around the world to get a good image. All that trouble because of diffraction... but it has its uses too.

Waves Go **Round Corners** and **Spread out** of **Gaps**

The way that **waves spread out** as they come through a **narrow gap** (aperture) or go round obstacles is called **diffraction**. **All** waves diffract, but it's not always easy to observe.

Use a Ripple Tank To Show Diffraction of Water Waves

You can make diffraction patterns in ripple tanks. The **amount** of diffraction depends on the **wavelength** of the wave compared with the **size of the gap**.

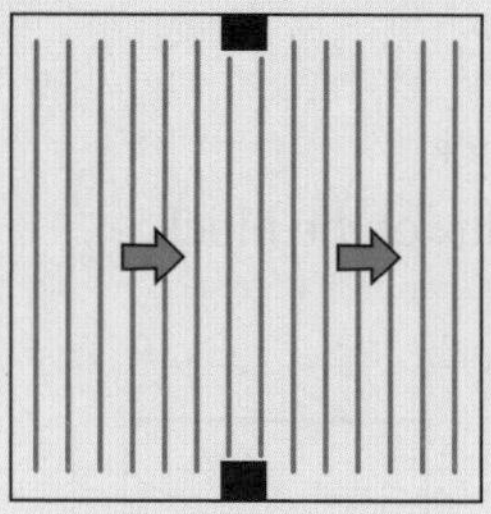

When the gap is **a lot bigger** than the **wavelength**, diffraction is **unnoticeable**.

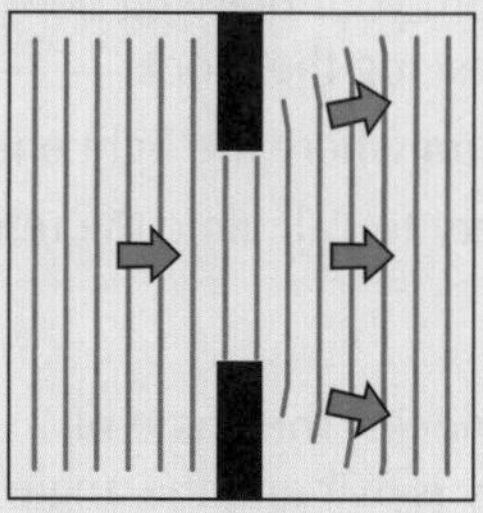

You get **noticeable diffraction** through a gap **several** wavelengths wide.

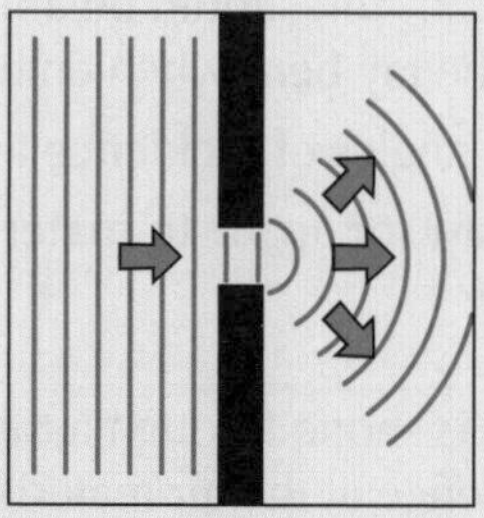

You get the **most** diffraction when the gap is **the same** size as the **wavelength**.

If the gap is **smaller** than the wavelength, the waves are mostly just **reflected back**.

When **sound** passes through a **doorway**, the **size of gap** and the **wavelength** are usually roughly **equal**, so **a lot** of **diffraction** occurs. That's why you have no trouble **hearing** someone through an **open door** to the next room, even if the other person is out of your **line of sight**. The reason that you can't **see** him or her is that when **light** passes through the doorway, it is passing through a **gap** around a **hundred million times bigger** than its wavelength — the amount of diffraction is **tiny**.

Demonstrate **Diffraction** in **Light** Using **Laser Light**

1) Diffraction in **light** can be demonstrated by shining a **laser light** through a very **narrow slit** onto a screen (see the next page). You can alter the amount of diffraction by changing the width of the slit.
2) You can do a similar experiment using a **white light** source instead of the laser (which is monochromatic) and a set of **colour filters**. The size of the slit can be kept constant while the **wavelength** is varied by putting different **colour filters** over the slit.

Warning. Use of coloured filters may result in excessive fun.

You Get a **Similar** Effect Around an Obstacle

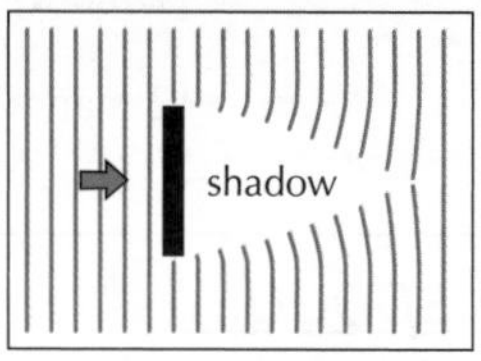

When a wave meets an **obstacle**, you get diffraction around the edges. Behind the obstacle is a '**shadow**', where the wave is blocked. The **wider** the obstacle compared with the wavelength of the wave, the less diffraction you get, and so the **longer** the shadow.

Diffraction

With **Light Waves** you get a **Pattern** of **Light** and **Dark Fringes**

1) If the **wavelength** of a **light wave** is roughly similar to the size of the **aperture**, you get a **diffraction pattern** of light and dark fringes.
2) The pattern has a **bright central fringe** with alternating **dark and bright fringes** on either side of it.
3) The central fringe is the most **intense** — there are more **incident photons per unit area** in the central fringe than in the other bright fringes. (See page 62 for more on light as **photons**).

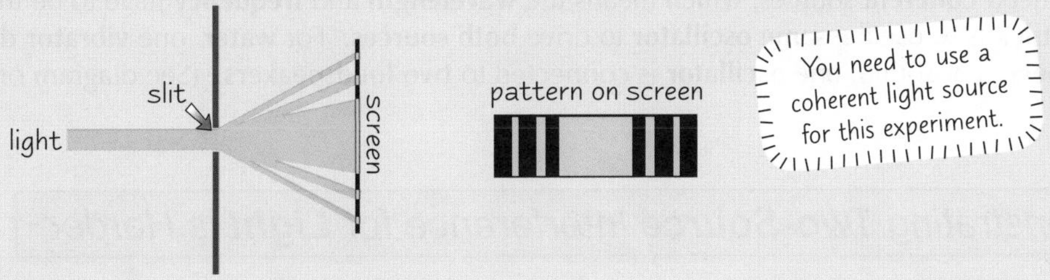

4) The **narrower** the slit, the **wider** the diffraction pattern.

You can Explain **Diffraction Patterns** Using **Phasors**

1) The **brightest** point of a diffraction pattern is where light passes in a straight line from the slit to the screen. All the light waves that arrive there are **in phase**.
2) At all other bright points where light hits the screen, there is a **constant phase difference** between the waves arriving there, so the phasors point in slightly different directions and form a **smaller resultant**.
3) **Dark fringes** on the screen are where the phase difference between the light waves means their phasors add to form a **loop**, giving a **resultant of zero**.

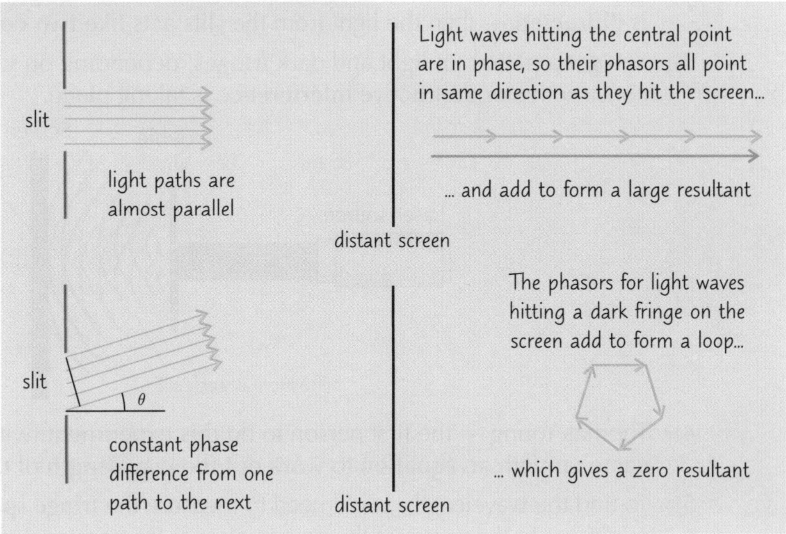

Practice Questions

Q1 What is diffraction?

Q2 Sketch what happens when plane waves meet an obstacle about as wide as one wavelength.

Q3 For a long time some scientists argued that light couldn't be a wave because it did not seem to diffract. Suggest why they might have got this impression.

Q4 Describe in terms of phasors why diffraction patterns are made up of bright and dark fringes.

Exam Question

Q1 A mountain lies directly between you and a radio transmitter.

Explain using diagrams why you can pick up long-wave radio broadcasts from the transmitter but not short-wave radio broadcasts. [4 marks]

Even hiding behind a mountain, you can't get away from long-wave radio...

Diffraction crops up again and again, so you really need to understand it — learn it, learn it, learn it. (And then learn it again.)

Two-Source Interference

That Young chap gets everywhere... and here he is again. Young was a doctor, and nowadays you probably wouldn't trust a doctor who started telling you he was right and other physicists including Newton were wrong... I mean Newton's Mr Gravity for goodness' sake. But it turned out he was right... and this was the experiment that helped him show it.

*Demonstrating Two-Source Interference in **Water** and **Sound** is Easy*

1) It's **easy** to demonstrate **two-source interference** for either **sound** or **water** because they've got **wavelengths** of a handy **size** that you can **measure**.
2) You need **coherent** sources, which means the **wavelength** and **frequency** have to be the **same**. The trick is to use the **same oscillator** to drive **both sources**. For **water**, one **vibrator drives two dippers**. For sound, **one oscillator** is connected to **two loudspeakers**. (See diagram on page 51).

*Demonstrating **Two-Source** Interference for **Light** is Harder*

Light is more difficult to demonstrate two-source interference with — you can either use **two coherent light sources**, or use a single **laser** and shine it through **two slits**... clever, huh. It's called **Young's double-slit experiment**, and you need to learn it...

1) Laser light is **coherent** and **monochromatic** (there's only **one wavelength** present).
2) The slits have to be about the same size as the wavelength of the laser light so that it is **diffracted** — then the light from the slits acts like **two coherent point sources**.
3) You get a pattern of light and dark **fringes**, depending on whether constructive or destructive **interference** is taking place.

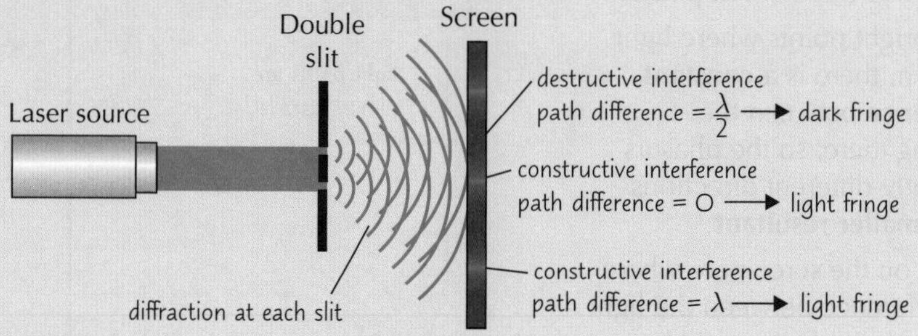

4) Thomas Young — the first person to do this experiment (with the Sun rather than a laser) — came up with an **equation** to **work out** the **wavelength** of the **light** from this experiment (see p.59).
5) To find the wavelength, you'll need to measure the **fringe spacing** — the distance from the **centre** of one **minimum** to the centre of the next minimum (or from one **maximum** centre to the next maximum centre).

*You Can Do a **Similar** Experiment with **Microwaves***

1) To see interference patterns with **microwaves**, you can **replace** the laser and slits with two microwave **transmitter cones** attached to the **same** signal generator.
2) You also need to replace the screen with a microwave **receiver probe**.
3) If you move the probe along the path of the green arrow, you'll get an **alternating pattern** of **strong** and **weak** signals — just like the light and dark fringes on the screen.

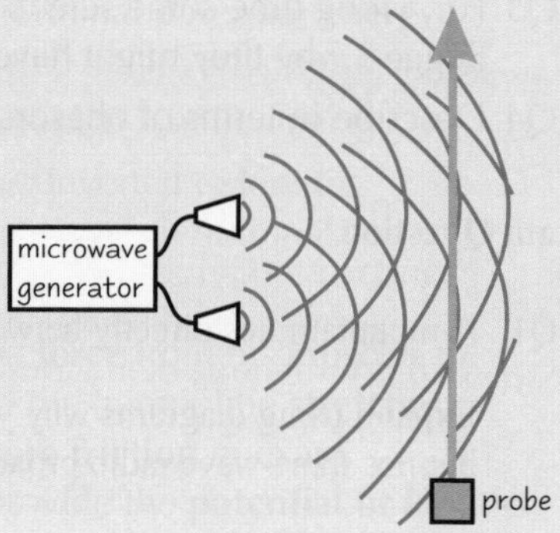

Two-Source Interference

Work Out the Wavelength with Young's Double-Slit Formula

1) The fringe spacing (**X**), wavelength (**λ**), spacing between slits (**d**) and the distance from slits to screen (**D**) are all related by **Young's double-slit formula**, which works for all waves (you need to be able to derive this, see p.61).

$$\text{Fringe spacing, } X = \frac{D\lambda}{d}$$

Always check your fringe spacing.

2) Since the wavelength of light is so small you can see from the formula that a high ratio of **D / d** is needed to make the fringe spacing **big enough to see**.
3) Rearranging, you can use **$\lambda = Xd / D$** to **calculate the wavelength** of light.
4) The fringes are **so tiny** that it's very hard to get an **accurate value of X**. It's easier to measure across **several** fringes then **divide** by the number of **fringe widths** between them. Doing this helps to lower the **percentage error** — see p.8 for more about this.

Young's Experiment was Evidence for the Wave Nature of Light

1) Towards the end of the **17th century**, two important **theories of light** were published — one by Isaac Newton and the other by a chap called Huygens. **Newton's** theory suggested that light was made up of tiny particles, which he called "**corpuscles**". And **Huygens** put forward a theory using **waves**.
2) The **corpuscular theory** could explain **reflection** and **refraction**, but **diffraction** and **interference** are both **uniquely** wave properties. If it could be **shown** that light showed interference patterns, that would help settle the argument once and for all.
3) **Young's** double-slit experiment (over 100 years later) provided the necessary evidence. It showed that light could both **diffract** (through the narrow slits) and **interfere** (to form the interference pattern on the screen).

Of course, this being Physics, nothing's ever simple — give it another 100 years or so and the debate would be raging again.

Practice Questions

Q1 In Young's experiment, why do you get a bright fringe at a point equidistant from both slits?

Q2 Write down Young's double-slit formula.

Q3 What does Young's experiment show about the nature of light?

Exam Questions

Q1 a) The diagram on the right shows waves from two slits on a screen, S_1 and S_2. Behind the screen is a laser light. Sketch the interference pattern, marking on constructive and destructive interference. [2 marks]

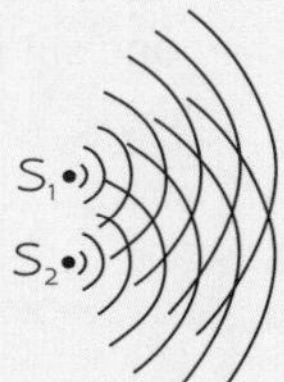

b) If S_1 and S_2 were changed to two separate light sources, what condition must be met in order to still observe an interference pattern? [1 mark]

Q2 In an experiment to study sound interference, two loudspeakers are connected to an oscillator emitting sound at 1320 Hz and set up as shown in the diagram below. They are 1.5 m apart and 7 m away from the line AC. A listener moving from A to C hears minimum sound at A and C and maximum sound at B. (You may assume that Young's double-slit formula can be used in this calculation).

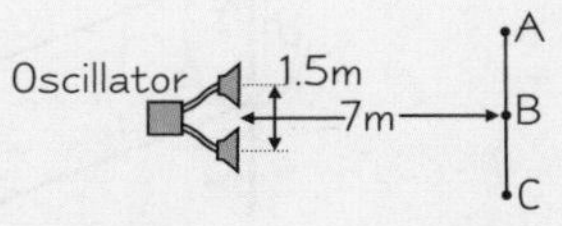

a) Calculate the wavelength of the sound waves if the speed of sound in air is taken to be 330 ms^{-1}. [1 mark]

b) Calculate the separation of points A and C. [2 marks]

Young's double-slit experiment — what bright spark came up with that name?

Be careful when you're calculating the fringe spacing by averaging over several fringes. Don't just divide by the number of bright lines. Ten bright lines will only have nine fringe-widths between them, not ten. You have been warned.

Diffraction Gratings

Diffraction gratings are pretty amazing. If you want to know what a star's made of you obviously can't just go there with your bucket and spade. Luckily astronomers can tell just by looking at light emitted from the star using one of these babies what the star's atmosphere's made of... genius.

Interference Patterns Get **Sharper** When You Diffract Through **More Slits**

1) You can repeat **Young's double-slit** experiment (see p.58) with **more than two equally spaced** slits. You get basically the **same shaped** pattern as for two slits — but the **bright bands** are **brighter** and **narrower** and the **dark areas** between are **darker**.
2) When **monochromatic light** (one wavelength) is passed through a **grating** with **hundreds** of slits per millimetre, the interference pattern is **really sharp** because there are so **many beams reinforcing** the **pattern**.
3) Sharper fringes make for more **accurate** measurements.

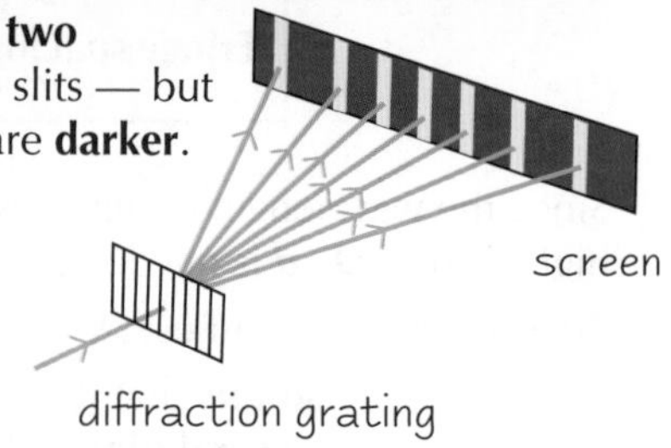

Monochromatic Light on a **Diffraction Grating** gives **Sharp Lines**

1) For **monochromatic** light, all the **maxima** are sharp lines. (It's different for white light — see next page.)
2) There's a line of **maximum brightness** at the centre called the **zero order** line.
3) The lines just **either side** of the central one are called **first order lines.** The **next pair out** are called **second order** lines and so on.
4) For a grating with slits a distance ***d*** apart, the angle between the **incident beam** and **the *n*th order maximum** is given by:

$$d \sin \theta = n\lambda$$

5) So by observing ***d***, ***θ*** and ***n*** you can **calculate the wavelength** of the light.

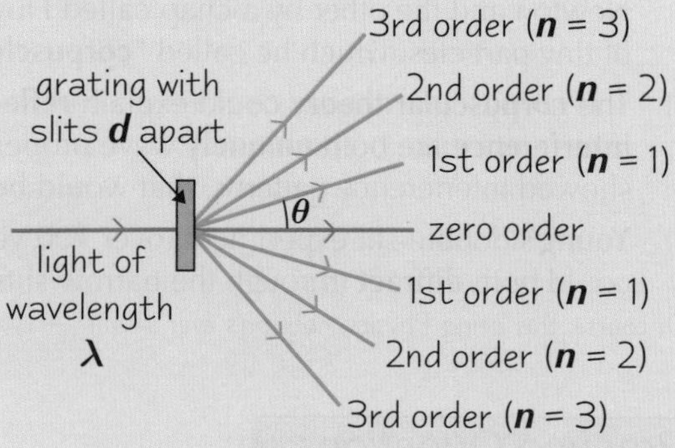

If the grating has N slits per metre, then the slit spacing, d, is just $1/N$ metres.

DERIVING THE EQUATION:

1) At **each slit**, the incoming waves are **diffracted**. These diffracted waves then **interfere** with each other to produce an **interference pattern**.
2) Consider the **first order maximum**. This happens at the **angle** when the waves from one slit line up with waves from the **next slit** that are **exactly one wavelength** behind.

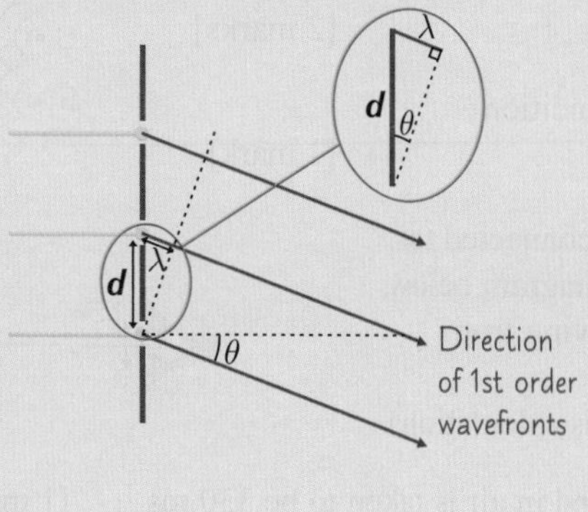

3) Call the **angle** between the **first order maximum** and the **incoming light *θ***.
4) Now, look at the **triangle** highlighted in the diagram. The angle is ***θ*** (using basic geometry), ***d*** is the slit spacing and the **path difference** is **λ**.
5) So, for the first maximum, using trig: $\boldsymbol{d \sin \theta = \lambda}$
6) The other maxima occur when the path difference is 2λ, 3λ, 4λ, etc. So to make the equation **general**, just replace λ with $n\lambda$, where ***n*** is an integer — the **order** of the maximum.

You can draw the following conclusions from $d \sin \theta = n\lambda$:

1) If **λ** is **bigger**, **sin *θ*** is **bigger**, and so ***θ*** is **bigger**. This means that the larger the **wavelength**, the more the pattern will **spread out**.
2) If ***d*** is **bigger**, **sin *θ*** is **smaller**. This means that the **coarser** the **grating**, the **less** the pattern will **spread out**.
3) Values of **sin *θ*** greater than **1** are **impossible**. So if for a certain ***n*** you get a result of **more than 1** for **sin *θ*** you know that that order **doesn't exist**.

Diffraction Gratings

You can **Derive** the **Fringe Spacing** from **$d \sin \theta = n\lambda$**

You have to be able to derive Young's double-slit formula for **fringe spacing** from page 59.

For the first order maximum ($n = 1$) the angle θ is small. This means you can use the **small angle approximations** of $\tan\theta \approx \theta$ and $\sin\theta \approx \theta$.

$\tan \theta$ is equal to $\frac{\text{opposite}}{\text{adjacent}}$, so in the triangle shown $\tan\theta = \frac{X}{D}$ $(\approx \theta \approx \sin\theta)$.
(X is fringe spacing and D is the distance from the grating to the screen).

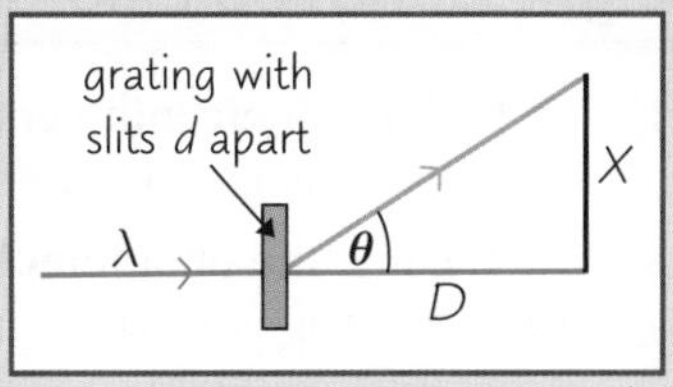

This means you can substitute $\frac{X}{D}$ into $d \sin \theta = n\lambda$ to get $\frac{Xd}{D} = \lambda$.

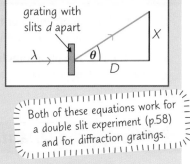

Remember, $n = 1$ here.

Rearrange for X and you get $\boxed{X = \frac{D\lambda}{d}}$

Both of these equations work for a double slit experiment (p.58) and for diffraction gratings.

Shining **White Light** Through a **Diffraction Grating** Produces **Spectra**

1) **White light** is really a **mixture** of **colours**. If you **diffract** white light through a **grating** then the patterns due to **different wavelengths** within the white light are **spread out** by **different** amounts.
2) Each **order** in the pattern becomes a **spectrum**, with **red** on the **outside** and **violet** on the **inside**. The **zero order maximum** stays **white** because all the wavelengths just pass straight through.
3) **Astronomers** and **chemists** often need to study spectra to help identify elements. They use diffraction gratings rather than prisms because they're **more accurate**.

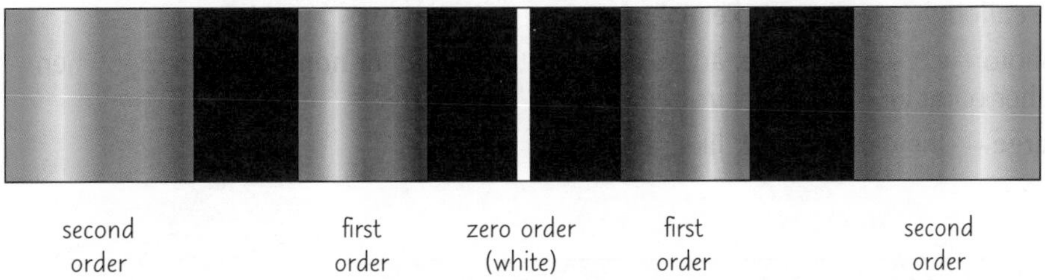

Practice Questions

Q1 How is the diffraction grating pattern for white light different from the pattern for laser light?

Q2 What difference does it make to the pattern if you use a finer grating?

Q3 What equation is used to find the angle between the nth order maximum and the incident beam for a diffraction grating?

Q4 From this, derive Young's double-slit formula.

Exam Questions

Q1 Yellow laser light of wavelength 600 nm (6.00×10^{-7} m) is transmitted through a diffraction grating of 4.0×10^5 lines per metre.

a) At what angle to the normal are the first and second order bright lines seen? [4 marks]

b) Is there a fifth order line? [1 mark]

Q2 Visible, monochromatic light is transmitted through a diffraction grating of 3.7×10^5 lines per metre. The first order maximum is at an angle of 14.2° to the incident beam.

Find the wavelength of the incident light. [2 marks]

Ooooooooooooo — pretty patterns...

Three important points for you to take away — the more slits you have, the sharper the image, one lovely equation to learn and white light makes a pretty spectrum. Make sure you get everything in this section — there's some good stuff coming up in the next one and I wouldn't want you to be distracted.

Light — Wave or Particle?

You probably already thought light was a bit weird — but oh no... being a wave that travels at the fastest speed possible isn't enough for light — it has to go one step further and act like a particle too...

Light Behaves Like a **Wave**... or a **Stream of Particles**

1) In the **late nineteenth century**, if you asked what light was, scientists would happily show you lots of nice experiments showing how light must be a **wave** (see pages 54–61).
2) Then came the **photoelectric effect** (pages 64–65), which mucked up everything. The only way you could explain this was if light acted as a **particle** — called a **photon**.

A **Photon** is a **Quantum** of **EM Radiation**

1) When Max Planck was investigating **black body radiation** (don't worry — you don't need to know about that right now), he suggested that **EM waves** can **only** be **released** in **discrete packets**, called **quanta**. A single packet of **EM radiation** is called a **quantum**.
   The **energy carried** by one of these **wave-packets** had to be:

$$E = hf = \frac{hc}{\lambda}$$

where h = the Planck constant = 6.63×10^{-34} Js, f = frequency (Hz), λ = wavelength (m) and c = speed of light in a vacuum = 3.00×10^{8} ms^{-1}

2) So, the **higher** the **frequency** of the electromagnetic radiation, the more **energy** its wave-packets carry.
3) **Einstein** went **further** by suggesting that **EM waves** (and the energy they carry) can only **exist** in discrete packets. He called these wave-packets **photons**.
4) He believed that a photon acts as a **particle**, and will either transfer **all** or **none** of its energy when interacting with another particle, e.g. an electron.
5) Photons have **no charge** — they are **neutral**, like neutrons.

Photon Energies are Usually Given in **Electronvolts**

1) The **energies involved** when you're talking about photons are **so tiny** that it makes sense to use a more **appropriate unit** than the **joule**. Bring on the **electronvolt**...
2) When you **accelerate** an electron between two electrodes, it transfers some electrical potential energy (eV) into kinetic energy.

$$eV = \frac{1}{2}mv^2$$

e is the size charge on an electron: 1.60×10^{-19} C.

3) An electronvolt is defined as:

   The **kinetic energy gained** by an **electron** when it is **accelerated** through a **potential difference** of **1 volt.**

4) So 1 electron volt = $e \times V = 1.60 \times 10^{-19}$ C $\times$ 1 JC^{-1}. ⟹ **1 eV = 1.60×10^{-19} J**

The **Threshold Voltage** is Used to Find the **Planck Constant**

1) The Planck constant comes up everywhere — but it's not just some random number plucked out of the air. You can find its value by doing a simple experiment with **light-emitting diodes** (**LEDs**).
2) Current will only pass through an LED after a **minimum voltage** is placed across it — **the threshold voltage V_0**.
3) This is the voltage needed to give the electrons the **same energy** as a photon emitted by the LED. **All** of the electron's **kinetic energy** after it is accelerated over this potential difference is **transferred** into a **photon**.
4) So by finding the threshold voltage for a particular wavelength LED, you can estimate the Planck constant.

$$E = \frac{hc}{\lambda} = eV_0 \Rightarrow h = \frac{(eV_0)\lambda}{c}$$

Light — Wave or Particle?

You can Use **LEDs** to **Estimate** the **Planck Constant**

You've just seen the **theory** of how to find the **Planck constant** — now it's time for the **practicalities**.

Experiment to Measure the Planck Constant

1) Connect an LED of **known wavelength** in the electrical circuit shown.
2) Close any **blackout blinds** and place a **shaded tube** over the LED to look through. The room should be as dark as possible so you can see when the LED **first** begins to emit light.
3) Start off with no **current** flowing through the circuit, then adjust the **variable power source** until a current **just** begins to flow through the circuit and the LED **lights up**.
4) Record the **voltage** (V_0) across the LED.
5) **Repeat** this experiment with a number of LEDs of different colours that emit light at different wavelengths.

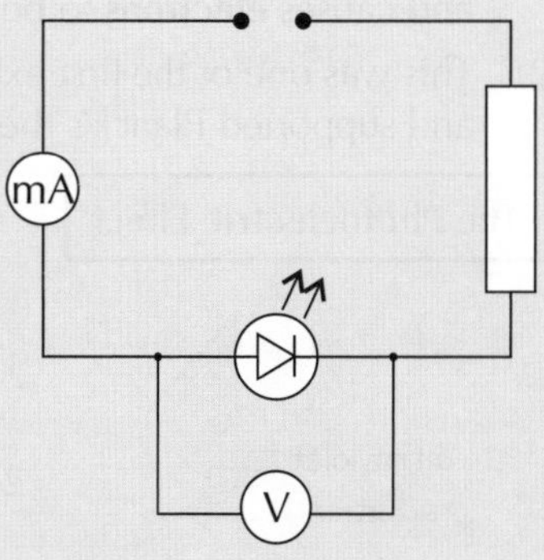

This is a milliammeter — used for measuring small currents.

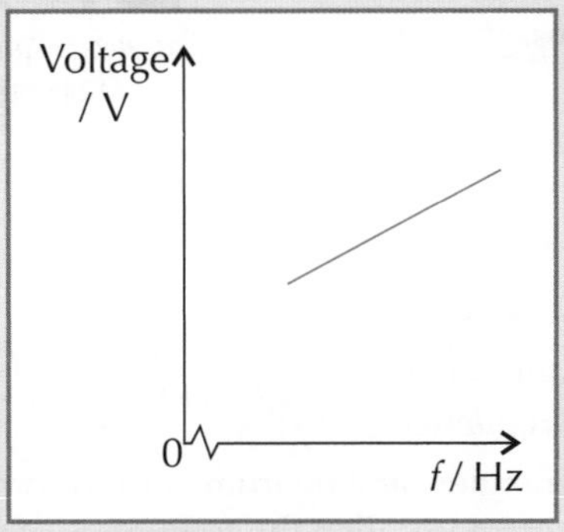

6) Plot a **graph** of **threshold voltages** (V_0) against frequency ($f = c/\lambda$) (where λ is the wavelength of light emitted by the LED in metres).
7) You should get a **straight line graph** with a **gradient** of h/e — which you can then use to find the value of h.

E.g. gradient $= \frac{h}{e} = 4.13 \times 10^{-15}$ so $h = 4.13 \times 10^{-15}e$

$= (4.13 \times 10^{-15}) \times (1.6 \times 10^{-19}) = 6.608 \times 10^{-34}$

$= \mathbf{6.6 \times 10^{-34}}$ **Js (to 2 s.f.)**

8) Repeat the experiment to find an **average** value of h.

If your straight line doesn't go through the origin, there could be some systematic errors you need to account for. You can do this by adding or taking away the difference between the origin and the vertical intercept from all of your data.

After careful measurements, Fluffles determined that her plank was indeed constant.

Practice Questions

Q1 Give two different ways to describe the nature of light.

Q2 What is a photon?

Q3 Write down the two formulas you can use to find the energy of a photon. Include the meanings of all the symbols you use.

Q4 What is an electronvolt? What is 1 eV in joules?

Q5 Describe an experiment to determine the Planck constant using different coloured LEDs.

Exam Question

Q1 An LED is tested and found to have a threshold voltage of 1.74 V.

a) Calculate the energy of the photons emitted by the LED. Give your answer in joules. [1 mark]

b) The LED emits light with a wavelength of 700 nm, given to 3 significant figures. Use your answer from a) to calculate an estimate for the value of the Planck constant. [2 marks]

c) Other LEDs are tested and a graph of threshold voltage against frequency is plotted. The intercept with the vertical axis is at 0.0400 V. Estimate the Planck constant taking this into account. [2 marks]

Millions of light particles are hitting your retinas as you read this... PANIC...

*I hate it in physics when they tell you lies, make you learn it, and just when you've got to grips with it they tell you it was all a load of codswallop. It just makes me doubt all the other things they say. I bet the Earth isn't even round. *Adjusts tin foil hat.* Ahem. This actually is the real deal folks — light isn't just the nice wave you've always known...*

The Photoelectric Effect

If light has enough energy, it can actually cause electrons to be kicked out of a metal. Parts of the experiment that shows this can't be explained with wave theory — but the photon model does a pretty good job...

The **Photoelectric Effect** Shows **Particle Behaviour** of Light

1) The **photoelectric effect** is when a light with a **high enough frequency** is shone onto the **surface of a metal**, and causes **electrons** to be **emitted**. For **most** metals, this **frequency** falls in the **U.V.** range.
2) This was one of the first experiments with light which couldn't be explained with **wave theory** and supported Planck's theory that light was **quantised** (p.62).

The Photoelectric Effect

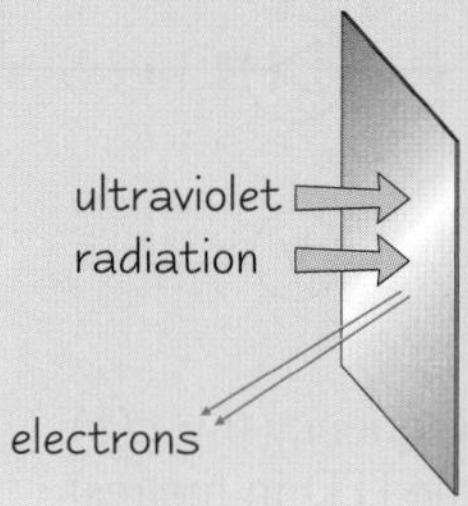

1) **Free electrons** on the **surface** of the metal **absorb energy** from the light, making them **vibrate**.
2) If an electron **absorbs enough** energy, the **bonds** holding it to the metal **break** and the electron is **released**.
3) This is called the **photoelectric effect** and the electrons emitted are called **photoelectrons**.

The electric photo effect is a whole other story.

You don't need to know the details of any experiments on this — you just need to learn the **three main conclusions**:

Conclusion 1: For a given metal, **no photoelectrons are emitted** if the radiation has a frequency **below** a certain value — called the **threshold frequency**.

Conclusion 2: The photoelectrons are emitted with a variety of kinetic energies ranging from zero to some maximum value. This value of **maximum kinetic energy** increases with the **frequency** of the radiation, and is **unaffected** by the **intensity** (photons per unit area) of the radiation.

Conclusion 3: The **number** of photoelectrons emitted per second is **proportional** to the **intensity** of the radiation.

These are the two that had scientists puzzled.

More on intensity of light on p.15.

The **Photoelectric Effect Couldn't** be Explained by **Wave Theory**

According to wave theory:
1) For a particular frequency of light, the **energy** carried is **proportional** to the **intensity** of the beam.
2) The energy carried by the light would be **spread evenly** over the wavefront.
3) **Each** free electron on the surface of the metal would gain a **bit of energy** from each incoming wave.
4) Gradually, each electron would gain **enough energy** to leave the metal.

For a comparison between wave theory and particle theory, see page 73.

SO...
- If the light had a **lower frequency** (i.e. was carrying less energy) it would take **longer** for the electrons to gain enough energy — but it would happen eventually. There is **no explanation** for the **threshold frequency**.
- The **higher the intensity** of the wave, the **more energy** it should transfer to each electron — the kinetic energy should increase with **intensity**. There's **no explanation** for the **kinetic energy** depending only on the **frequency**.

The Photoelectric Effect

The *Photon Model* Explained the *Photoelectric Effect* Nicely

According to the photon model (see page 62):

1) When light hits its surface, the metal is **bombarded** by photons.
2) If one of these photons is **absorbed** by a free electron, the electron will gain energy equal to ***hf***. So a higher **frequency** will result in a **higher kinetic energy**.
3) Each electron only **absorbs one** photon at a time, so all the **energy** it needs to gain before it can be released must come from that **one photon**.
4) So an **increase** in the **intensity** of the light (i.e. **more photons**) won't affect the **kinetic energy** of the electrons — only the **frequency** will.

Before an electron can **leave** the surface of the metal, it needs enough energy to **break the bonds holding it there**. This energy is called the **work function energy** (symbol ϕ, phi) and its **value** depends on the **metal**.

It also Explained the *Threshold Frequency*

Remember, h is the Planck constant — 6.63×10^{-34} Js^{-1}.

1) If the energy **gained** by an electron (on the surface of the metal) from a photon is **greater** than the **work function**, the electron is **emitted**.
2) If it **isn't**, the metal will heat up, but **no electrons** will be emitted.
3) Since, for **electrons** to be released, $hf \geq \phi$, the **threshold frequency** must be:

$$f = \frac{\phi}{h}$$

Example: A metal has a work function of 3.2 eV. Light is incident on the metal which has just enough energy to release electrons. Calculate the energy of the incoming light and the threshold frequency.

$$E = hf = \phi, \text{ so } f = \frac{\phi}{h} = \frac{3.2 \times 1.60 \times 10^{-19}}{6.63 \times 10^{-34}}$$

$f = 7.72... \times 10^{14} = \mathbf{7.7 \times 10^{14}}$ **Hz (to 2 s.f.)**

The energy must **equal** the work function as it's **just** enough to release electrons.

Remember to convert back to joules. 1 eV = 1.60×10^{-19} J.

Practice Questions

Q1 State the main three conclusions which can be drawn from the photoelectric effect.

Q2 Briefly describe the wave theory of light.

Q3 Explain why the photoelectric effect suggested light wasn't a wave.

Q4 What is the equation for calculating the threshold frequency of a metal?

Exam Questions

$h = 6.63 \times 10^{-34}$ Js; 1 eV = 1.60×10^{-19} J

Q1 The work function of calcium is 2.9 eV. Calculate the threshold frequency of radiation needed for the photoelectric effect to take place. [2 marks]

Q2 Photons with an energy E of 9.0 eV strike a metal, causing it to emit electrons with kinetic energies of 3.6 eV.

a) Define the work function of a metal. [1 mark]

b) Calculate the threshold frequency of the metal. [3 marks]

Q3 Explain why the photoelectric effect only occurs after the incident light has reached a certain frequency. [3 marks]

I'm so glad we got that all cleared up...

Yep, the photoelectric effect is a bit tricky. The most important bit here is why wave theory doesn't explain the phenomenon, and why photon theory does. A good way to learn conceptual stuff like this is to try to explain it to someone else. If you need to use any formulas (e.g. for frequency), they'll be in your handy data and formulae booklet.

Energy Levels and Photon Emission

Hot gas doesn't sound like one of the nicest discussion points, but look how pretty it is. All together now: red and yellow and pink and green, orange and purple and bluuuuuuuuuuuuuuuuuuuue...

Electrons in Atoms Exist in Discrete Energy Levels

1) **Electrons** in an **atom** can **only exist** in certain **well-defined energy levels**. Each level is given a **number**, with ***n* = 1** representing the **ground state**.
2) Electrons can **move down** an energy level by **emitting** a **photon**.
3) Since these **transitions** are between **definite energy levels**, the **energy** of **each photon** emitted can **only** take a **certain allowed value**.
4) The diagram on the right shows the **energy levels** for **atomic hydrogen**.
5) The **energy** carried by each **photon** is **equal** to the **difference in energies** between the **two levels**. The equation below shows a **transition** between levels ***n* = 2** and ***n* = 1**:

$$\Delta E = E_2 - E_1 = hf = \frac{hc}{\lambda}$$

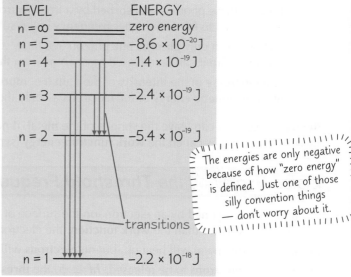

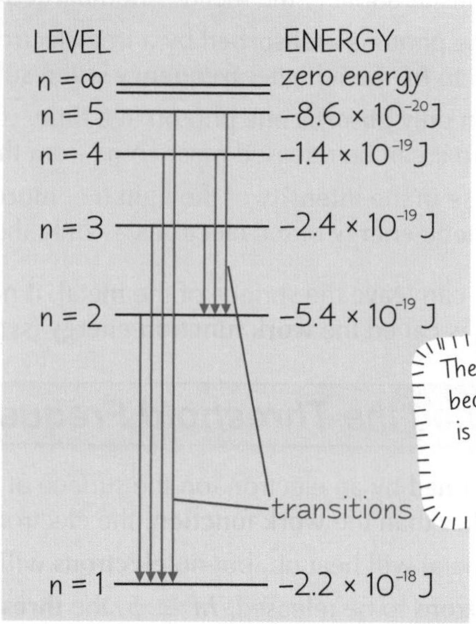

The energies are only negative because of how "zero energy" is defined. Just one of those silly convention things — don't worry about it.

Example: An excited electron moves from the $n = 2$ level of an atom, which has an energy of $E = -1.2$ eV, to the ground state, which has an energy of −6.6 eV. Calculate the wavelength of the photon that is emitted as the electron makes this transition.

$1\text{ eV} = 1.60 \times 10^{-19}\text{ J}$
$c = 3.00 \times 10^{8}\text{ ms}^{-1}$
$h = 6.63 \times 10^{-34}\text{ Js}$.

$\Delta E = E_2 - E_1 = -1.2\text{ eV} - -6.6\text{ eV} = 5.4\text{ eV}$

Convert this to joules: $5.4 \times 1.60 \times 10^{-19} = 8.64 \times 10^{-19}$ J

$$\Delta E = \frac{hc}{\lambda} \text{ so } \lambda = \frac{hc}{\Delta E} = \frac{6.63 \times 10^{-34} \times 3.00 \times 10^{8}}{8.64 \times 10^{-19}} = 2.302... \times 10^{-7} = \mathbf{2.3 \times 10^{-7}\,m\ (to\ 2\ s.f.)}$$

Hot Gases Produce Line Emission Spectra

1) If you heat a gas to a **high temperature**, many of its **electrons** move to higher **energy levels** (this is known as **excitation** — the **atom** becomes excited).
2) As they **fall** back to the **ground state**, these electrons **emit energy** as **photons**.
3) If you **split** the light from a **hot gas** with a **prism** or a **diffraction grating** (see pages 60-61), you get a **line spectrum**.
4) A line spectrum is seen as a **series** of **bright lines** against a **black background**, as shown on the right.
5) Each **line** on the spectrum corresponds to a **particular wavelength** of light **emitted** by the source. Since only **certain photon energies** are **allowed**, you only see the **corresponding wavelengths**.

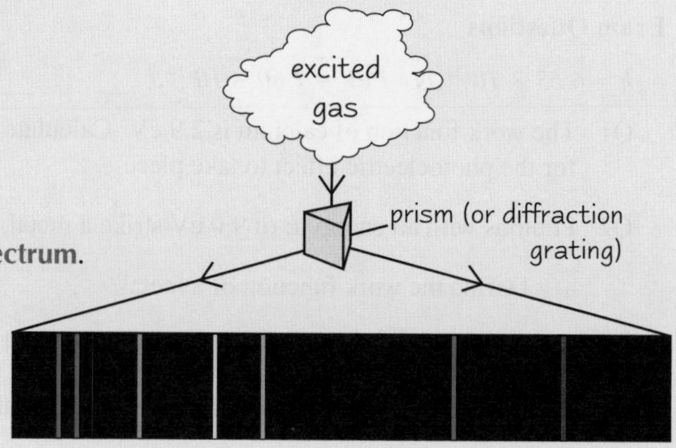

Energy Levels and Photon Emission

*Shining **White Light** through a **Cool Gas** gives an **Absorption Spectrum***

Continuous Spectra** Contain **All** Possible **Wavelengths

1) The **spectrum** of **white light** is **continuous**.
2) If you **split** the **light** up with a **prism**, the **colours** all **merge** into each other — there **aren't** any **gaps** in the spectrum.
3) **Hot things** emit a **continuous spectrum** in the visible and infrared parts of the **spectrum**.

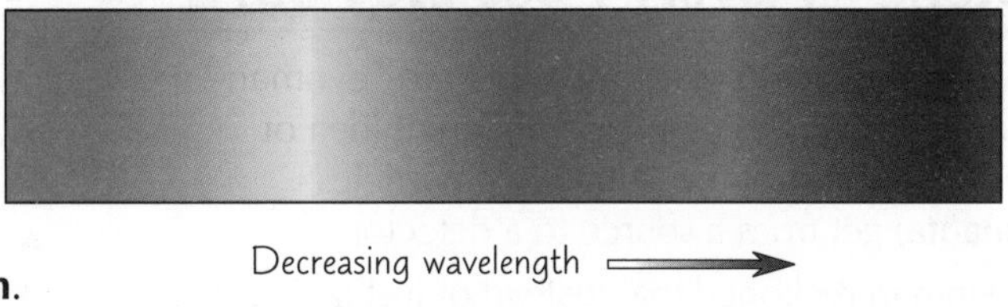

***Cool** Gases **Remove** Certain **Wavelengths** from the Continuous Spectrum*

1) You get a **line absorption spectrum** when **light** with a **continuous spectrum** of **energy** (white light) passes through a cool gas.
2) At **low temperatures**, **most** of the **electrons** in the **gas atoms** will be in their **ground states**.
3) **Photons** of the **correct wavelength** are **absorbed** by the **electrons** to **excite** them to **higher energy levels**.
4) These **wavelengths** are then **missing** from the **continuous spectrum** when it **comes out** the other side of the gas.
5) You see a **continuous spectrum** with **black lines** in it corresponding to the **absorbed wavelengths**.
6) If you **compare** the **absorption** and **emission spectra** of a **particular gas**, the **black lines** in the **absorption spectrum match up** to the **bright lines** in the **emission spectrum**.

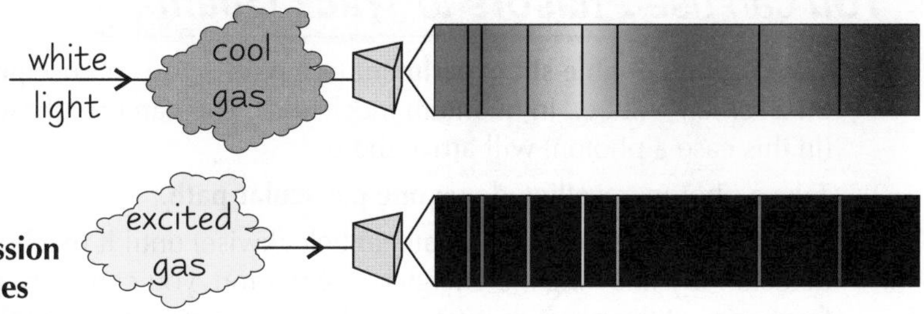

Practice Questions

Q1 Describe line absorption and line emission spectra. How are these two types of spectra produced?

Q2 Why do different excited gases glow different colours?

Exam Question

Q1 An electron has a kinetic energy of 2.04×10^{-18} J. This electron hits a hydrogen atom and excites it.

a) Explain what is meant by excitation. [1 mark]

b) Using the energy values on the right, work out to which energy level the electron in the hydrogen atom is excited. [1 mark]

c) Draw all the possible transitions the atom might undergo to return to a de-excited state. [2 marks]

d) Assume multiple electrons excite multiple atoms and all of the transitions you drew in c) occur. State how many spectral lines would appear on the emission spectra. [1 mark]

e) Calculate the frequency of the photon produced as an atom transitions from the $n = 3$ level to the $n = 1$ level. [2 marks]

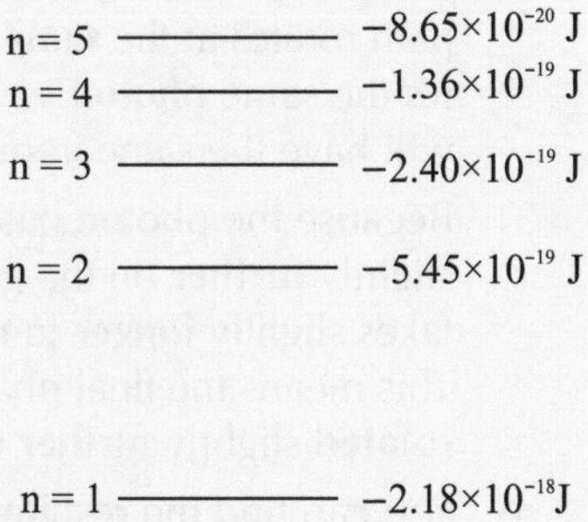

I can honestly say I've never got so excited that I've produced light...

This is heavy stuff, it really is. Quite interesting though, as I was just saying to Dom a moment ago. He's doing a psychology book. Psychology's probably quite interesting too — but it won't help you become an astrophysicist.

The "Sum Over Paths" Theory

So... you've got to grips with phasors... now here's where the really weird stuff kicks in. Buckle your seatbelts... and prepare to be amazed as the magical world of quantum reveals why light travels in straight lines, and why probability is a bit more useful than guessing what coloured ball you're likely to pick out of a bag...

Photons try Every Possible Path

1) A rather clever bloke called Richard Feynman came up with a completely different idea of how photons (or any subatomic particles, **quanta**) get from a source to a detector.
2) Feynman reckoned that instead of just taking one route to the detector, a photon will take **all** of the **possible paths** to the detector in one go. You can keep track of this photon whizzing along every possible route using **phasors** (see p.50).

A phasor shows the amplitude (size) and phase (direction) of a point on a wave.

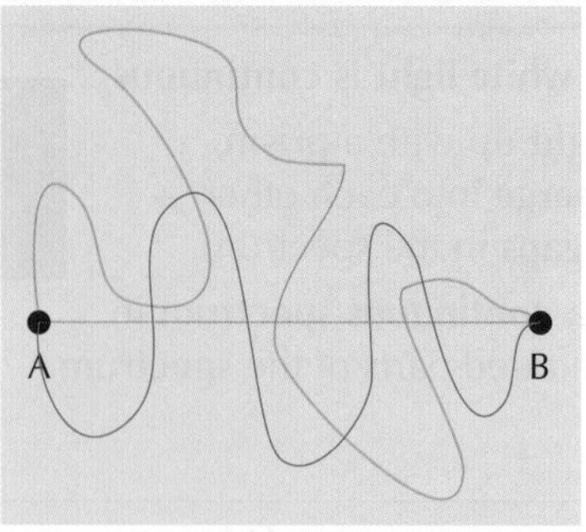

And all means <u>all</u> — the paths between A and B can be as squiggly as you like.

Andrew wasn't lost, he was just trying every path.

You can use Phasors to Track Quanta

1) Take **Young's double-slit experiment** (see p.58). You can use **phasors** to show how light or dark a certain spot on a screen will be. In quantum mechanics, you can use phasors to tell you how **probable** it is that a quantum (in this case a photon) will arrive there.
2) Take a photon travelling down **one particular path**.
3) As it travels, its phasor will rotate (anticlockwise) until it reaches the detector. By knowing the energy of the photon, you can work out the **frequency** of the phasor's rotation, *f*, by rearranging Planck's formula.

$$f = \frac{E}{h}$$

Remember — *E* is the photon's energy and *h* is Planck's constant.

4) You want to **record** the position of the phasor at the **end** of every path — you could then **sum** these phasors to find the **resultant phasor** for the photon making the journey from a source to a detector.
5) Of course you can't find the final phasor for every path as there's an **infinite** number of them. When you do the maths, nearly all the phasors cancel each other out — so you only need to consider the straightest/quickest possible paths (see next page).

Young's Double-Slit Experiment (again...)

1) Imagine that a photon is emitted by the source and hits point X on the screen. Take two of its possible paths and say it follows **both** of them, as shown.
2) The **phasor** of the photon along each path rotates at the **same rate** (because it's the **same photon** so the phasors will have the same frequency).
3) Because the photon has to travel slightly **further** on the green path, it takes slightly **longer** to reach point X. This means the final phasor for the green path will have **rotated** slightly **further** than that for the blue path.
4) You can find the **resultant** phasor arrow for the photon reaching point X by **adding** the final phasor position for each path, **tip-to-tail** (just like a normal vector sum (see p.74)).

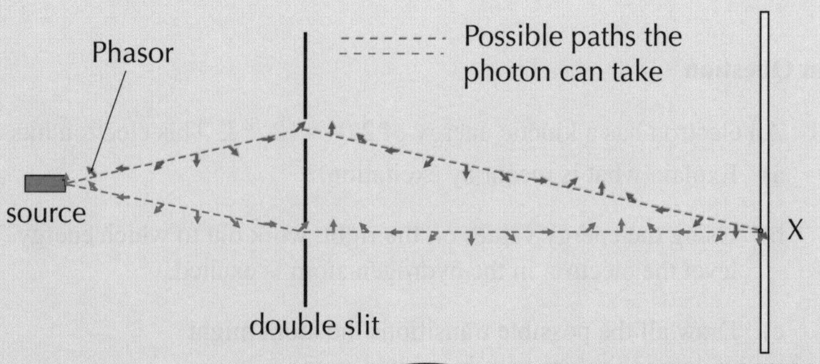

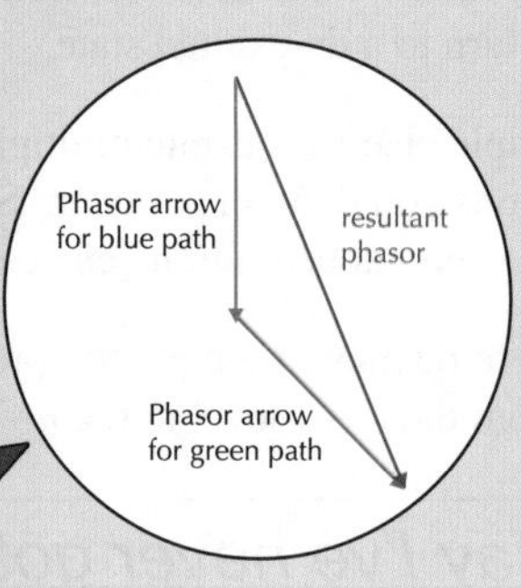

The "Sum Over Paths" Theory

*You can Calculate **Probability** from the **Resultant Phasor***

1) You can find the **probability** that a quantum will arrive at a point from **squaring** the **resultant phasor amplitude**.

Probability $\propto$ (Resultant phasor)^2

2) The **resultant phasor amplitude** has nothing to do with the **amplitude** of the light wave hitting the area, only the **probability** that a particle will arrive there.
3) The **higher** the probability, the **more likely** the particle will arrive there (well duh....).
4) If the **photon** is your quantum of choice, you can think of the **probability** and the **brightness** of the area as pretty much the same thing — the more **probable** it is that a photon will arrive at a point, the **brighter** it will appear.

Example: The resultant phasor amplitudes are shown for the paths a photon could take to points X and Y. How many times brighter does point X appear than point Y? Explain your answer.

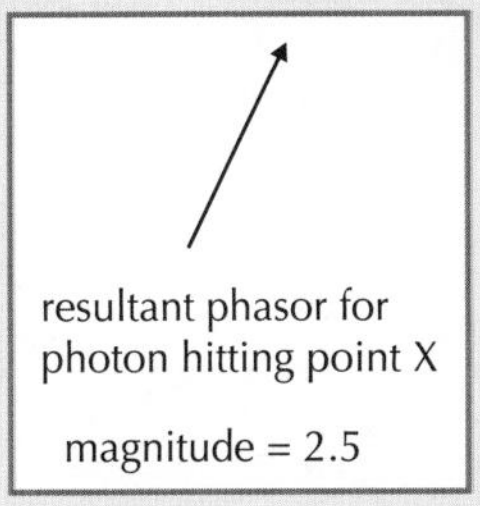

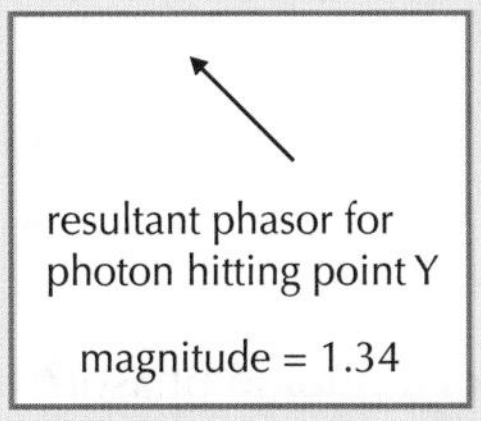

Square the magnitude of each phasor to find a number proportional to the probability of the photon arriving at each point.

Probability of photon hitting point X $\propto (2.5)^2 = \mathbf{6.25}$

Probability of photon hitting point Y $\propto (1.34)^2 = 1.7956$
$= \mathbf{1.80}$ **(to 3 s.f.)**

The more probable a photon will arrive at a point, the brighter it will be. So the relative probability of a photon arriving at the two points will be the relative brightness between the points.
So, point X appears $6.25 \div 1.7956 = 3.48... =$ **3.5 times (to 2 s.f.)** brighter than point Y.

*The **Path** that gives the **Highest Probability** is the **Quickest Route***

1) The sum over paths rule (finding the path with the **highest probability**) predicts all sorts of physics laws we take for granted. And each time it seems to be down to the **same reason**:

The final phasor of the **quickest path** will contribute the **most** to the **resultant amplitude** and the **probability** of a quantum arriving at a point.

2) It even predicts one of the most fundamental light behaviours — that **light** travels in a **straight line**. As a **straight line** is the shortest (and therefore **quickest**) path between two points — it provides the largest probability of a photon arriving at a particular point.
3) Obviously there are times when light **doesn't** travel in a straight line, like when it's being **refracted** — but quantum behaviour predicts that as well...

Refraction is also Predicted by Quantum Behaviour

1) Imagine spotting a pineapple at the bottom of a swimming pool. What **route** does the light take from the pineapple to your eye? Altogether now... it takes **all of them**.
2) When light travels in water, it **slows down**, but its **frequency stays the same**. This means the photons still have the **same energy**, and a photon's phasor will still have the **same amplitude** and **frequency** of rotation **whatever** material it's travelling through.
3) If you **add** up all the phasors for all the possible paths, it's the path that takes the **shortest time** that contributes the most to the **resultant amplitude** (and so gives the **highest probability** that the photon will get to your eye).

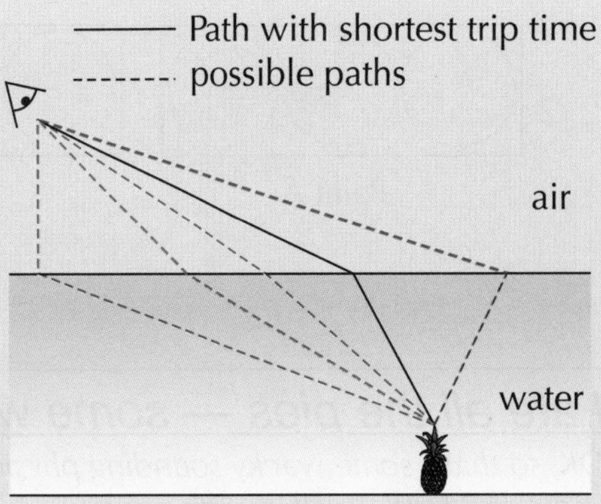

The "Sum Over Paths" Theory

You Need **All Paths** to Take the **Same Time** to Focus **Quanta**

To **focus** photons (or any other quanta), you need to make sure all straight line paths (that follow the reflection or refraction rule) from the source to the focus point take the **same amount of time** — so the final phasors for every path will be in the same direction.

A Convex Lens

The paths towards the edges of the lens are **longer** than those that go through the middle. You make the time taken for each path the same by **increasing** the amount of **glass** in the **middle part** of the lens to increase the time it takes to travel along the shorter paths between the source and detector.

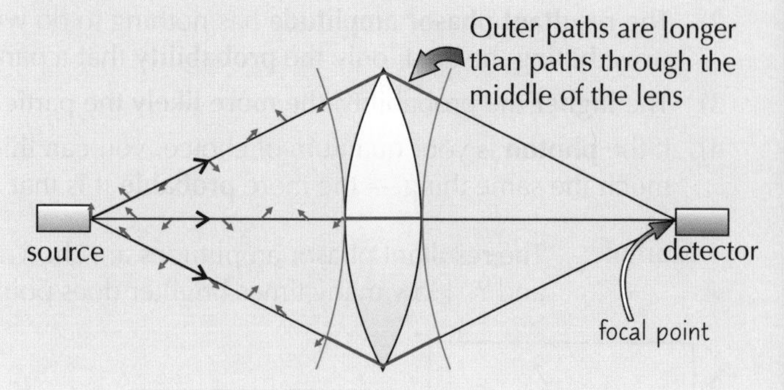

Practice Questions

Q1 What equation would you use to find the frequency of rotation of a photon phasor?

Q2 How are two phasor arrows combined to give a resultant?

Q3 How will a point appear if the probability for a light photon is zero there?

Q4 What path gives the highest probability?

Q5 Explain why light travels in straight lines.

Q6 Describe in terms of phasors how light is focused through a convex lens.

Exam Questions

Q1 The resultant phasors for an electron reaching points A and B have magnitudes of 6.3 and 4.5 respectively. How many times more likely is it that an electron will arrive at point A than point B? [3 marks]

Q2 A light photon has a frequency of 6.0×10^{14} Hz. How many times does the photon's phasor arrow rotate as it moves along a path 120 mm long from a source to a detector? ($c = 3.0 \times 10^8$ ms^{-1}.) [2 marks]

Q3 Using the idea of phasors and the "sum over paths theory", explain why very little (if any) light would be detected around the corner from the source in the diagram shown. [3 marks]

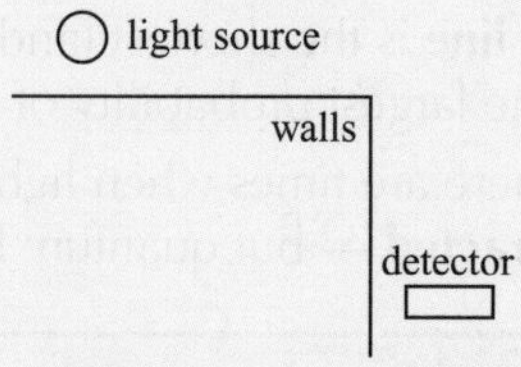

Q4 A photon takes all possible paths through a convex lens. By considering three possible straight line paths (that can reflect and refract), choose the option which correctly describes the phasors of each path at the focal point of the lens.

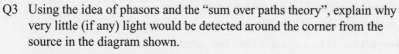

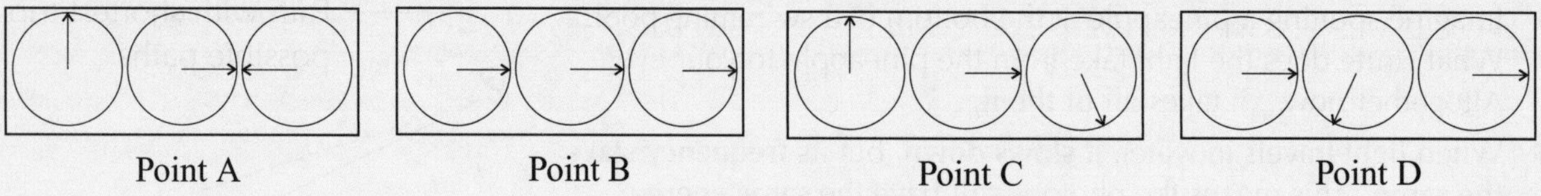

[1 mark]

I ate all the pies — some would call it greed, I say it's photon thinking...

OK, so that's some wacky sounding physics... but it does seem to work and agree with the standard physics laws we know and love... well, maybe not love. It's tricky, but you just need to follow the same method each time: sum the final phasors for all possible paths to get the resultant, then use the resultant to find the probability the quanta will get there.

Quantum Behaviour of Electrons

Light isn't the only thing that shows quantum behaviour — electrons do too...

De Broglie** Suggested **Electrons** were **Quantum Objects

1) Louis de Broglie made a **bold suggestion** in his **PhD thesis**:

> If '**wave-like' light** showed **particle properties** (photons), **'particles'** like **electrons** should be expected to show **wave-like properties**.

2) The **de Broglie equation** relates a **wave property** (**wavelength**, λ) to a **moving particle property** (**momentum**, p). h = Planck's constant = 6.63×10^{-34} Js.

$$\lambda = \frac{h}{p} \quad \text{or} \quad \lambda = \frac{h}{mv}$$

3) The **de Broglie wave** of a particle can be interpreted as a **'probability wave'**. You can use it to find the probability of finding an electron at a particular point (hmm, sounds familiar...).
4) Many physicists at the time **weren't very impressed** — his ideas were just **speculation**. But later experiments **confirmed** the wave nature of electrons.

De Broglie's
Controversial
PhD

I'm not impressed — this is just speculation. What do you think Dad?

Example: Electrons in a beam are travelling at a speed of 3.50×10^6 ms^{-1} and are exhibiting quantum behaviour. Calculate the de Broglie wavelength of the particles, and the speed at which protons would need to travel to have an equal de Broglie wavelength. $m_e = 9.11 \times 10^{-31}$ kg, $m_p = 1.673 \times 10^{-27}$ kg, $h = 6.63 \times 10^{-34}$ Js.

The momentum of the electrons is:

$$p = mv = 9.11 \times 10^{-31} \times 3.50 \times 10^{6} = 3.1885 \times 10^{-24} \text{ kgms}^{-1}$$

So the de Broglie wavelength of the electrons is:

$$\lambda = \frac{h}{p} = \frac{6.63 \times 10^{-34}}{3.1885 \times 10^{-24}} = 2.079... \times 10^{-10} = \mathbf{2.08 \times 10^{-10}\ m\ (to\ 3\ s.f.)}$$

For the protons:

$$v = \frac{h}{m\lambda} = \frac{6.63 \times 10^{-34}}{1.673 \times 10^{-27} \times 2.079... \times 10^{-10}} = 1905.8... = \mathbf{1910\ ms^{-1} (to\ 3\ s.f.)}$$

Rearranging $\lambda = \frac{h}{mv}$.

The Evidence: Electron Interference** and **Superposition

1) You can repeat experiments like **Young's double-slit** experiment (p.58) with **electrons**. They show the same kind of **interference** and **superposition** effects as you get with photons.
2) You usually show interference and superposition patterns using a **fluorescent screen**. As an electron hits the screen, it causes a photon to be released, so you can see the location of the electron.
3) Just like photons, the **electrons try every path**:

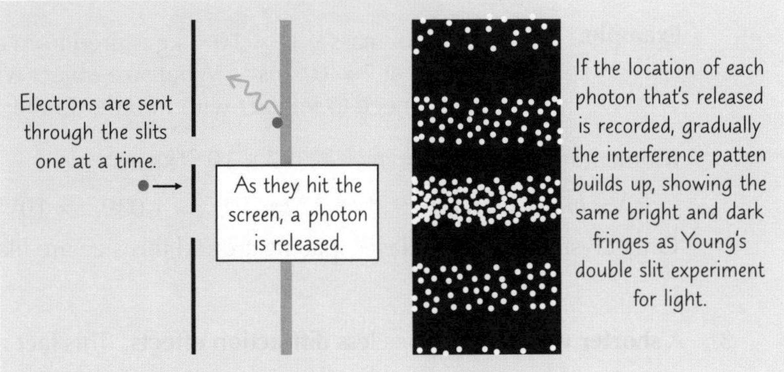

Electrons are sent through the slits one at a time.
As they hit the screen, a photon is released.
If the location of each photon that's released is recorded, gradually the interference patten builds up, showing the same bright and dark fringes as Young's double slit experiment for light.

> **Bright fringes** in an electron interference pattern show where the **probability** of an electron arriving is **high**. **Dark fringes** show where the **probability** of an electron hitting the screen is **low**.

Quantum Behaviour of Electrons

Electron Diffraction Also Supports Electrons Being Quantum Objects

1) **Diffraction patterns** are observed when **accelerated electrons** in a vacuum tube **interact** with the **spaces** in a graphite **crystal**.
2) You can think of it in exactly the same way as photon diffraction. By summing the final phasor for every possible path, you can find how **likely** it is an electron will hit the fluorescent screen at a particular point. The **higher** the **probability**, the **brighter** the point on the screen.
3) The only difference is that when finding the **frequency** and **amplitude** of the electron phasor, ***E*** is the **kinetic energy** of the electron.

Electron diffraction patterns look like this.

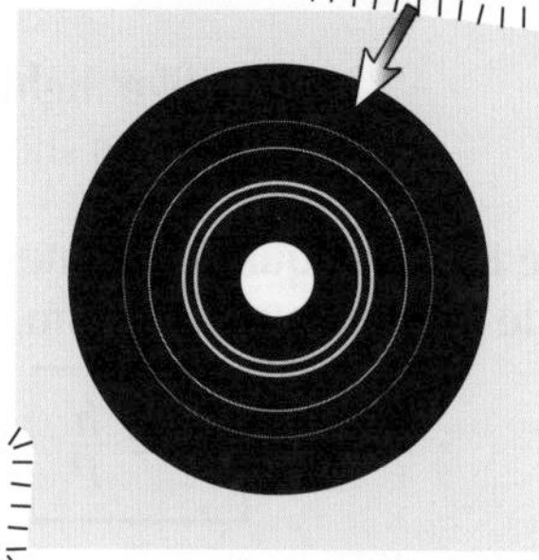

$$f = \frac{E_{kinetic}}{h}$$

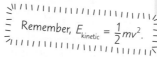

Remember, $E_{kinetic} = \frac{1}{2}mv^2$.

4) This **confirms** that **electrons** show **quantum behaviour**.
5) This was a **huge** discovery. A few years earlier, **Louis de Broglie** had **hypothesised** that electrons would show **quantum behaviour** just like **light**, but this was the first **direct evidence** for it.
6) **Increasing** the **accelerating voltage** also **increases** the **electron speed**. The diffraction pattern circles will **squash together** towards the **middle**. This fits in with the **de Broglie** equation on the previous page — if the **velocity** is **higher**, the **wavelength** is **shorter** and the **spread** of lines is **smaller**.

The race was on to squash into the best sunbathing spot.

Example: An electron has a velocity of 8.42×10^5 ms^{-1}. Calculate the frequency of the electron phasor. Electron mass = 9.11×10^{-31} kg.

$E_{kinetic} = ½ \times m \times v^2 = ½ \times 9.11 \times 10^{-31} \times (8.42 \times 10^5)^2 = 3.229... \times 10^{-19}$

$f = E_{kinetic} / h = (3.229... \times 10^{-19}) / (6.63 \times 10^{-34})$

$= 4.870... \times 10^{14}$ = **4.87×10^{14} Hz (to 3 s.f.)**

Electrons Don't show Quantum Behaviour All the Time

1) You **only** get **diffraction** if a particle interacts with an object of about the **same size** as its **de Broglie wavelength**.
2) A **tennis ball**, for example, with **mass 0.058 kg** and **speed 100 ms^{-1}** has a **de Broglie wavelength** of **10^{-34} m**. That's **10^{19} times smaller** than the **nucleus** of an **atom**! There's nothing that small for it to interact with.

Example: An electron of mass 9.11×10^{-31} kg is fired from an electron gun at 7×10^6 ms^{-1}. What size object will the electron need to interact with in order to diffract?

You need the de Broglie equation from the previous page, $\lambda = \frac{h}{mv}$.

Momentum of electron = $mv = 6.377 \times 10^{-24}$ kg ms^{-1}

$\lambda = h/mv = 6.63 \times 10^{-34} / 6.377 \times 10^{-24} = 1.039... \times 10^{-10}$ = **1×10^{-10} m (to 1 s.f.)**

Only crystals with atom layer spacing around this size are likely to cause the diffraction of this electron.

3) A **shorter wavelength** gives **less diffraction effects**. This fact is used in the **electron microscope**.

Diffraction effects **blur detail** on an image. If you want to **resolve tiny detail** in an **image**, you need a **shorter wavelength**. **Light** blurs out detail more than **electrons** do, so an **electron microscope** can resolve **finer detail** than a **light microscope**. They can let you look at things as tiny as a single strand of DNA... which is nice.

Quantum Behaviour of Electrons

All this Couldn't Be Explained By **Particle Theory**

1) Particle theory says that particles are **physical** objects which cannot **superpose** with other particles. To have **interference** patterns, you need superposition.
2) You also need at least **two slits** to create an interference pattern — classic particles would either go through **one slit** or the other, not both. However, interference patterns can be seen when only a **single electron** at a time is sent through narrow slits.
3) These experiments showed how electrons exhibited **wave-like** properties as theorised by de Broglie.

The table shows which observations are explained by each theory of light.

Phenomenon	Is it explained by...	
	...wave theory?	...particle theory?
Diffraction	Yes	No
Superposition and Interference	Yes	No
Refraction	Yes	No
Photoelectric effect	No	Yes

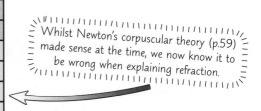

Whilst Newton's corpuscular theory (p.59) made sense at the time, we now know it to be wrong when explaining refraction.

Practice Questions

Q1 State the two equations for calculating the de Broglie wavelength and explain all of the symbols used.
Q2 What happens to the de Broglie wavelength of a particle if its velocity increases?
Q3 State one observable phenomena which supported de Broglie's theory that electrons were quantum objects.
Q4 What is the formula for calculating the phasor frequency of electrons?
Q5 What conditions must be met for electron diffraction to occur?
Q6 What were the limitations of particle theory which showed that electrons must display wave-like properties?

Exam Questions

Q1 An electron has a kinetic energy of 5.22×10^{-19} J.

a) Calculate the frequency of the electron phasor. [1 mark]

b) Calculate the atomic spacing needed to cause diffraction of the electron. [2 marks]

c) Calculate how much the velocity of the electron would need to be increased by for it to be diffracted by a lattice spacing of 2.3×10^{-10} m. [2 marks]

Q2 Electrons are accelerated through a potential difference and diffracted through a crystal lattice. The diffraction pattern is shown in Figure 1. The potential difference is then altered, and a second diffraction pattern is created, as shown in Figure 2.

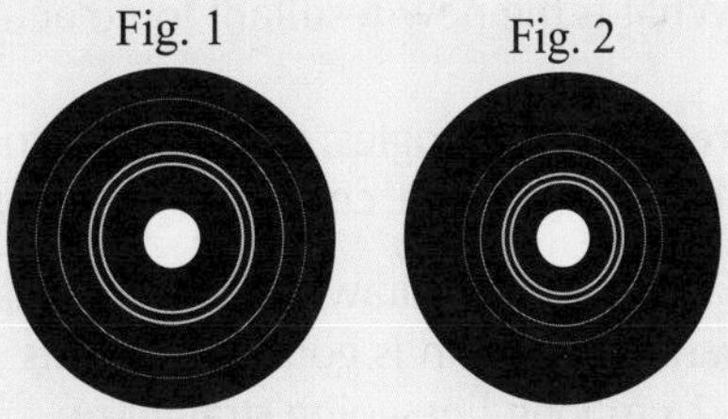

a) State whether the accelerating voltage was increased or decreased. [1 mark]

b) Explain why the rings are closer together on the second diffraction pattern. [2 marks]

Don't look now, but... it's the ENDOFTHESECTION — YAY...

Right — I think we'll all agree that quantum physics is a wee bit strange when you come to think about it. What it's saying is that electrons and photons aren't really waves, and they aren't really particles — they're both... at the same time. It's what quantum physicists like to call a 'juxtaposition of states'. Well they would, wouldn't they...

Scalars and Vectors

Time to draw some lovely triangles. Please, don't all thank me at once...

Scalars Only Have Size, but Vectors Have Size and Direction

1) A **scalar** has **no direction** — it's **just an amount** of something, like the **mass** of a **sack of meaty dog food**.
2) A **vector** has magnitude (**size**) and **direction** — like the **velocity** (**speed and direction**) of next door's **cat** running away.
3) **Force, velocity and momentum** are all **vectors** — you need to know **which way** they're going as well as **how big** they are. Here are some of the common scalars and vectors that you'll come across in your exams:

Scalars	Vectors
mass, time, temperature, length, speed, energy	displacement, force, velocity, acceleration, momentum

You can Add Vectors to Find the Resultant

1) Adding two or more vectors is called finding the **resultant** of them. Whatever the quantity is — displacement, force, momentum, the procedure is the same.
2) You should always start by drawing a **diagram**. Draw the vectors '**tip-to-tail**'. If you're doing a **vector subtraction**, draw the vector you're subtracting with the same magnitude but pointing in the **opposite direction**.
3) If the vectors are at **right angles** to each other, then you can use **Pythagoras** and **trigonometry** to find the resultant vector.
4) If the vectors aren't at right angles, you may need to draw a **scale diagram**.

Trig's really useful in physics, so make sure you're completely okay with it. Remember SOH CAH TOA.

Example 1: Jemima goes for a walk. She walks 3.0 m north and 4.0 m east. She has walked 7.0 m but she isn't 7.0 m from her starting point. Find the magnitude and direction of her displacement.

Jemima's 'displacement' gives her position <u>relative</u> to her starting point, see p.76.

First, draw the vectors **tip-to-tail**. Then draw a line from the **tail** of the first vector to the **tip** of the last vector to give the **resultant**:

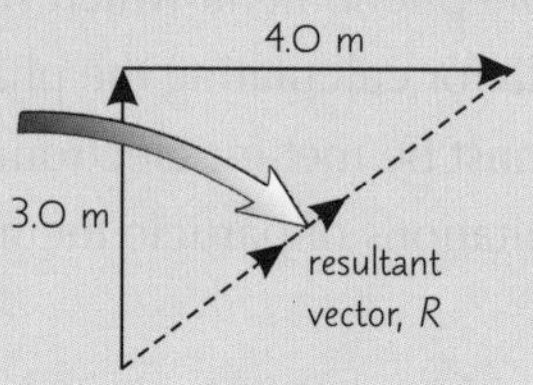

Because the vectors are at right angles, you get the **magnitude** of the resultant using Pythagoras:

$R^2 = 3.0^2 + 4.0^2 = 25.0$ So $R = \mathbf{5.0\ m}$

Now find the **bearing** of Jemima's new position from her original position. You use the triangle again, but this time you need to use trigonometry. You know the opposite and the adjacent sides, so you can use:

$\tan\theta = 4.0 / 3.0$ So $\theta = \mathbf{053°}$ **(to 2 s.f.)**

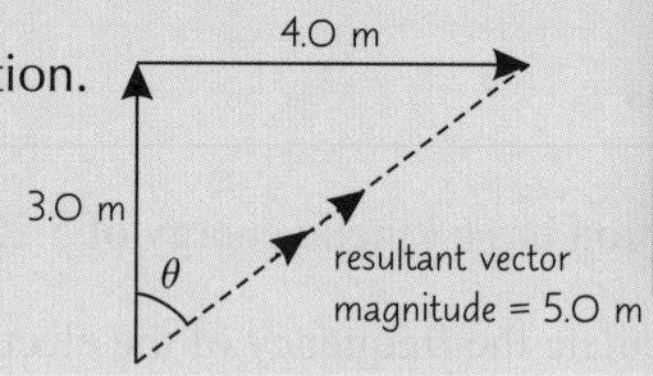

Jemima

A bearing is just an angle measured clockwise from the north line, represented by three digits, e.g. 10° = 010°.

Example 2: A van is accelerating north, with a resultant force of 510 N. A wind begins to blow on a bearing of 150°. It exerts a force of 200 N on the van. What is the new resultant force acting on the van?

The vectors **aren't** at right angles, so you need to do a scale drawing. Pick a sensible scale. Here, 1 cm = 100 N seems good.

Using a really sharp pencil, draw the initial resultant force on the van. As the van is going north, this should be a 5.1 cm long line going straight up.

The force of the wind acts on a bearing of 150°, so add this to your diagram. Using the same scale, this vector has a length of 2.0 cm.

Then you can draw on the new resultant force and measure its length. Measure the angle carefully to get the bearing.

The resultant force has a magnitude of 350 N (to 2 s.f.), acting on a bearing of 017° (to 2 s.f.).

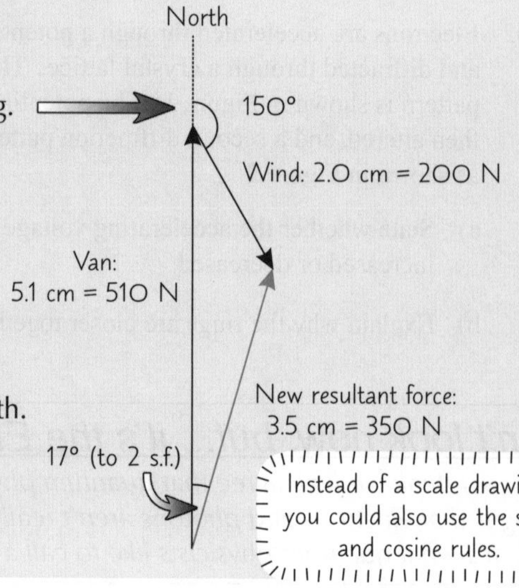

Instead of a scale drawing, you could also use the sine and cosine rules.

Scalars and Vectors

It's Useful to Split a **Vector** *into* **Horizontal** *and* **Vertical Components**

This is the opposite of finding the resultant — you start from the resultant vector and split it into two **components** at right angles to each other. You're basically **working backwards** from Example 1 on the last page.

Resolving a vector v into horizontal and vertical components:

You get the **horizontal** component v_h like this:

$$\cos\theta = v_h / v$$

$$\mathbf{v_h = v\cos\theta}$$

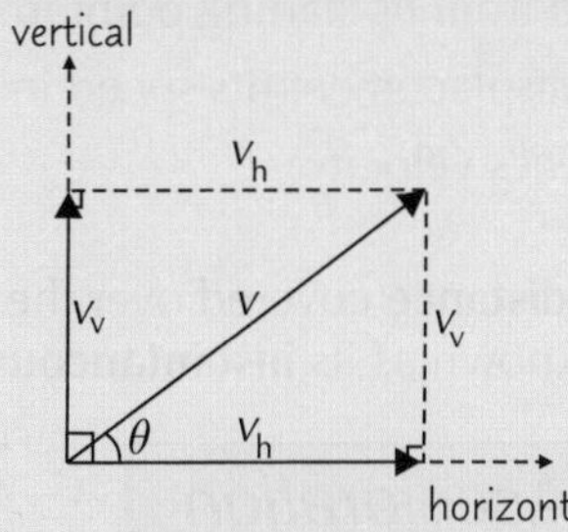

...and the **vertical** component v_v like this:

$$\sin\theta = v_v / v$$

$$\mathbf{v_v = v\sin\theta}$$

Where θ is the angle from the horizontal.

Example: Charley's amazing floating home is travelling at a speed of 5 ms^{-1} at an angle of 60° to the horizontal. Find the vertical and horizontal components.

The **horizontal** component v_h is:

$v_h = v\cos\theta = 5\cos 60° = \mathbf{2.5\ ms^{-1}}$

The **vertical** component v_v is:

$v_v = v\sin\theta = 5\sin 60° = \mathbf{4.3\ ms^{-1}}$ **(to 2 s.f.)**

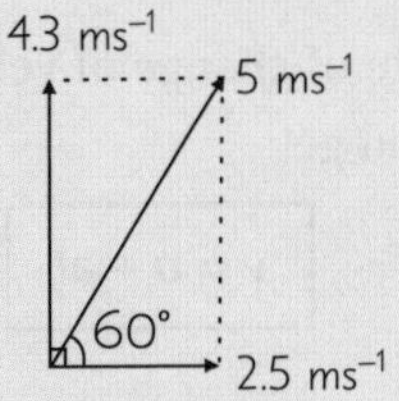

Charley's mobile home was the envy of all his friends.

Resolving is dead useful because the two components of a vector **don't affect each other**. This means you can deal with the two directions **completely separately**.

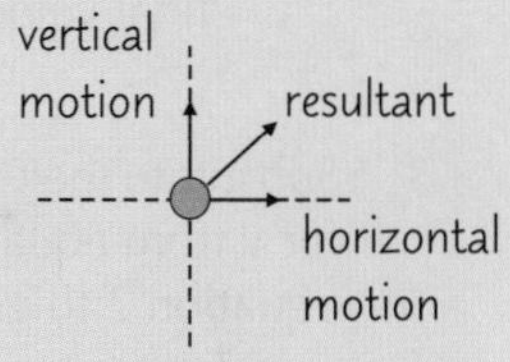

Only the vertical component is affected by gravity.

See pages 80–81 for more on resolving.

Practice Questions

Q1 What is the difference between a vector and a scalar?

Q2 Name three vector quantities and three scalar quantities.

Q3 Describe how to find a resultant vector using a scale diagram.

Q4 If a vector of magnitude L makes an angle of 30° to the horizontal, what are the horizontal and vertical components of the vector?

Exam Questions

Q1 The wind applies a horizontal force of 20 N on a falling rock of weight 75 N.
Calculate the magnitude and direction of the resultant force. [2 marks]

Q2 A glider is travelling at a velocity of 20.0 ms^{-1} at an angle of 15.0° below the horizontal.
Calculate the horizontal and vertical components of the glider's velocity. [2 marks]

Q3 A remote controlled boat is placed in a river. The boat produces a driving speed of 1.54 ms^{-1} at an angle of 60° to the current (travelling with the current). The river is flowing at 0.20 ms^{-1}.
By resolving the vectors into their horizontal and vertical components, show that the resultant velocity of the boat is 1.6 ms^{-1} at an angle of 54° to the current. [4 marks]

I think I'm a scalar quantity, my Mum says I'm completely direction-less...

Lots of different ways to solve vector problems on these pages, it must be your lucky day. Personally, I avoid doing scale drawings unless I absolutely have to (too fiddly for my liking), but if they work for you that's great. And you may get told to draw one in your exams, so you need to be prepared in case they come up.

Motion with Constant Acceleration

All the equations on this page are for motion with constant acceleration. It makes life a whole lot easier, trust me.

Learn the **Definitions** of **Speed**, **Displacement**, **Velocity** and **Acceleration**

Displacement, velocity and acceleration are all **vector** quantities (page 74), so the **direction** matters.

Speed — How fast something is moving, regardless of direction (i.e. the magnitude of velocity).
Displacement (s) — How far an object's travelled from its starting point in a given direction.
Velocity (v) — The rate of change of an object's displacement (its speed in a given direction).
Acceleration (a) — The rate of change of an object's velocity.

During a journey, the **average speed** is just the **total distance** covered over the **total time** elapsed.
The speed of an object at any given point in time is known as its **instantaneous** speed.

Uniform Acceleration is **Constant** Acceleration

Acceleration could mean a change in speed or direction or both.

Uniform means **constant** here. It's nothing to do with what you wear.
There are **four main equations** that you use to solve problems involving **uniform acceleration**.
You need to be able to **derive them** so make sure you learn all of these steps.

1) **Acceleration is the rate of change of velocity.**
From this definition you get:

$$a = \frac{(v-u)}{t} \quad \text{so} \quad \boldsymbol{v = u + at}$$

where:
u = initial velocity a = acceleration
v = final velocity t = time taken

2) **displacement = average velocity × time**
If acceleration is constant, the average velocity is just the average of the initial and final velocities, so:

$$\textbf{average velocity} = \frac{(u+v)}{2} \qquad s = \frac{(u+v)}{2} \times t$$

s = displacement

3) Substitute the expression for v from equation 1 into equation 2 to give:

$$s = \frac{(u + u + at) \times t}{2} = \frac{2ut + at^2}{2}$$

$$\boldsymbol{s = ut + \tfrac{1}{2}at^2}$$

4) You can **derive** the fourth equation from equations **1** and **2**:

Use equation **1** in the form: $a = \frac{v-u}{t}$ Multiply both sides by s, where: $s = \frac{(u+v)}{2} \times t$

This gives us: $as = \frac{(v-u)}{t} \times \frac{(u+v)t}{2}$

The t's on the right cancel, so:
$2as = (v - u)(v + u)$
$2as = v^2 - uv + uv - u^2$

so: $\boldsymbol{v^2 = u^2 + 2as}$

Example: A tile falls from the edge of a roof 25.0 m above ground level. Assuming it was initially at rest, calculate its speed when it hits the ground and how long it takes to fall. Take $g = 9.81\ \text{ms}^{-2}$.

First of all, write out what you know:
$s = 25.0$ m
$u = 0\ \text{ms}^{-1}$ since the tile's stationary to start with
$a = 9.81\ \text{ms}^{-2}$ due to gravity
$v = ?$ $t = ?$

Usually you take upwards as the positive direction. In this question it's probably easier to take downwards as positive, so you get $g = +9.81\ \text{ms}^{-2}$ instead of $g = -9.81\ \text{ms}^{-2}$.

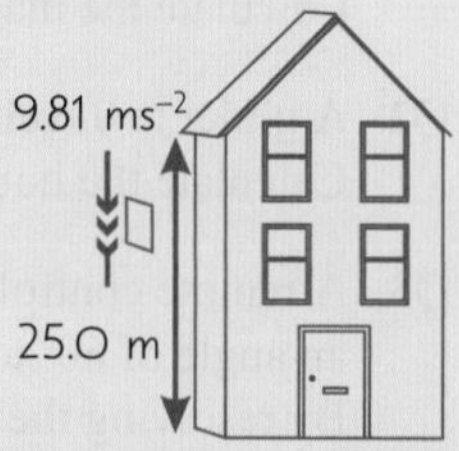

Then, choose an equation with only **one unknown quantity**.
So start with $v^2 = u^2 + 2as$
$v^2 = 0 + 2 \times 9.81 \times 25.0$
$v^2 = 490.5$ $v = \mathbf{22.1\ ms^{-1}}$ **(to 3 s.f.)**

Now, find t using:
$s = ut + \tfrac{1}{2}at^2$
$25.0 = 0 + \tfrac{1}{2} \times 9.81 \times t^2$
$t^2 = \frac{25.0}{4.905}$

Final answers:
t = **2.26 s (to 3 s.f.)**
v = **22.1 ms⁻¹ (to 3 s.f.)**

Motion with Constant Acceleration

Example: A car accelerates steadily from rest at a rate of 4.2 ms^{-2} for 6.0 seconds.
a) Calculate the car's final speed.
b) Calculate the distance travelled by the car during the 6.0 seconds.

Remember — always start by writing down what you know.

a) $a = 4.2\ ms^{-2}$
$u = 0\ ms^{-1}$
$t = 6.0\ s$
$v = ?$

choose the right equation... $v = u + at$

$v = 0 + 4.2 \times 6.0$

Final answer: $v = \mathbf{25.2\ ms^{-1}}$

b) $s = ?$
$t = 6.0\ s$
$u = 0\ ms^{-1}$
$a = 4.2\ ms^{-2}$
$v = 25.2\ ms^{-1}$

you can use: $s = \frac{(u + v)}{2} \times t$ **or:** $s = ut + \frac{1}{2}at^2$

$s = \frac{(0 + 25.2)}{2} \times 6.0$ $\qquad$ $s = 0 + \frac{1}{2} \times 4.2 \times (6.0)^2$

Final answer: $s = \mathbf{75.6\ m}$ $\qquad$ $s = \mathbf{75.6\ m}$

It's always better to use an equation which doesn't use a value you've previously calculated.

Practice Questions

Q1 Write down the definitions of speed, velocity and displacement.

Q2 Define average speed.

Q3 Define acceleration and write down the equation that links acceleration, initial and final velocity and time.

Q4 Give the equation for calculating the average velocity.

Q5 Write down another equation of motion for constant acceleration.

Exam Questions

Q1 A skydiver steps out of an aeroplane when it is flying horizontally. She accelerates due to gravity for 5 s.
a) Calculate her maximum vertical velocity. (Assume no air resistance.) [2 marks]
b) Calculate how far she falls in this time. [2 marks]

Q2 A motorcyclist slows down uniformly as he approaches a red light.
He takes 3.2 seconds to come to a halt and travels 40 m in this time.
a) Calculate how fast he was travelling initially. [2 marks]
b) Calculate his acceleration. (N.B. a negative value shows a deceleration.) [2 marks]

Q3 The flow of a section of river provides a constant acceleration of 6 ms^{-2}. A remote controlled boat is travelling upstream. 1.2 m upstream from the edge of a waterfall, the boat's motor cuts out. Just before it reaches the waterfall, it is travelling at a speed of 5 ms^{-1}.
a) Calculate the boat's velocity when the motor cuts out. [2 marks]
b) Calculate the maximum distance upstream from the waterfall the boat reaches. [2 marks]

Q4 A cyclist is travelling at a constant speed of 3 ms^{-1} as he starts to roll down a hill. He rolls down the hill with a constant acceleration. During the third second, he travels a distance of 6 m.
a) Calculate the cyclist's acceleration. [3 marks]
b) Calculate how far he travels during the fourth second. [2 marks]

Constant acceleration — it'll end in tears...

If a question talks about "uniform" or "constant" acceleration, it's a dead giveaway they want you to use one of these equations. The tricky bit is working out which one to use — start every question by writing out what you know and what you need to know. That makes it much easier to see which equation you need. To be sure. Arrr.

Acceleration of Free Fall

Ahhh acceleration due to gravity. The reason falling apples whack you on the head.

Free Fall is When There's Only **Gravity** and Nothing Else

Free fall is defined as the motion of an object undergoing an acceleration of 'g'. You need to remember:

1) Acceleration is a **vector quantity** — and 'g' acts **vertically downwards**.
2) The magnitude of 'g' is usually taken as **9.81 ms^{-2}**, though it varies slightly at different points above the Earth's surface.
3) The **only force** acting on an object in free fall is its **weight**.
4) **All** objects free fall at the **same rate**.
5) Objects can have an initial velocity in any direction and still undergo **free fall** as long as the **force** providing the initial velocity is **no longer acting**.

You Can Calculate **g** By Doing an **Experiment**...

1) Set up the equipment shown in the diagram on the right.
2) Measure the height h from the **bottom** of the ball bearing to the **trapdoor**.
3) Flick the switch to simultaneously **start the timer** and **disconnect the electromagnet**, releasing the ball bearing.
4) The ball bearing falls, knocking the trapdoor down and **breaking the circuit** — which **stops the timer**. Record the time t shown on the timer.
5) **Repeat** this experiment three times and **average** the time taken to fall from this height. Do this for a range of **different heights**.
6) You can then use these results to find g using a **graph**.

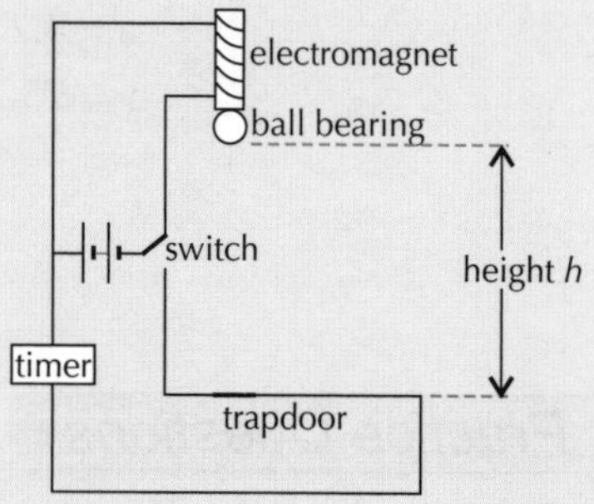

1) Use your data from the experiment to plot a graph of **height** (s) against the **time** it takes the ball to fall, **squared** (t^2). Then draw a **line of best fit**.
2) You know that with constant acceleration: $s = ut + \frac{1}{2}at^2$.
3) If you drop the ball, initial speed $u = 0$, so $s = \frac{1}{2}at^2$.
4) Rearranging this gives $\frac{1}{2}a = \frac{s}{t^2}$, or $\frac{1}{2}g = \frac{s}{t^2}$ (remember the acceleration is all due to gravity).
5) The gradient of the line of best fit $\frac{\Delta s}{\Delta t^2}$, is equal to $\frac{1}{2}g$:

$$g = 2 \times \frac{\Delta s}{\Delta t^2} = 2 \times \frac{0.44}{0.09} = \mathbf{9.8\ ms^{-2}}\ \text{(to 2 s.f.)}$$

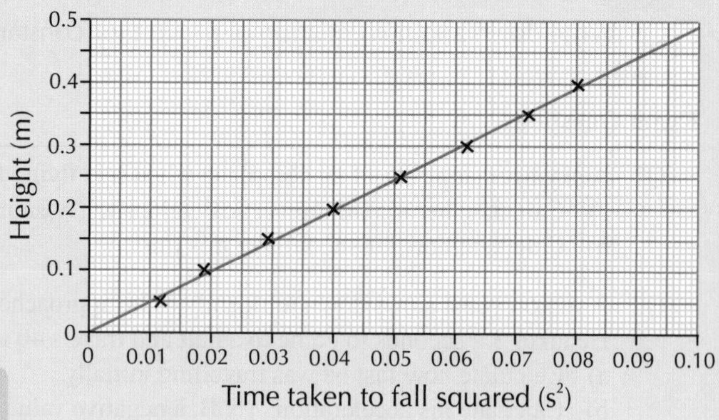

To increase the **accuracy** (see page 8) of the measurements you take you can:

- Use a **small** and **heavy** ball bearing so you can assume air resistance is so small that you can **ignore it**.
- Use a ruler with **smaller increments** and pick a certain **point** on the ball bearing to measure from to reduce the errors in measuring the **height**.

In the experiment above, using a computer to **automatically release** and **time** the ball bearing's fall **removes random error** that might arise if you timed the ball bearing manually by eye with a stopwatch, **reducing** the **uncertainty** (see page 8) in **time** measurement.

You could also do a **similar** experiment with **light gates**. **Drop** the ball bearing from a height h so it falls through a light gate. The light gate **automatically** calculates the **velocity** of the falling object.

You can then use $\mathbf{v^2 = u^2 + 2as}$ to calculate the acceleration due to gravity, g.

Both methods give less **uncertainty** when calculating g than measuring the time manually by eye would. The light gates can calculate the velocity automatically, instead of it being calculated from time measurements, which could reduce **systematic error**. This means the main uncertainty would be caused by measuring h.

Acceleration of Free Fall

You Can Also Use **Video Techniques** to find *g*

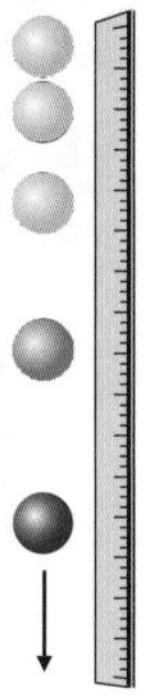

1) Set up a **video camera** in front of a **metre rule** and record the ball as it is dropped from the top of the ruler.
2) Once the ball hits the floor, you can stop recording and analyse the video with video editing software.
3) Go through **frame by frame**, making a note of the **distance** the ball has travelled every **0.1 seconds**.
4) Create a table to calculate the ball's **velocity**. You can then calculate an average value for g from the **table** or plot a **graph** of **velocity** against **distance**. The **gradient** of this graph will give the **acceleration** due to gravity.

Your table should have the headings shown below:

Time (s)	Total distance fallen (m)	Change in distance (m)	Velocity (ms^{-1})	Change in velocity (ms^{-1})	Acceleration (ms^{-2})
You'll be measuring every 0.1 s.	This is what you measure.	This is the distance fallen in the 0.1 s interval.	This is change in distance ÷ change in time. (Which is the previous column ÷ 0.1)	This is the difference in the velocities in the current row and the previous one.	This is the change in velocity ÷ change in time (i.e. the previous column ÷ 0.1)

You can also use a **regular camera** in a **dark** room and a **strobe light** to find g.

Set the camera to take a **long exposure**. While the camera is taking the photo, turn on the strobe light and **drop** the ball. As the ball falls, it will be **lit up** at regular intervals by the strobe light.
This means that ball will appear **multiple times** in the photograph, in a different position each time.
Calculate the **change in distance** between each location of the ball and create the same **table** as above.
The **frequency** that the strobe light flashes at gives you the **time interval** between distances.

1) The **main cause** of uncertainty in this experiment is in measuring the **distance** fallen by the ball — other sources of uncertainty are small because you're not timing the ball yourself (see previous page).
2) **Parallax** (systematic error due to looking at the ruler at an angle) will also affect your **distance** measurements, so make sure your camera is at a **right angle** to the ruler (and use **multiple cameras** if the ruler is large).
3) Uncertainty caused by the **time interval** between pictures can be reduced by either **increasing** the **frequency** of the strobe light, or using a camera with a **higher frame rate**.
4) **Repeating** the experiment and calculating an **average value** of g can also increases the accuracy of the experiment.
5) Measuring over a **larger distance** or using **smaller time increments** means you will **average** over more values, which is likely to give a more **accurate** value for g.

Practice Questions

Q1 What is meant by free fall?

Q2 How does the velocity of a free-falling object change with time?

Q3 Describe an experiment that uses an electromagnet and a trapdoor to calculate the value of g.

Q4 Describe how video techniques could be used to calculate a value of g.

Exam Questions

Q1 In an experiment to determine the value of g, a small steel ball is dropped from a range of heights. The time it takes to reach the ground when dropped from each height is recorded.

a) Explain why using a small steel ball is better than using a beach ball in this experiment. [1 mark]

b) State one random and one systematic error that could arise from this experiment and suggest ways to reduce or remove them. [4 marks]

c) A graph of the distance travelled by the ball against time taken squared is plotted. Show that the gradient of the graph is equal to half the value of g. [3 marks]

Q2 A video camera with a frame rate of 4 Hz is used to record the motion of a ball dropped from the edge of a tall building. Frame 2 immediately follows Frame 1. Calculate the acceleration due to gravity if the ball is travelling at 13.51 ms^{-1} when Frame 1 is recorded. [4 marks]

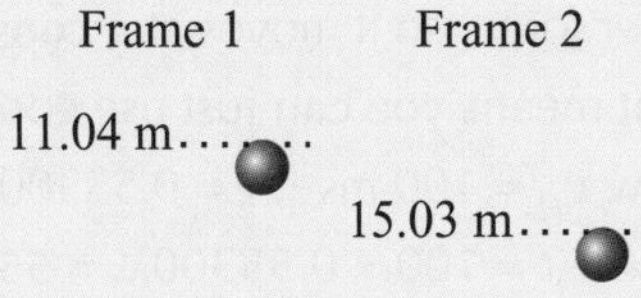

It's not the falling that hurts — it's the being pelted with rotten vegetables... okay, okay...

Make sure you know about all of these methods, including the uncertainties they cause and how you can fix them.

Projectile Motion

Calculators at the ready — it's time to resolve some more things into vertical and horizontal components. It can be a bit tricky at first, but you'll soon get the hang of it. Chop chop, no time to lose.

You can just Replace a with g in the Equations of Motion

You need to be able to work out **speeds**, **distances** and **times** for objects moving vertically with an **acceleration** of g. As g is a **constant acceleration** you can use the **equations of motion**. But because g acts downwards, you need to be careful about directions, here we've taken **upwards as positive** and **downwards as negative**.

Case 1: No initial velocity (it's just free falling)

Initial velocity $u = 0$

Acceleration $a = g = -9.81\ \text{ms}^{-2}$. Hence the equations of motion become:

$$v = gt \qquad v^2 = 2gs$$
$$s = \frac{1}{2}gt^2 \qquad s = \frac{vt}{2}$$

Case 2: An initial velocity upwards (it's thrown up into the air)

The equations of motion are just as normal, but with $a = g = -9.81\ \text{ms}^{-2}$.

Sign Conventions — Learn Them:
g is always downwards so it's usually negative
t is always positive
u and v can be either positive or negative
s can be either positive or negative

Case 3: An initial velocity downwards (it's thrown down)

Example: Alex throws a stone downwards from the top of a cliff. She throws it with a downwards velocity of $2.0\ \text{ms}^{-1}$. It takes 3.0 s to reach the water below. How high is the cliff?

1) You know: $u = -2.0\ \text{ms}^{-1}$, $a = g = -9.81\ \text{ms}^{-2}$ and $t = 3.0$ s. You need to find s.
2) Use $s = ut + \frac{1}{2}gt^2 = (-2.0 \times 3.0) + \left(\frac{1}{2} \times -9.81 \times 3.0^2\right) = -50.145$ m. The cliff is **50 m (to 2 s.f.)** high.

s is negative because the stone ends up further down than it started. Height is a scalar quantity, so is always positive.

You Have to Think of Horizontal and Vertical Motion Separately

Example: Sharon fires a scale model of a TV talent show presenter horizontally with a velocity of $100\ \text{ms}^{-1}$ (to 3 s.f.) from 1.5 m above the ground. How long does it take to hit the ground, and how far does it travel horizontally? Assume the model acts as a particle, the ground is horizontal and there is no air resistance.

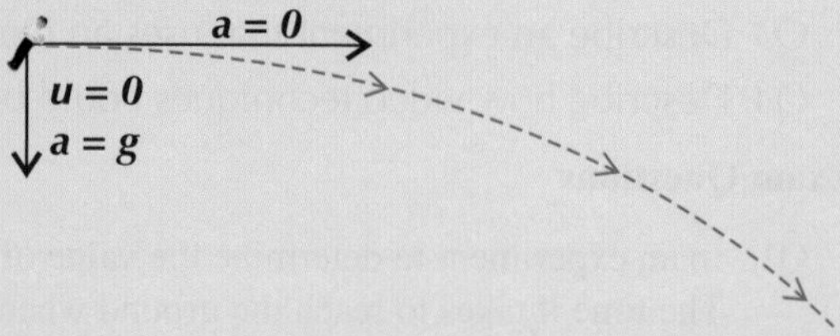

Think about the vertical motion first:

1) It's **constant acceleration** under gravity...
2) You know $u = 0$ (no vertical velocity at first), $s = -1.5$ m and $a = g = -9.81\ \text{ms}^{-2}$. You need to find t.
3) Use $s = \frac{1}{2}gt^2 \Rightarrow t = \sqrt{\frac{2s}{g}} = \sqrt{\frac{2 \times -1.5}{-9.81}} = 0.55300...$ s
4) So the model hits the ground after **0.55 seconds (to 2 s.f.)**.

Then do the horizontal motion:

1) The horizontal motion isn't affected by gravity or any other force, so it moves at a **constant speed**.
2) That means you can just use good old **speed = distance / time**.
3) Now $v_H = 100\ \text{ms}^{-1}$, $t = 0.55300...$ s and $a = 0$. You need to find s_H.
4) $s_H = v_H t = 100 \times 0.55300... = $ **55 m (to 2 s.f.)**

Where v_H is the horizontal velocity, and s_H is the horizontal distance travelled (rather than the height fallen).

Projectile Motion

It's Slightly Trickier if it Starts Off at an Angle

If something's projected at an angle (like, say, a javelin) you start off with both horizontal and vertical velocity:

Method:
1) Resolve the initial velocity into horizontal and vertical components.
2) Use the vertical component to work out how long it's in the air and/or how high it goes.
3) Use the horizontal component to work out how far it goes horizontally while it's in the air.

Example: A cannonball is fired from ground height at an angle of exactly 40° to the horizontal with an initial velocity of 15 ms^{-1}. Calculate how far the cannonball travels horizontally before it hits the ground. Assume no air resistance and that the ground is level.

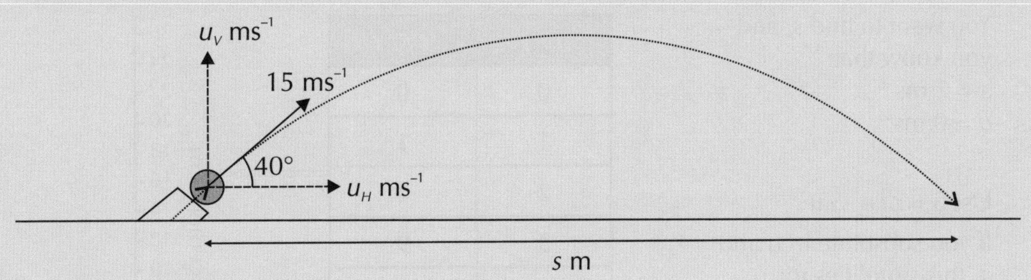

Resolve the velocity into horizontal and vertical components:
1) Horizontal component $u_H = 15\cos 40° = 11.49...\ ms^{-1}$
2) Vertical component $u_V = 15\sin 40° = 9.64...\ ms^{-1}$

Use the vertical component to work out how long the cannonball is in the air:
1) Halfway through the ball's flight, v_V will be zero. $u_V = 9.64...\ ms^{-1}$, $a = -9.81\ ms^{-2}$, $t = ?$.

   Use $v_V = u_V + at$: $0 = 9.64... + (-9.81 \times t) \Rightarrow t = \frac{9.64...}{9.81} = 0.98...\ s$
2) So the time it takes to reach the ground again $= 2 \times 0.98... = 1.96...\ s$

You know this because of the symmetrical shape of the cannonball's path — it will reach its highest point halfway through its flight.

Use the horizontal component to work out how far it goes while it's in the air:
1) There's no horizontal acceleration, so $u_H = v_H = 11.49...\ ms^{-1}$.
2) Distance = constant speed × time = 11.49... × 1.96... = 22.58... = **23 m (to 2 s.f.)**

Practice Questions

Q1 What is the initial vertical velocity for an object projected horizontally with a velocity of 5 ms^{-1}?

Q2 What is the initial horizontal component of velocity of an object projected at 45° to the ground with a speed of 25 ms^{-1}?

Exam Questions

Q1 Jason stands on the edge of a vertical cliff, throwing stones into the sea below. He throws a stone horizontally with a speed of exactly 8.0 ms^{-1}, from a point 230 m above sea level.

a) Calculate the time taken for the stone to hit the water from leaving Jason's hand. Use $g = -9.81\ ms^{-2}$ and ignore air resistance. [2 marks]

b) Calculate the distance of the stone from the base of the cliff when it hits the water. [2 marks]

Q2 Robin fires an arrow into the air with a vertical component of velocity of exactly 30 ms^{-1}, and a horizontal component of velocity of exactly 20 ms^{-1}, from 1 m above the ground. Calculate the maximum height from the ground reached by his arrow to the nearest metre. Use $g = -9.81\ ms^{-2}$ and ignore air resistance. [3 marks]

All this physics makes me want to create projectile motions...

...by throwing my revision books out of the window. The maths on this page can be tricky, but take it slowly step by step and all will be fine. Don't worry about making Norman (the lion) wait on the next page — he's very patient.

Displacement-Time Graphs

Drawing graphs by hand — oh joy. You'd think examiners had never heard of the graphical calculator. Ah well, until they manage to drag themselves out of the Dark Ages, you'll just have to grit your teeth and get on with it.

Acceleration Means a Curved Displacement-Time Graph

A graph of displacement against time for an **accelerating object** always produces a **curve**.
If the object is accelerating at a **uniform rate**, then the **rate of change** of the **gradient** will be constant.

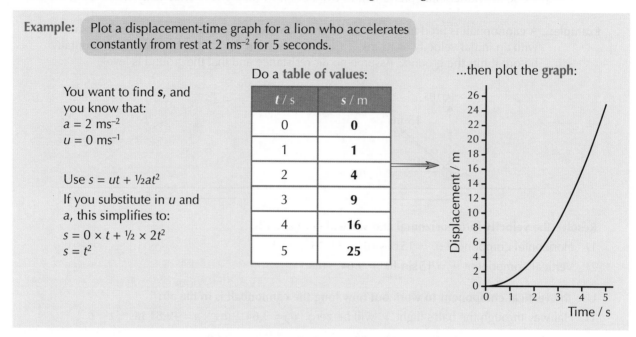

Example: Plot a displacement-time graph for a lion who accelerates constantly from rest at 2 ms^{-2} for 5 seconds.

You want to find **s**, and you know that:
$a = 2\ ms^{-2}$
$u = 0\ ms^{-1}$

Use $s = ut + ½at^2$
If you substitute in u and a, this simplifies to:
$s = 0 \times t + ½ \times 2t^2$
$s = t^2$

Do a **table of values:**

t / s	s / m
0	**0**
1	**1**
2	**4**
3	**9**
4	**16**
5	**25**

...then plot the **graph**:

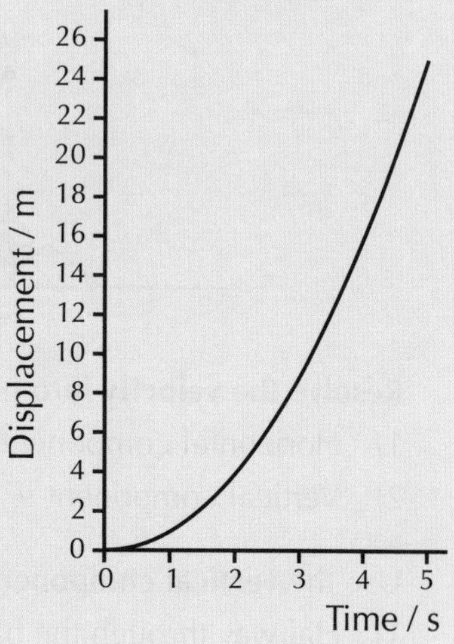

Different Accelerations Have Different Gradients

In the example above, if the lion has a **different acceleration** it'll change the **gradient** of the curve like this:

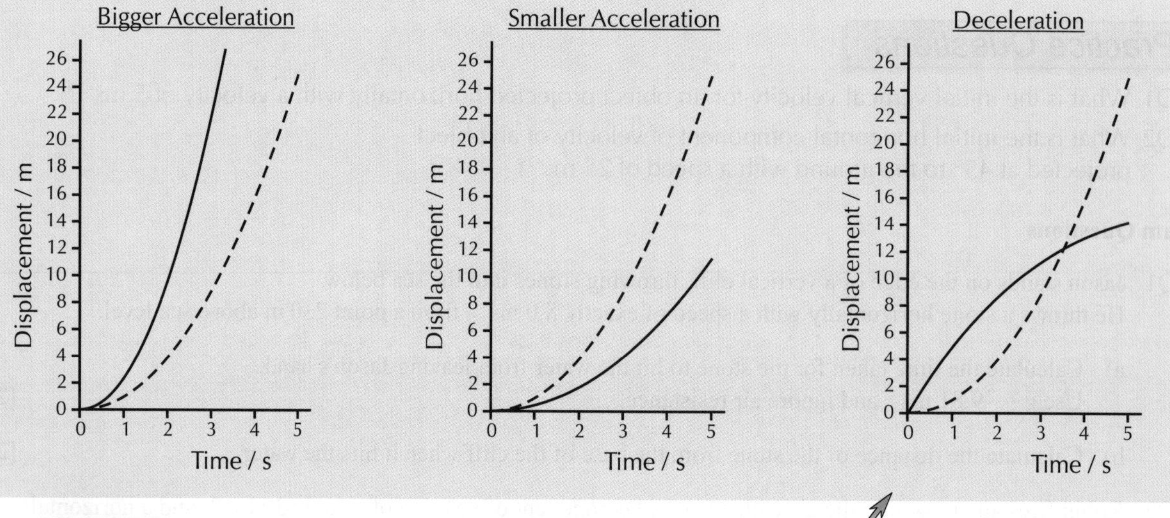

Norman (the lion).
Ooo, he's mean...

Displacement-Time Graphs

The **Gradient** of a **Displacement-Time Graph** Tells You the Velocity

When the velocity is constant, the graph's a **straight line**.
Velocity is defined as...

$$\textbf{velocity} = \frac{\textbf{change in displacement}}{\textbf{change in time}}$$

On the graph, this is $\frac{\text{change in } y\ (\Delta y)}{\text{change in } x\ (\Delta x)}$, i.e. the gradient.

So to get the velocity from a displacement-time graph, just find the gradient.

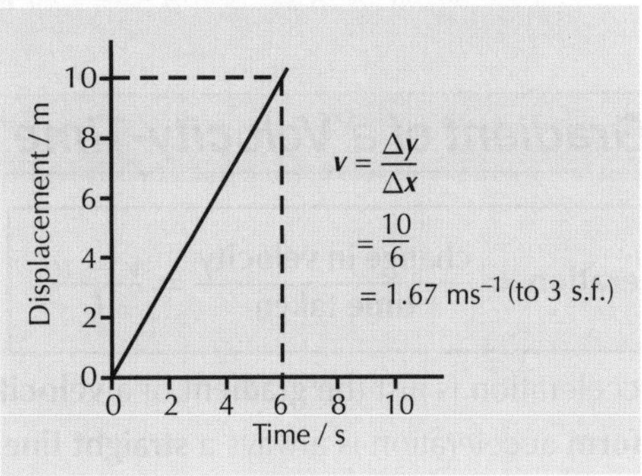

It's the Same with **Curved Graphs**

If the graph is a **curve**, (i.e. the object is accelerating) then you can find its **instantaneous velocity** (i.e. its velocity at a certain point).

To find the **instantaneous velocity** at a certain point, you need to draw a **tangent** to the curve at that point and find its gradient.

To find the **average velocity** over a period of time, just divide the final (change in) displacement by the final (change in) time — it doesn't matter whether or not the graph is curved.

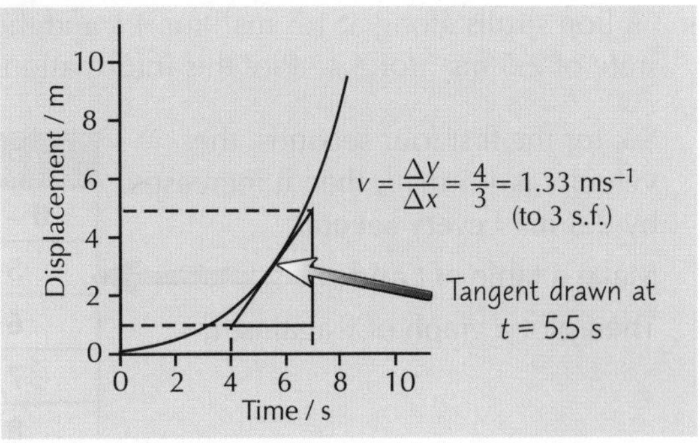

Practice Questions

Q1 What is given by the gradient of a displacement-time graph?

Q2 Sketch a displacement-time graph to show: a) constant velocity, b) acceleration, c) deceleration.

Exam Questions

Q1 Describe the motion of a cyclist whose journey is shown by the graph below. [4 marks]

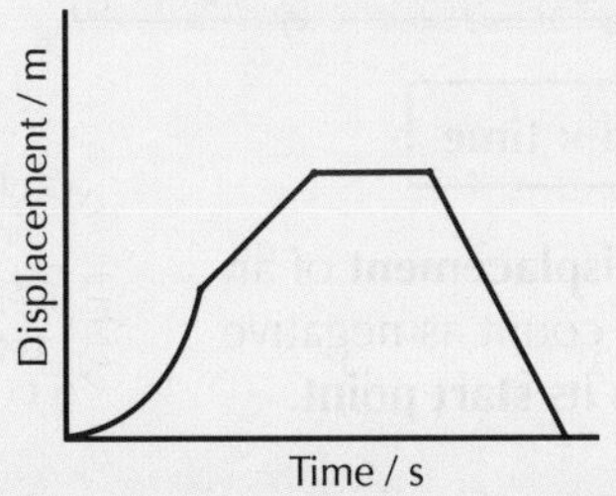

Q2 A baby crawls in a straight line. At first she crawls 5 m over 8 seconds at a constant velocity. She then rests for 5 seconds before crawling a further 3 m in 5 seconds at a constant velocity. Finally, she makes her way back to her starting point in 10 seconds, travelling at a constant speed all the way.

a) Draw a displacement-time graph to show the baby's journey. [4 marks]

b) Calculate her velocity during each of the four stages of her journey. [2 marks]

Be ahead of the curve, get to grips with this stuff now...

Whether it's a straight line or a curve, the steeper it is, the greater the velocity. There's nothing difficult about these graphs — the problem is that it's easy to confuse them with velocity-time graphs (next page). If in doubt, think about the gradient — is it velocity or acceleration, is it changing (curve), is it constant (straight line), is it 0 (horizontal line)...

Velocity-Time Graphs

Speed-time graphs and velocity-time graphs are pretty similar. The big difference is that velocity-time graphs can have a negative part to show something travelling in the opposite direction:

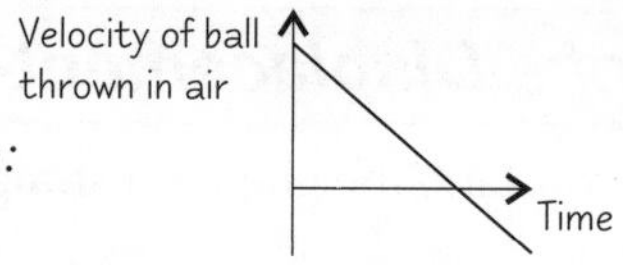

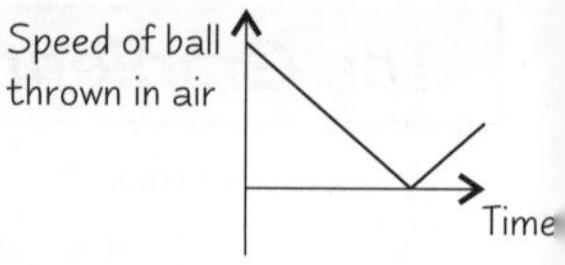

The **Gradient** of a **Velocity-Time Graph** tells you the **Acceleration**

$$\textbf{acceleration} = \frac{\textbf{change in velocity}}{\textbf{time taken}} = \frac{v - u}{t}$$

likewise for a speed-time graph

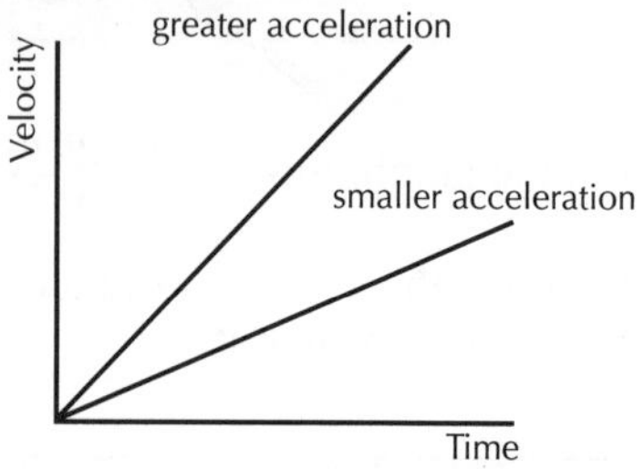

So the acceleration is just the **gradient** of a **velocity-time graph.**

1) **Uniform** acceleration is always a **straight line.**
2) The **steeper** the **gradient**, the **greater** the **acceleration**.

The equation for a straight line is $\boldsymbol{y = mx + c}$. You can rearrange the acceleration equation into the same form, getting $\boldsymbol{v = at + u}$. So on a linear *v-t* graph, **acceleration**, *a*, is the **gradient** (*m*) and the **initial speed**, *u*, is the ***y*-intercept** (*c*).

You've seen $v = u + at$ before (p.76).

Example: A lion strolls along at 1.5 ms^{-1} for 4 s and then accelerates uniformly at a rate of 2.5 ms^{-2} for 4 s. Plot this information on a velocity-time graph.

So, for the first four seconds, the velocity is 1.5 ms^{-1}, then it increases by **2.5 ms^{-1} every second.**

Make a table of *t* and *v*:

Then plot a graph of *v* against *t*.

t (s)	*v* (ms^{-1})
0 – 4	**1.5**
5	**4.0**
6	**6.5**
7	**9.0**
8	**11.5**

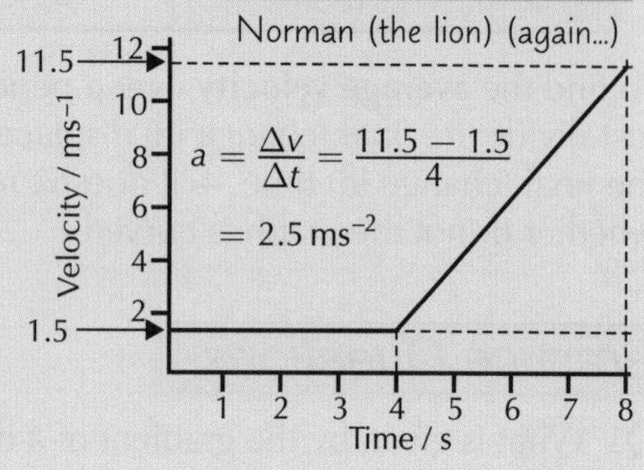

You can see that the **gradient of the line** is **constant** between 4 s and 8 s and has a value of 2.5 ms^{-2}, representing the **acceleration of the lion.**

You could also draw this graph in two parts. Draw a straight horizontal line for the first 4 s, then work out his final velocity at 8 s using the equations of motion for constant acceleration. Plot this value and connect the two points with another straight line.

Displacement = **Area** under **Velocity-Time Graph**

You know that: **distance travelled = average speed × time**

The **area** under a velocity-time graph tells you the **displacement** of an object. Areas under any **negative** parts of the graph count as negative areas, as they show the object moving **back** towards its **start point**.

Similarly, the area under a speed-time graph is the total distance travelled.

Example: A racing car on a straight track accelerates uniformly from rest to 40 ms^{-1} in 10 s. It maintains this speed for a further 20 s before coming to rest by decelerating at a constant rate over the next 15 s. Draw a velocity-time graph for this journey and use it to calculate the final displacement of the racing car.

Plot a graph of the information and split it into **sections:** A, B and C.

Calculate the **area** of each and **add** the three results together.

A: Area = ½ base × height = ½ × 10 × 40 = 200 m

B: Area = *b* × *h* = 20 × 40 = 800 m

C: Area = ½ *b* × *h* = ½ × 15 × 40 = 300 m

Final displacement = 200 + 800 + 300 = 1300 m

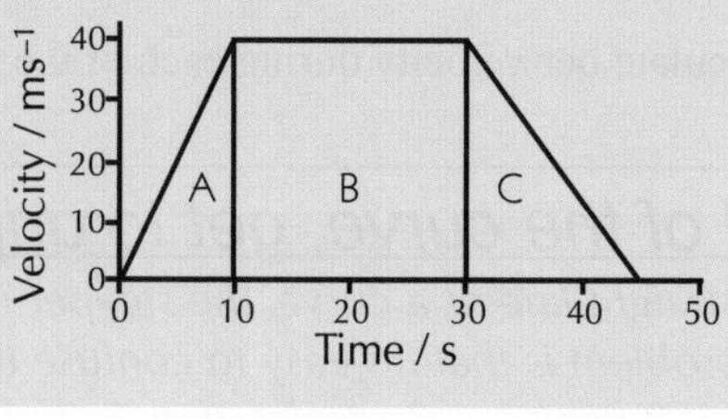

Velocity-Time Graphs

Non-Uniform Acceleration is a Curve on a V-T Graph

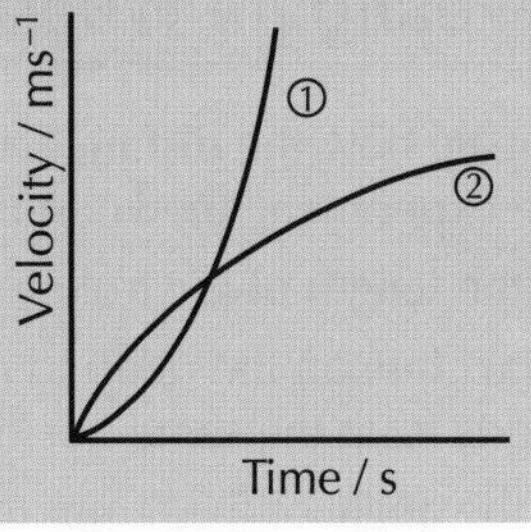

1) If the acceleration is changing, the gradient of the velocity-time graph will also be changing — so you **won't** get a **straight line.**
2) **Increasing acceleration** is shown by an **increasing gradient** — like in curve ①.
3) **Decreasing acceleration** is shown by a **decreasing gradient** — like in curve ②.

Simple enough...

Estimate the Area to Find Displacement from a Curved V-T Graph

As the velocity-time graph is no longer a simple straight line, you have to **estimate** the area under the curve. If the graph is on **squared paper**, an easy way to do this is just **count** the squares under the curve. Another way is to split the curve up into **trapeziums**, calculate the **area** of each one and then **add** them all up.

Example: A car accelerates from rest. It decreases its acceleration as it approaches 15 ms^{-1}. Estimate the car's displacement between 0 and 3 seconds, using the velocity-time graph.

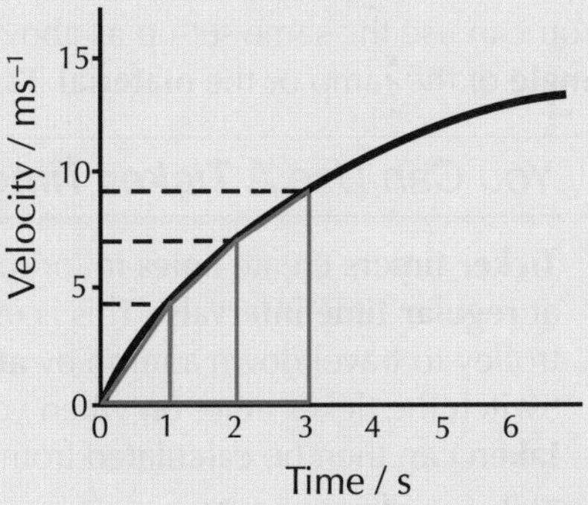

Split the area under the curve up into trapeziums and a triangle.

0-1 s — estimate the area using a triangle.
The height of the triangle is about 4.
The base of the triangle is 1.
$A = \frac{1}{2}(1 \times 4) = 2\,\text{m}$

1-2 s — estimate the area using a trapezium. Area $= \frac{1}{2}(a + b)h$
a is the length of the first side, $a \approx 4$
b is the length of the second side, $b \approx 7$
h is the width of each strip, so $h = 1$
$A = \frac{1}{2}(4 + 7) \times 1 = 5.5\,\text{m}$

2-3 s — another trapezium, $a \approx 7$, $b \approx 9$, $h = 1$ $A = \frac{1}{2}(7 + 9) \times 1 = 8\,\text{m}$

Now add the areas together — total area = 2 + 5.5 + 8 = 15.5 m

So the estimated overall displacement of the car is 15.5 m = **16 m (to 2 s.f.)**

Practice Questions

Q1 How do you calculate acceleration from a velocity-time graph?

Q2 How do you calculate the distance travelled from a speed-time graph?

Q3 Sketch velocity-time graphs for constant velocity and constant acceleration.

Q4 Three trapeziums are drawn side by side on a v-t graph to estimate the area under a curve. They have equal widths of 2 s, and side lengths of 1, 3, 7 and 9 ms^{-1}. Show that the displacement shown by this area is about 30 m.

Exam Question

Q1 A skier accelerates uniformly from rest at 2 ms^{-2} down a straight slope.

a) Sketch a velocity-time graph for the first 5 s of his journey. [2 marks]

b) Use a constant acceleration equation to calculate his displacement at t = 1, 2, 3, 4 and 5 s, and plot this information onto a displacement-time graph. [4 marks]

c) Suggest another method of calculating the skier's displacement after each second and use this to check your answers to part b). [2 marks]

Still awake — I'll give you five more minutes...

There's a lovely sunset outside my window. It's one of those ones that makes the whole landscape go pinky-yellowish. And that's about as much interest as I can muster on this topic. Normal service will be resumed on page 87, I hope.

Motion Experiments and Models

It's all getting a bit hi-tech now — using light gates and video cameras to look at how an object's velocity changes as it rolls down a ramp or crashes into something. Who doesn't love a good motion experiment...

You Can **Investigate** What **Affects** the **Motion** of a Trolley on a Slope

1) To investigate how the **distance** a trolley has rolled affects its speed, set up the experiment shown in the diagram.
2) Measure the **length** of the trolley.
3) Mark a **start line** on the ramp to make sure the trolley always starts from the **same position**.
4) Measure the **angle** of the ramp, θ, and the **distance** from the **start line** to the **light gate**, d.
5) Place the trolley on the **ramp** and **line it up** with the start line. Let go of it so its **initial velocity**, u, is **0**.
6) The **data logger** will record the **time** taken for the trolley to pass through the light gate and calculate the **velocity** of the trolley as it passes through the gate.
7) Change the **starting position** of the trolley, so d is varied.
8) **Repeat** this experiment for each distance 3 times and average the recorded velocities to reduce the **error** in your final result.

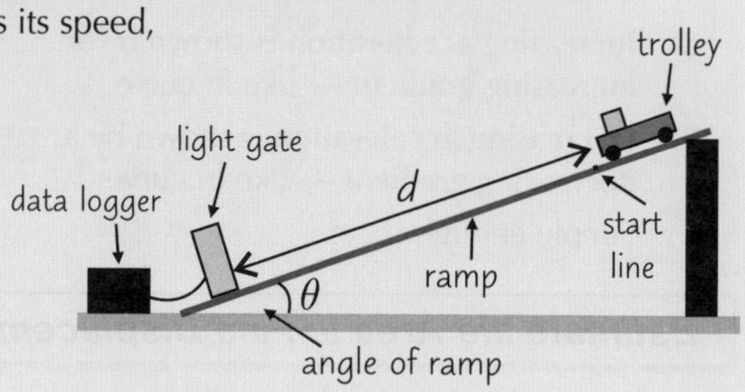

Using a light gate gives a much lower uncertainty in the measurement than using a stopwatch and calculating the velocity manually.

You can use the same set-up as above to investigate other factors. For example, you could change the **angle** of the ramp or the **material** it's made from, or change the **mass**, **size** or **shape** of the trolley.

You Can Use A **Ticker Timer** Instead of a **Data Logger**

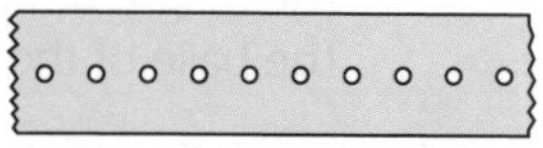

10 dots = 1/5th of a second.

Ticker timers create **holes** in (or make **dots** on) a long piece of **paper** (**ticker tape**) at **regular time intervals**. This is usually about **every 50th** of a second. You can **calculate** how long it takes a trolley to travel down a ramp by **attaching ticker tape** to the back of the trolley and threading it through the timer. Switch the ticker timer **on** when you **release** the trolley, and **off** when it reaches the **end** of the **ramp**. The **time taken** can then be calculated from the **number of holes** punched into the ticker tape (50 holes = 1 second).

Ticker timers are able to measure time very **accurately** but rely on **manually** turning on and off the machine, which will add **uncertainty** to the measurements e.g. human error/reaction time. Uncertainty can also be introduced when having to **count** the **total number** of dots.

Data loggers do not have this **human error** and can calculate the **velocity** and display it in **real time** — saving **time** and allowing **comparisons** between experiments to be easily made.

You Can Also **Investigate** How **Collisions** Affect the **Motion** of an Air Glider

Air gliders have **minimal friction**, as they're not in contact with a surface as they move. You can investigate what happens when **two** gliders collide using the experiment below.

- Set up the experiment shown in the diagram below, with a **video camera** positioned side-on to the motion of the gliders.
- Measure the **length** and **mass** of both gliders.
- Turn on the video camera and **start recording**.
- **Push** one glider so it hits the second glider.
- When both gliders have come to a stop, stop recording.

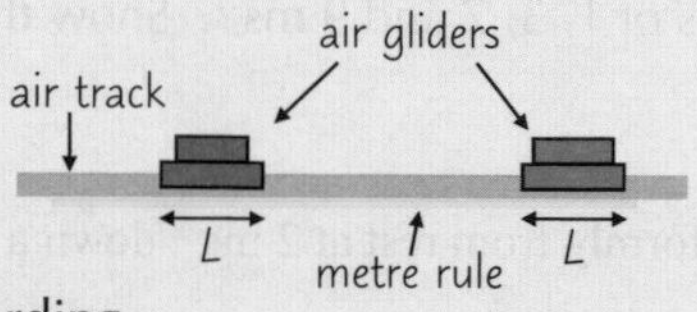

If you use the velocities you find to work out the total momentum before and after the collision, you should find it is the same (see p.92).

1) You can use this experiment to investigate how the **mass** and **velocity** of a glider just **before** a collision **affect** the **velocities** of both gliders after the **collision**.
2) Using **video analysis** software, you can view your videos **frame by frame**. Pick a **point of reference** on the metre rule and count how many **frames** it takes a glider to pass that point.
3) By knowing how many **frames per second** the video is shot at (the frame rate of the video), you can calculate the **time taken** (t) for a whole glider to pass that point. You recorded the **length** (L) of each glider, and so you can calculate their **velocities**.

$$\text{Time taken } (t) \text{ for a glider to pass a point} = \text{Number of frames for glider to pass a point} \times \frac{1 \text{ second}}{\text{Frame rate of camera}}$$

$$\text{velocity} = \frac{L}{t}$$

Motion Experiments and Models

*Motion can be **Modelled** Using **Iterative Methods***

*You can **Model** Using a **Spreadsheet...***

Using the **equations of motion** for **constant acceleration** (p.76) you can **model** how a uniformly accelerating body's **velocity** and **displacement** vary over time. To do this, use an **iterative method**, where **velocity** and **displacement** are calculated over **lots** of **small time increments** to model their behaviour over a **longer time period**. Create a **spreadsheet** like the one shown (which models motion for a body accelerating from rest at 4 ms^{-2} over increments of 1 s).

t (s)	Δt (s)	Δv (ms^{-1})	v (ms^{-1})	Δx (m)	x (m)
0	-	-	0	-	0
1	1	4	4	2	2
2	1	4	8	6	8
3	1	4	12	10	18

1) For each row, the change in velocity, $\Delta \boldsymbol{v}$ will be constant (as $\Delta \boldsymbol{v} = \boldsymbol{a}\Delta \boldsymbol{t} = 4 \times 1 = 4$ ms^{-1}).
2) **Add** this $\Delta \boldsymbol{v}$ to the velocity, $\boldsymbol{v}$, from the **previous** row, giving you the **new velocity** for each increment.
3) To find the **change in displacement**, $\Delta \boldsymbol{x}$, for each row use $\Delta \boldsymbol{x} = \boldsymbol{u}\Delta t + \frac{1}{2}\boldsymbol{a}(\Delta t)^2$ (where $\boldsymbol{u}$ is the value of $\boldsymbol{v}$ from the previous row). Add this to the previous $\boldsymbol{x}$ value to get the new **displacement** at the **end** of each time interval.
4) **Repeat** this to build up a full model of the body's motion over time. If you enter the correct formulas into the spreadsheet, then it can automatically complete as many rows (iterations) as you want.
5) You can then **plot a graph** of $\boldsymbol{v}$ against t (which should be a **straight line** through the origin with **gradient** equal to the body's **acceleration**) and $\boldsymbol{x}$ against t (which should be a **curve** similar to the one shown on page 82).

*...Or by **Drawing Vectors***

(This method is useful for visualising motion in 2 dimensions.)

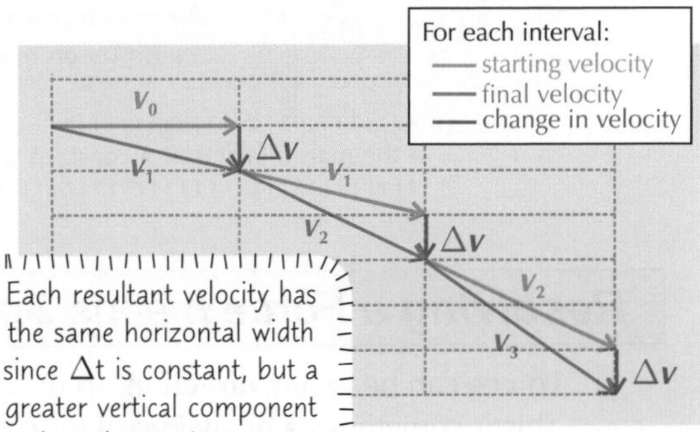

1) Consider an object fired horizontally, so that it begins to move with **projectile motion** (see p.80) under the influence of gravity.
2) Initially, the object has horizontal speed v_0 and vertical speed 0. Following the first time increment, the object still has horizontal speed v_0, but its **vertical speed** has **increased by Δv**. This gives a resultant velocity of $\boldsymbol{v}_1$, as shown.
3) Following the second increment, the horizontal speed has remained constant and the vertical speed has again **increased by Δv**. The new resultant velocity is $\boldsymbol{v}_1 + \Delta \boldsymbol{v} = \boldsymbol{v}_2$.
4) This pattern **continues** for each time increment. The resultant velocity **increases** for each increment (the blue arrow gets longer each time), as the object is **accelerating**.

Each resultant velocity has the same horizontal width since Δt is constant, but a greater vertical component than the previous one.

Draw a grid (or use graph paper). Each horizontal increment represents an increment of time. The increments on the vertical axes often represent Δv.

Practice Questions

Q1 Describe an experiment you could do to investigate the motion of a trolley on a slope.

Q2 Explain how a ticker timer works. State one advantage of using a data logger instead of a ticker timer.

Q3 Describe how you could use a spreadsheet to model displacement and velocity of a constantly accelerating object.

Exam Questions

Q1 A video recording is made of two 15 cm long trollies. Trolley 1 is pushed and then allowed to collide with trolley 2. The frame rate of the camera is 26 frames per second.

a) The video is analysed and after the collision, trolley 2 takes a little less than one frame to fully pass a reference point. It is assumed the trolley takes exactly one frame to pass the reference point. Estimate the velocity of trolley 2. [3 marks]

b) Suggest and explain one change which could be made to the experiment that could give more precise velocity measurements. [2 marks]

Q2 A projectile is fired diagonally upwards from ground level, with an initial vertical velocity of 35 ms^{-1} and an initial horizontal velocity of 20 ms^{-1}. Taking the acceleration due to gravity to be 10 ms^{-2} downwards, sketch a series of velocity vectors at 1 second intervals to model the first 6 seconds of the motion of the projectile. [3 marks]

Investigating motion — not an excuse to throw out your physics books...

So many ways to investigate motion. You can roll trolleys, push air gliders, use ticker tape or video techniques, or decide to theoretically model it on a spreadsheet... just make sure you can explain all of them.

Forces

Remember the vector stuff from the beginning of the section? Good, you're going to need it...

Free-Body Force Diagrams** show **All Forces** on a **Single Body

1) **Free-body force** diagrams show a **single body** on its own.
2) The diagram should include all the **forces** that **act on** the body, but **not** the **forces it exerts** on the rest of the world.
3) Remember **forces** are **vector quantities** and so the **arrow labels** should show the **size** and **direction** of the forces.
4) If a body is in **equilibrium** (i.e. not accelerating) the **forces** acting on it will be **balanced**.

Drawing free-body force diagrams isn't too hard — you just need practice. Here are a few **examples**:

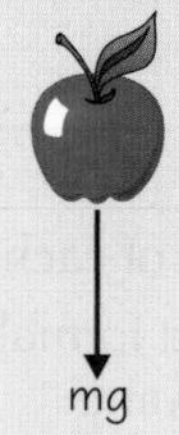

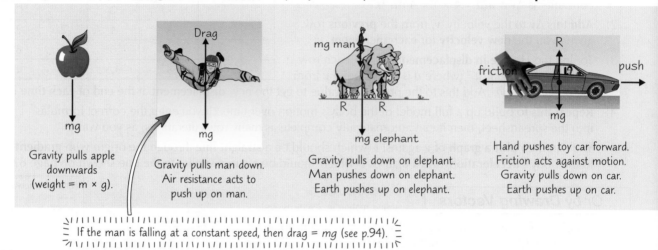

Gravity pulls apple downwards (weight = m × g).

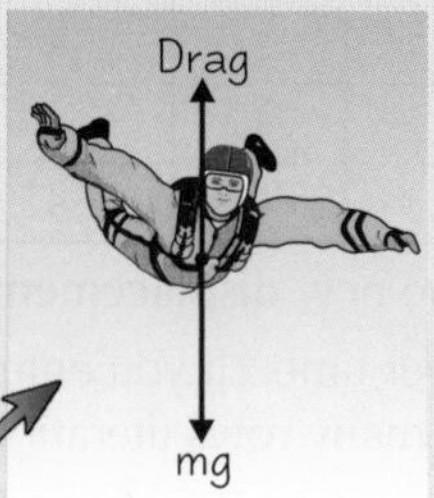

Gravity pulls man down. Air resistance acts to push up on man.

Gravity pulls down on elephant. Man pushes down on elephant. Earth pushes up on elephant.

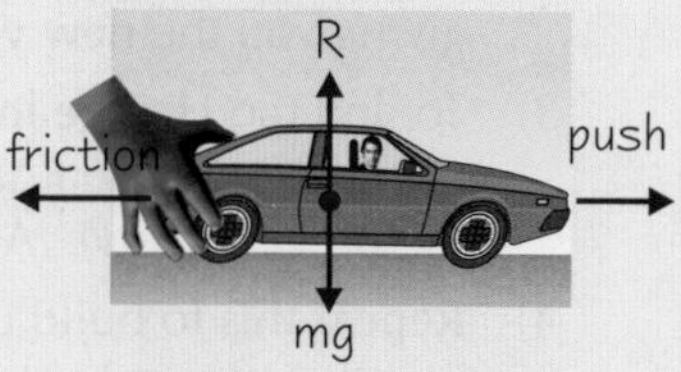

Hand pushes toy car forward. Friction acts against motion. Gravity pulls down on car. Earth pushes up on car.

If the man is falling at a constant speed, then drag = *mg* (see p.94).

Resolving** a **Force** means **Splitting** it into **Components

1) Forces can be in **any direction**, so they're not always at right angles to each other. This is sometimes a bit **awkward** for **calculations**.
2) To make an 'awkward' force easier to deal with, you can think of it as two **separate**, **independent** forces, acting at **right angles** to each other.
3) These two forces have **no effect** on each other as they are **perpendicular**. E.g. a horizontal force will have no vertical effect, and vice-versa.

The force F has exactly the same effect as the horizontal and vertical forces, F_H and F_V.
Replacing F with F_H and F_V is called **resolving the force F.**

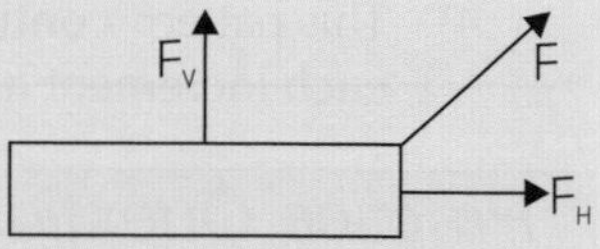

4) To find the **size** of a **component** force in a particular **direction**, you need to use trigonometry (see page 74). Forces are vectors, so you treat them in the same way as velocity or displacement — put them end to end.

So this...

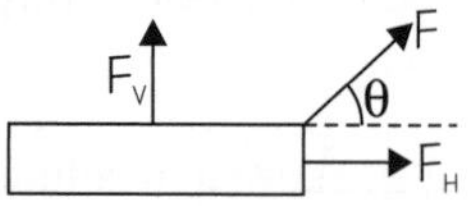

...could be drawn like this:

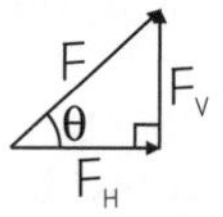

Using trigonometry you get:

$$\frac{F_H}{F} = \cos\theta \quad \text{or} \quad F_H = F\cos\theta$$

And:

$$\frac{F_V}{F} = \sin\theta \quad \text{or} \quad F_V = F\sin\theta$$

Remember that cos 90° = 0, so forces which act at an angle of **90°** to each other are **independent** (i.e. they have **no effect** on each other).

Example: A tree trunk is pulled along the ground by an elephant exerting a force of 1200 N at an angle of 25° to the horizontal. Calculate the components of this force in the horizontal and vertical directions.

Horizontal force:
1200 × cos 25° = 1087.5...
= **1100 N (to 2 s.f.)**

Vertical force:
1200 × sin 25° = 507.1...
= **510 N (to 2 s.f.)**

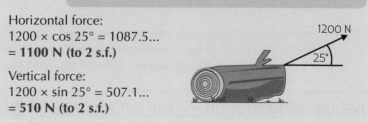

Forces

You Add the Components Back Together to get the Resultant Force

1) If **two forces** act on an object, you find the **resultant** (total) **force** by adding the **vectors** together and creating a **closed triangle**, with the resultant force represented by the **third side**.
2) Forces are vectors (as you know), so use **vector addition** — draw the forces as vector arrows 'tip-to-tail'.
3) Then it's yet more trigonometry to find the **angle** and the **length** of the third side.

Example: Two dung beetles roll a dung ball along the ground at a constant velocity. Beetle A applies a force of 0.5 N northwards while beetle B exerts a force of only 0.2 N eastwards. What is the resultant force on the dung ball?

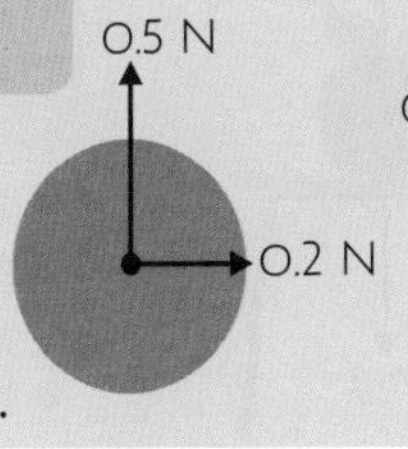

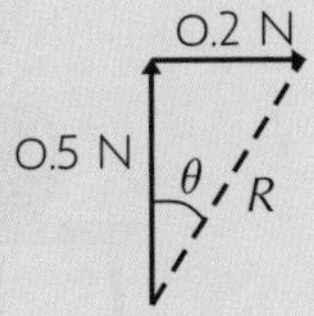

By Pythagoras, $R^2 = 0.5^2 + 0.2^2 = 0.29$
$R = \sqrt{0.29} = 0.538... =$ **0.54 N (to 2 s.f.)**

$\tan\theta = \frac{0.2}{0.5}$ so $\theta = \tan^{-1}\left(\frac{0.2}{0.5}\right) = 21.8°... =$ **22° (to 2 s.f.)**

So the resultant force is **0.54 N** at an angle of **22° to the vertical** (a bearing of 022°).

Choose Sensible Axes for Resolving

Use directions that **make sense** for the situation you're dealing with. If you've got an object on a slope, choose your directions **along the slope** and **at right angles to it**. You can turn the paper to an angle if that helps.

Always choose sensible axes

Examiners like to call a slope an "inclined plane".

Example

The component of the bone's weight down the slope is 2.5 N so you'd need 2.5 N of friction to stop it sliding down.

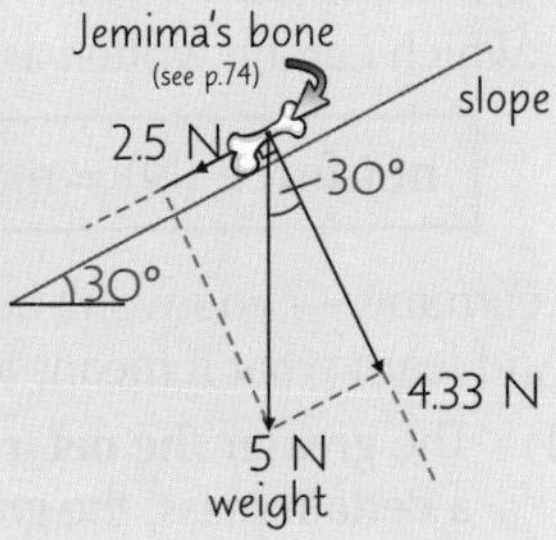

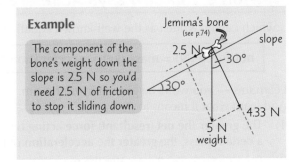

Practice Questions

Q1 Sketch a free-body force diagram for an ice hockey puck moving across horizontal ice (assuming no friction).

Q2 What are the horizontal and vertical components of a force F if it is applied at an angle of θ to the horizontal?

Q3 Explain why perpendicular forces are independent of each other.

Exam Questions

Q1 An 8 kg picture is suspended from a hook as shown in the diagram. Calculate the tension force, T, in the string. [2 marks]

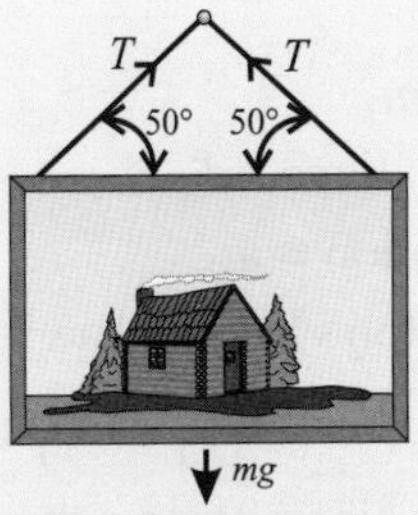

Q2 Two elephants pull a tree trunk as shown in the diagram. Calculate the resultant force on the tree trunk. Both values given are correct to 3 s.f. [2 marks]

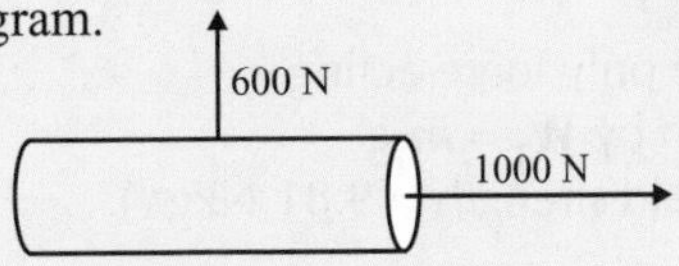

Free-body force diagram — sounds like a dance competition...

Remember those $F\cos\theta$ and $F\sin\theta$ bits. Write them on bits of paper and stick them to your wall. Scrawl them on your pillow. Tattoo them on your brain. Whatever it takes — you just have to learn them.

Newton's Laws of Motion

You did most of this at GCSE, but that doesn't mean you can just skip over it now.
You'll be kicking yourself if you forget this stuff in the exam — it's easy marks...

Newton's **1st Law** says that a **Force** is Needed to Change Velocity

1) **Newton's 1st law of motion** states the **velocity** of an object will **not change** unless a **resultant force** acts on it.
2) This means a body will remain at rest or moving in a **straight line** at a **constant speed**, unless acted on by a **resultant force**.

An apple sitting on a table won't go anywhere because the **forces** on it are **balanced**.

reaction (R) = **weight** (mg)

(table pushing up on apple) (gravity pulling apple down)

3) If any forces acting on a body **aren't balanced**, the **overall resultant force** will cause the body to **accelerate**. If you gave the apple on the left a shove, there'd be a resultant force acting on it and it would roll off the table.
4) Acceleration can mean a change in **direction**, or **speed**, or both.

Newton's 2nd Law says **Acceleration** is **Proportional** to **Force**

...which can be written as the well-known equation:

net force (N) = mass (kg) × acceleration (ms^{-2}) or $F = ma$

From this equation, $1\ N = 1\ kg\,ms^{-2}$. This is the definition of a newton. $F = ma$ is a special case of Newton's second law — the mass is constant. For the momentum version see p.93.

Learn this — you won't be given it in your exam.
And learn what it means too:

1) The **greater the net** (**resultant**) **force** acting on a body of a certain mass, the **greater** the **acceleration** of the body.
2) For a given force, the **greater** the **mass** of the body it acts on, the **less acceleration** the body will experience.

REMEMBER:
1) The **resultant force** is the **vector sum** of all the forces.
2) The force is **always** measured in **newtons**.
3) The **mass** is always measured in **kilograms**.
4) The **acceleration** is always in the **same direction** as the **resultant force** and is measured in **ms^{-2}**.

All Objects Fall at the **Same Rate** (if you **Ignore Air Resistance**)

1) On Earth, the force that causes objects to accelerate towards the ground is the **gravitational pull** of the Earth. The gravitational field strength on Earth, g, is pretty much **constant** — so all objects should **accelerate** towards the ground at the **same rate**, no matter what their mass is.
2) Newton's 2nd law explains it neatly — consider two balls dropped at the same time — ball **1** being heavy, and ball **2** being light. Then use Newton's 2nd law to find their acceleration.

You've already seen free fall on p.78–79.

mass = m_1
resultant force = F_1
acceleration = a_1

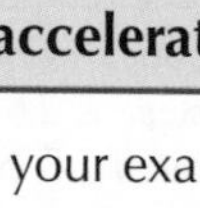

By Newton's Second Law:

$$F_1 = m_1 a_1$$

Ignoring air resistance, the only force acting on the ball is weight, given by $W_1 = m_1 g$ (where g = gravitational field strength = 9.81 Nkg^{-1}).

So: $F_1 = m_1 a_1 = W_1 = m_1 g$
So: $m_1 a_1 = m_1 g$
m_1 cancels out to give: $a_1 = g$

mass = m_2
resultant force = F_2
acceleration = a_2

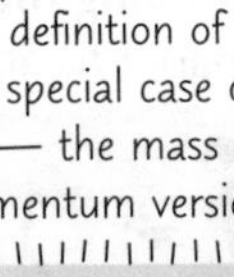

By Newton's Second Law:

$$F_2 = m_2 a_2$$

Ignoring air resistance, the only force acting on the ball is weight, given by $W_2 = m_2 g$ (where g = gravitational field strength = 9.81 Nkg^{-1}).

So: $F_2 = m_2 a_2 = W_2 = m_2 g$
So: $m_2 a_2 = m_2 g$
m_2 cancels out to give: $a_2 = g$

Newton's Laws of Motion

Newton's **3rd Law** is a **Consequence** of the **Conservation of Momentum**

There are a few different ways of stating Newton's 3rd law, but the clearest way is:

If an object A EXERTS a FORCE on object B, then object B exerts AN EQUAL BUT OPPOSITE FORCE on object A.

You'll also hear the law as "every action has an equal and opposite reaction". But this confuses people who wrongly think the forces are both applied to the same object. (If that were the case, you'd get a resultant force of zero and nothing would ever move anywhere...)

The two forces actually represent the **same interaction**, just seen from two **different perspectives**:

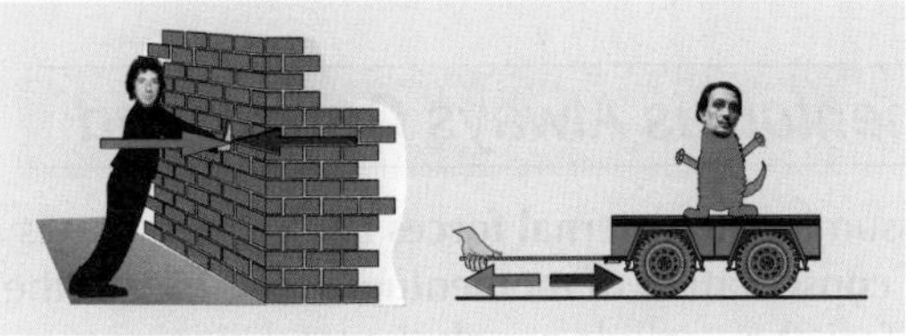

1) If you **push against a wall**, the wall will **push back** against you, **just as hard**. As soon as you stop pushing, so does the wall. Amazing...
2) If you **pull a cart**, whatever force **you exert** on the rope, the rope exerts the **exact opposite** pull on you.
3) When you go **swimming**, you push **back** against the water with your arms and legs, and the water pushes you **forwards** with an equal-sized force. So, the **backward momentum** of the water is equal to your **forward momentum**.

Newton's 3rd law applies in **all situations** and to all **types of force**. But the pairs of forces are always the **same type**, e.g. both gravitational or both electrical.

This looks like Newton's 3rd law...

But it's NOT.

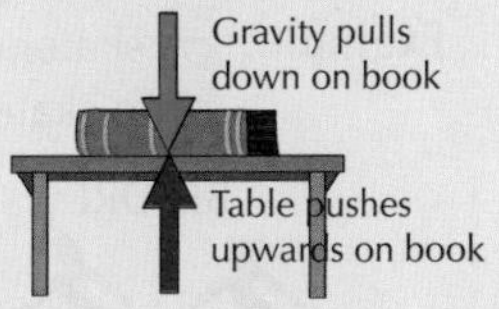

...because both forces are acting on the book, and they're not of the same type. This is two separate interactions. The forces are equal and opposite, resulting in zero acceleration, so this is showing Newton's 1st law.

Newton's 3rd law is a consequence of the **conservation of momentum** (page 92). A **resultant force** acting means a change in **mass** or **acceleration** (***F*** = ***ma***) — which means a **change in momentum**.

Momentum is always **conserved** when no external force acts, so whenever one object exerts a force on another (and changes its momentum), the second object must exert an **equal-sized** force back on the first object so that the **overall** change in momentum is **zero**.

Practice Questions

Q1 State Newton's 1st, 2nd and 3rd laws of motion, and explain what they mean.

Q2 Write out the formula which describes a special case of Newton's 2nd law.

Q3 Sketch a force diagram of a book resting on a table to illustrate Newton's 3rd law.

Exam Questions

Q1 A parachutist with a mass of 78 kg steps out of a plane. As she falls, she accelerates.

a) Use Newton's 2nd law to explain why she initially accelerates. [2 marks]

b) What is the initial vertical force on the parachutist? Use $g = 9.81$ ms^{-2}. [1 mark]

Q2 A 250 kg boat is moving across a river. The engines provide a force of 500 N at right angles to the flow of the river, and the boat experiences a drag of 100 N in the opposite direction. The force on the boat due to the flow of the river is 300 N. Show that the magnitude of the acceleration of the boat is 2 ms^{-2}. [3 marks]

Newton's three incredibly important laws of motion...

These equations may not really fill you with a huge amount of excitement (and I hardly blame you if they don't)... but it was pretty fantastic at the time — suddenly people actually understood how forces work, and how they affect motion.

Momentum and Impulse

Linear momentum is just momentum in a straight line (not a circle or anything complicated like that).

Understanding **Momentum** helps you do **Calculations** on **Collisions**

The **momentum** of an object depends on two things — its **mass** and **velocity**:

momentum (in kg ms^{-1}) = **mass** (in kg) × **velocity** (in ms^{-1})
or in symbols: $p = mv$

Momentum is a vector quantity (see p.74), so just like velocity, it has size and direction.

Momentum is Always **Conserved**

1) Assuming **no external forces** act, momentum is always **conserved** (this is the **principle of conservation of momentum**). This means the **total momentum** of two objects **before** they collide **equals** the total momentum **after** the collision.
2) This is really handy for working out the **velocity** of objects after a collision (as you do...):

Example: A skater of mass 75 kg and velocity 4 ms^{-1} collides with a stationary skater of mass 50 kg. The skaters join together and move off in the same direction. Calculate their velocity after impact.

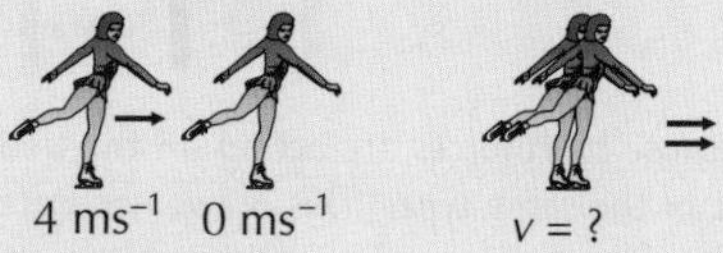

Before you start a momentum calculation, always draw a quick sketch.

Momentum of skaters before = Momentum of skaters after

$(75 \times 4) + (50 \times 0) = 125v$

$300 = 125v$

So... v = **2.4 ms^{-1}**

3) The same principle can be applied in **explosions**. E.g. if you fire an **air rifle**, the **forward momentum** gained by the pellet **equals** the **backward momentum** of the rifle, and you feel the rifle recoiling into your shoulder.

Collisions can be **Elastic** or **Inelastic**

A **perfectly elastic** collision is one where **momentum** is **conserved** and **kinetic energy** is **conserved** — i.e. no energy is dissipated as heat, sound, etc. If a collision is **inelastic** it means that some of the kinetic energy is converted into other forms during the collision. But **momentum is always conserved.**

You can use the **principle of conservation of momentum**, (and the conservation of kinetic energy in elastic collisions) to predict the behaviour of real-world objects, for example balls in sports games.

Example: A toy lorry (mass 2.0 kg) travelling at 3.0 ms^{-1} crashes into a smaller toy car (mass 800 g to 2 s.f.), travelling in the same direction at 2.0 ms^{-1}. The velocity of the lorry after the collision is 2.6 ms^{-1} in the same direction. Calculate the new velocity of the car and the total kinetic energy (KE) before and after the collision.

Momentum before collision = Momentum after collision

$(2.0 \times 3.0) + (0.80 \times 2.0) = (2.0 \times 2.6) + (0.80v)$

$7.6 = 5.2 + 0.80v$

$2.4 = 0.80v$ so v = **3.0 ms^{-1}**

KE before = KE of lorry + KE of car

$= \frac{1}{2}mv^2_{(lorry)} + \frac{1}{2}mv^2_{(car)}$

$= \frac{1}{2}(2.0 \times 3.0^2) + \frac{1}{2}(0.80 \times 2.0^2)$

$= 9 + 1.6 =$ **10.6 J**

KE after $= \frac{1}{2}(2.0 \times 2.6^2) + \frac{1}{2}(0.80 \times 3.0^2)$

$= 6.76 + 3.6 =$ **10.4 J (to 3 s.f.)**

The KE before is different to the KE after — so this is an inelastic collision. The difference in the two values is the amount of energy dissipated as heat or sound, or in damaging the vehicles.

Momentum and Impulse

Newton's 2nd Law says that Force is the Rate of Change of Momentum

Newton's 2nd law states that:

"The **rate of change of momentum** of an object is **directly proportional** to the **net force** which acts on the object." or $F = \frac{\Delta(mv)}{\Delta t}$

If mass is constant, this can be written as:

net force = mass × acceleration or $F = ma$

Remember this equation — it's not given in the exam. If you forget, the equation above is given and you should know that acceleration is rate of change of velocity.

(As you saw on page 90.)

F = ma Doesn't Apply if the Mass is Changing

$F = ma$ is a special case of Newton's 2nd law. If the **mass** of the object is **changing** — e.g. if it is accelerating at close to the **speed of light** — then you **can't** use $F = ma$.
(You don't need to know why this happens.)

Don't worry though — **Newton's 2nd law still applies**, it's just that the 'rate of **change of momentum**' bit refers to a **change in mass and velocity**.

Daisy always knew she was special.

Impulse = Change in Momentum

1) Newton's second law says **force = rate of change of momentum** (see above), or $F = \Delta mv \div \Delta t$.
2) **Rearranging** Newton's 2nd law gives: $F\Delta t = \Delta mv$, so **impulse = change of momentum**.
   Impulse is defined as **average force × time**, $F\Delta t$.
   The units of impulse are **newton seconds**, Ns.
3) Impulse is the change in momentum of **one** object, whilst conservation of momentum applies to the **whole system**. So the **impulse** of an object can **change** while **momentum** is **conserved**.

Practice Questions

Q1 Write down the formula for calculating momentum.

Q2 What is the difference between elastic and inelastic collisions?

Q3 Give the equation for calculating the net force on an object which relates mass, velocity and time.

Q4 What is impulse? Write down the equation for calculating impulse, defining all symbols used.

Q5 A 20 N force acting on a moving mass causes an impulse of 80 Ns. Show that the force acts for 4 seconds.

Exam Question

Q1 A snooker ball of mass 0.145 kg moving at 1.94 ms^{-1} collides with a stationary snooker ball of mass 0.148 kg. The first ball rebounds along its initial path at 0.005 ms^{-1}, and the second ball moves off in the opposite direction.

a) Calculate the velocity of the second ball immediately after the collision. [2 marks]

b) State whether or not the collision is perfectly elastic. Support your answer with a calculation. [3 marks]

c) The first ball then hits the cushion at the edge of the table and comes to a stop. The collision takes 0.15 seconds. Calculate the average force experienced by the ball in this collision. [2 marks]

Momentum will never be an endangered species — it's always conserved...

...unlike exams which, one day, will be done forever and you'll never have to revise ever again. But if you don't get momentum and impulse nailed now, you'll forever be looking back and wishing you had — so go learn it well good like.

Terminal Velocity

If you jump out of a plane at 2000 metres, you want to know that you're not going to be accelerating all the way.

Friction is a *Force* that *Opposes Motion*

There are two main types of friction:

1) **Contact friction** between **solid surfaces** (which is what we usually mean when we just use the word 'friction'). You don't need to worry about that too much for now.
2) **Fluid friction** (known as **drag** or fluid resistance or air resistance).

Fluid Friction or Drag:

1) 'Fluid' is a word that means either a **liquid or a gas** — something that can **flow**.
2) The force depends on the thickness (or **viscosity**) of the fluid.
3) It **increases** as the **speed increases** (for simple situations it's directly proportional, but you don't need to worry about the mathematical relationship).
4) It also depends on the **shape** and **size** of the object moving through it — the larger the **area** pushing against the fluid, the greater the resistance force.

Things you need to remember about frictional forces:

1) They **always** act in the **opposite direction** to the **motion** of the object.
2) They can **never** speed things up or start something moving.
3) They convert **kinetic energy** into **heat**.

Terminal Velocity — when the *Friction* Force *Equals* the *Driving Force*

You will reach a **terminal velocity** at some point, if you have:

1) a **driving force** that stays the **same** all the time
2) a **frictional** or **drag force** (or collection of forces) that increases with speed

There are **three main stages** to reaching terminal velocity:

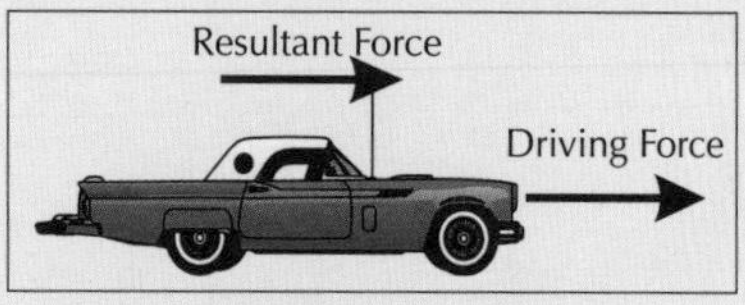

The car **accelerates** from **rest** using a constant driving force.

As the **velocity increases**, the **resistance forces increase** (because of things like turbulence — you don't need the details). This **reduces the resultant force** on the car and hence **reduces its acceleration**.

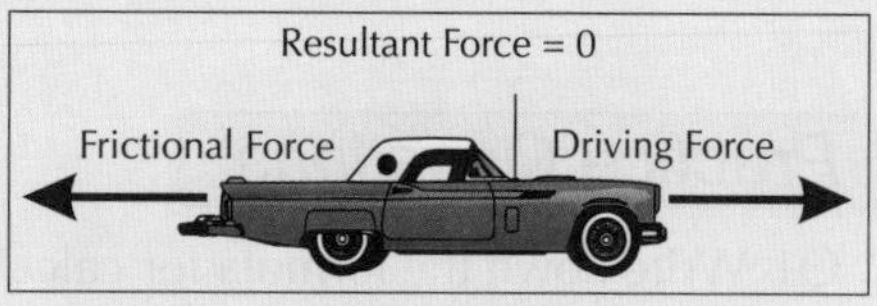

Eventually the car reaches a velocity at which the **resistance forces are equal to the driving force**. There is now **no resultant force** and **no acceleration**, so the car carries on at **constant velocity**.

Sketching a *Graph* for *Terminal Velocity*

You need to be able to **recognise** and **sketch** the graphs for **velocity against time** and **acceleration against time** for the **terminal velocity** situation.

Nothing for it but practice — shut the book and sketch them from memory. Keep doing it till you get them right every time.

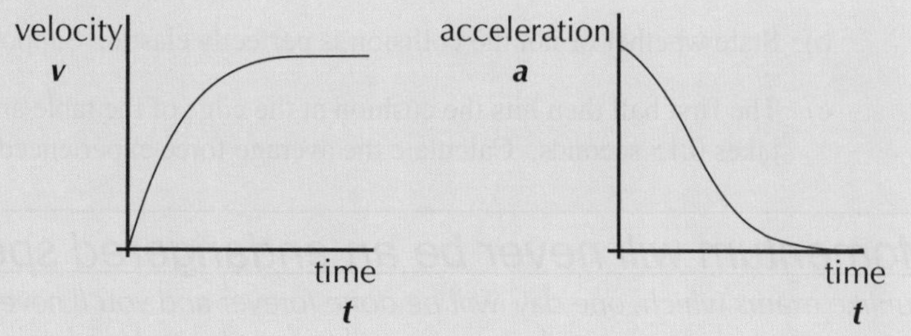

Terminal Velocity

*Things **Falling** through **Air** or **Water** Reach a **Terminal Velocity** too*

When something's falling through air, the weight of the object is a **constant** force accelerating the object downwards. Air resistance is a frictional force opposing this motion, which **increases** with **speed**.

So before a parachutist opens the parachute, exactly the same thing happens as with the car example:

1) A skydiver leaves a plane and will **accelerate** until the **air resistance** equals his **weight**.

2) He will then be travelling at a **terminal velocity**.

But... the terminal velocity of a person in free fall is too great to land **safely**. The **parachute increases** the **air resistance massively**, which slows him down to a lower terminal velocity:

3) Before reaching the ground he will **open his parachute**, which immediately **increases the air resistance** so it is now **bigger** than his **weight**.

4) This **slows him down** until his speed has dropped enough for the **air resistance** to be **equal to his weight** again. This new terminal velocity is small enough to survive landing.

The *v-t* graph is a bit different, because you have a new terminal velocity being reached after the parachute is opened:

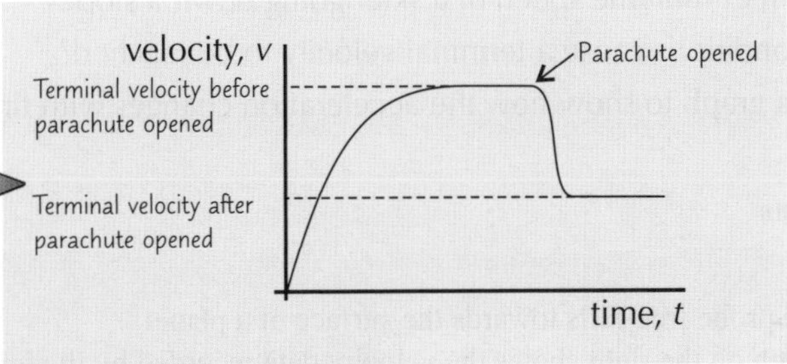

*Measure the **Terminal Velocity** of a **Ball Bearing***

You don't have to use elastic bands — you could also use insulation tape or another marker for your intervals.

You can calculate the terminal velocity of a **ball bearing** (a little steel ball) in a **viscous** (thick) liquid by setting up an experiment like this:

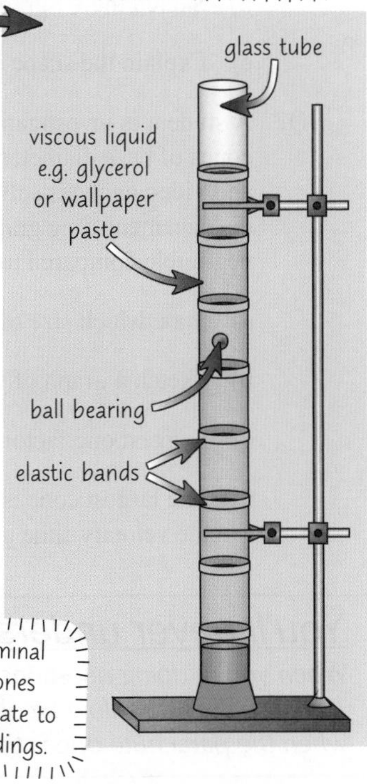

1) Put **elastic bands** around the tube of viscous liquid at **fixed distances** using a **ruler**.
2) **Drop** a ball bearing into the tube, and use a **stopwatch** to record the time at which it reaches **each band**. Record your results in a **table** (see below).
3) **Repeat** this a few times to reduce the effect of **random errors** (see p.12) on your results. You can use a **strong magnet** to remove the ball bearing from the tube.
4) **Calculate** the times taken by the ball bearing to travel between consecutive elastic bands and calculate an **average** for each reading. Use the **average times** and the **distance between bands** to calculate the **average velocity** between **each pair** of elastic bands.
5) You should find that the average velocity **increases** at first, then **stays constant** — this is the ball bearing's **terminal velocity** in the viscous liquid used.

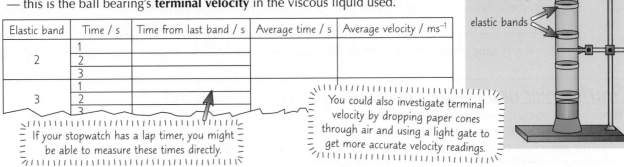

Elastic band	Time / s	Time from last band / s	Average time / s	Average velocity / ms^{-1}
2	1			
	2			
	3			
3	1			
	2			
	3			

If your stopwatch has a lap timer, you might be able to measure these times directly.

You could also investigate terminal velocity by dropping paper cones through air and using a light gate to get more accurate velocity readings.

Terminal Velocity

You can Work Out what **Affects** Terminal Velocity

Prof. Fraise dedicated his life to investigating terminal velocity in fluids.

1) Use your average velocity data from the experiment on page 95 to plot a graph of **velocity** against **time**. Draw a smooth curve and use it to estimate the terminal velocity.
2) You might be asked to draw **force diagrams** for the ball bearing as it falls. Remember that the forces are balanced when the ball reaches terminal velocity.
3) You can change parts of your experiment to see what effect they have on terminal velocity and the time taken to reach terminal velocity. For example you could:
   - Change the **liquid** — the terminal velocity will be **lower** in more viscous (thicker) liquids because the drag is **greater**. Try mixing water into wallpaper paste and see how much the terminal velocity increases when the drag is lower.
   - Change the **size** of the ball. What happens if the ball is larger? Or smaller?
   - Change the **shape** of the thing you are dropping. The drag force will be greater on **less streamlined** shapes.
   - Change the **mass** of the thing you are dropping, while keeping the **size** the **same** (this might be a bit tricky). You should find that **heavier objects** reach a **faster** terminal velocity because a **greater drag force** is needed to balance the extra weight. (Remember, objects with different masses only fall at the same rate if drag is ignored — p.90.)

Turn back to p.84–85 for more on velocity-time graphs.

Practice Questions

Q1 What forces limit the speed of a skier going down a slope?

Q2 What conditions cause a terminal velocity to be reached?

Q3 Sketch a graph to show how the acceleration changes with time for an object falling through air.

Exam Questions

Q1 A space probe free-falls towards the surface of a planet.
The graph on the right shows the velocity data recorded by the probe as it falls.

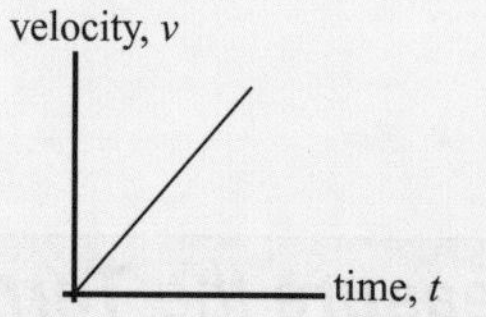

a) The planet does not have an atmosphere. Explain how you can tell this from the graph. [2 marks]

b) Sketch the *v-t* graph you would expect to see if the planet did have an atmosphere. [2 marks]

c) Explain the shape of the graph you have drawn. [3 marks]

Q2 A student is investigating how the terminal velocity of paper cones varies with cone size. She drops weighted cones of base diameter 5 cm, 10 cm and 15 cm point-down from a height of 2 m and uses a video camera and video analysis software to obtain data on the displacement of the cone at certain times. She then plots a displacement-time graph to calculate the terminal velocity. You may assume that the weights of the cones are negligible compared to that of the weights used to stabilise them, and that each cone is weighted by the same amount.

a) State which size of cone you expect to have the lowest terminal velocity. Explain your answer. [2 marks]

b) Sketch a graph of velocity against time for the three cones. Put all three curves on the same axes. [3 marks]

c) Suggest one factor the student must keep the same in her experiment and explain why. [1 mark]

d) The largest cone is crushed into a ball and used in the experiment. Describe and explain how the velocity-time graph for the ball would differ from the original cone's velocity-time graph. [3 marks]

You'll never understand this without going parachuting...*

When you're doing questions about terminal velocity, remember the frictional forces reduce acceleration, not speed. They usually don't slow an object down, apart from in the parachute example, where the skydiver is travelling faster when the parachute opens than the terminal velocity for the parachute-skydiver combination.

* No. 37 in a series of the 100 least convincing excuses for an interesting holiday.

Work and Power

As everyone knows, work in Physics isn't like normal work. It's harder. Work also has a specific meaning that's to do with movement and forces. You'll have seen this at GCSE — now it's time to have a look at it in more detail.

Work is Done Whenever Energy is Transferred

This table gives you some examples of **work being done** and the **energy changes** that happen.

Activity	Work Done Against	Final Energy Form
Lifting up a box.	Gravity	Gravitational potential energy
Pushing a chair across a level floor.	Friction	Heat and sound
Pushing two magnetic north poles together.	Magnetic force	Magnetic Energy
Stretching a spring.	Stiffness of spring	Elastic potential energy

1) Usually you need a force to move something because you're having to **overcome another force**.
2) The thing being moved has **kinetic energy** while it's **moving**.
3) The kinetic energy has been transferred to **another form of energy** when the movement stops.

The word **'work'** in Physics means the **amount of energy transferred** from one form to another when a force causes a movement of some sort.

Work = Force × Distance

When a car tows a caravan, it applies a force to the caravan to move it to where it's wanted.
To **find out** how much **work** has been **done**, you need to use the **equation**:

$$\Delta E = F\Delta s$$ or **work done = force causing motion × distance moved**

...where ΔE is measured in joules (J), F is measured in newtons (N) and Δs is measured in metres (m).

You might also see the equation for work written as $W = Fx$, where W is work, F is the force and x is the distance moved.

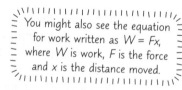

Example: A student moves a book from a shelf to the shelf above. She exerts 1.96 N to do this. The shelves are 0.30 metres apart. Calculate the work done by the student in moving the book and state what the work was done against.

$\Delta E = F \times \Delta s$ so $\Delta E = 1.96 \times 0.30 = 0.588$
$= \mathbf{0.59\ J}$ **(to 2 s.f.)**

As the book was lifted through a gravitational field, the work was done against gravity.

Points to remember:

1) **Work** is the **energy** that's been **changed** from one form to another — it's not necessarily the **total** energy. E.g. moving a book from a low shelf to a higher one will increase its gravitational potential energy, but it had some potential energy to start with. Here, the **work done** would be the **increase** in potential energy, **not the total** potential energy.
2) Remember the distance needs to be measured in metres — if you have **distance in centimetres or kilometres**, you need to **convert** it to metres first.
3) The force ***F*** will be a **fixed** value in any calculations, either because it's **constant** or because it's the **average** force.
4) The equation assumes that the **direction of the force** is the **same** as the **direction of movement**.
5) The equation gives you the **definition** of the joule (symbol J):
'One joule is the work done when a force of 1 newton moves an object through a distance of 1 metre'.

Work and Power

The **Force** isn't always in the **Same Direction** as the **Displacement**

Sometimes the **direction of movement** is **different** from the **direction of the force**.

1) To **calculate the work done** in a situation like the one on the right, you need to consider the **horizontal** and **vertical components** of the **force**.
2) The only **displacement** is in the **horizontal** direction. This means the **vertical force** is not causing any displacement (and hence not doing any work) — it's just **balancing** out some of the **weight**, meaning there's a **smaller reaction force**.
3) The horizontal force is causing the displacement — so to **calculate** the **work done**, this is the **only force** you need to consider. Which means you get:

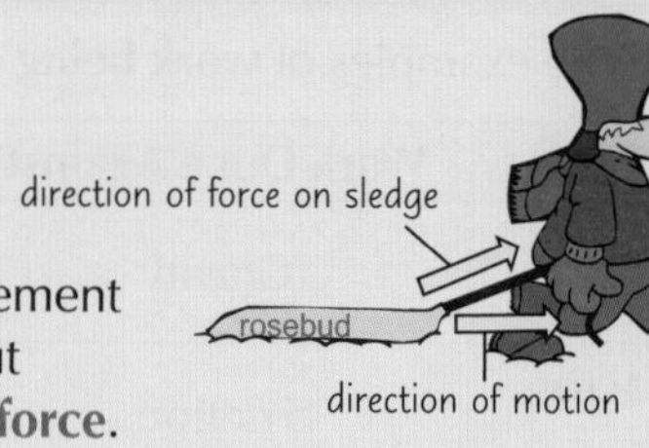

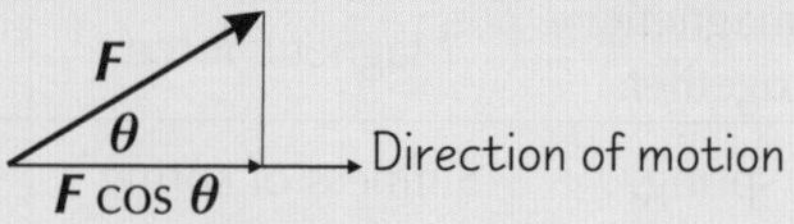

$$\Delta E = F\Delta s\cos\theta$$

Where θ is the angle between the direction of the force and the direction of displacement. See page 88–89 for more on resolving forces.

Power = Rate of Energy Transfer

Power means many things in everyday speech, but in physics (of course!) it has a special meaning. Power is the **rate of doing work** — in other words it's the **amount of energy transferred** from one form to another **per second.** You **calculate power** from this equation:

$$P = \frac{\Delta E}{t}$$

Power = work done ÷ time

...where P is measured in watts (W), ΔE is measured in joules (J) and t is measured in seconds (s).

The **watt** (symbol W) is defined as a **rate of energy transfer** equal to **1 joule per second** (Js^{-1}).

Example: a) Brian is doing the shopping. He pushes a 15 kg cart with a force of 45 N and his arms make an angle of 20.0° to the horizontal. If it takes him 7 seconds to reach the end of a 10.0 m aisle, calculate the power he outputs to do so.

The horizontal component of the pushing force is given by $F\cos\theta$

So $\Delta E = F \times \Delta s \times \cos\theta = 45 \times 10.0 \times \cos(20°)$

$= 422.861...$ J

Power is $P = \frac{\Delta E}{t} = \frac{422.861...}{7}$

$= 60.408... =$ **60 W (to 2 s.f.)**

b) Brian later sees that chocolate biscuits are on sale on a shelf 5.0 m away. He races to get the last pack, exerting the twice as much force as in part a) and keeping his arms in the same position as before. He outputs 211 W of power to get to the biscuits. Calculate the time it takes him to reach them.

The force applied is doubled, but the distance over which it is applied is halved, so the work is still $\Delta E = 422.861...$

The time taken, $t = \frac{\Delta E}{P} = \frac{422.861...}{211}$

$= 2.004... =$ **2.0 s (to 2 s.f.)**

Work and Power

Power is also Force × Velocity (P = Fv)

Sometimes, it's **easier** to use **this version** of the power equation. This is how you get it:

1) You **know** $P = \Delta E \div t$.
2) You also **know** $\Delta E = F\Delta s$, which gives $\boldsymbol{P = F\Delta s \div t}$.
3) But $v = \Delta s \div t$, which you can substitute into the above equation to give: **$P = Fv$**
4) It's easier to use this if you're given the **speed** in the question.
   Learn this equation as a **shortcut** to link **power** and **speed**.

Example: A car is travelling at a speed of 10 ms^{-1} and is kept going against frictional forces by a driving force of 500 N in the direction of motion. Find the power supplied by the engine to keep the car moving.

Use the shortcut $P = Fv$, which gives: $P = 500 \times 10 =$ **5000 W**

If the force and motion are in different directions, you can replace F with $F\cos\theta$ to get: $\boldsymbol{P = Fv\cos\theta}$

You **aren't** expected to **remember** this equation, but it's made up of bits that you **are supposed to know**, so be ready for the possibility of calculating **power** in a situation where the **direction of the force and direction of motion are different**.

Practice Questions

Q1 Define 'work' in terms of transferring energy.

Q2 Write down the equation for calculating work when the force, F, acts in the same direction as the change in displacement, Δs.

Q3 An engine applies a force perpendicular to a change in displacement. How much work does it do?

Q4 Write down the equation for calculating work when the motion is horizontal and the applied force is at an angle θ to the horizontal.

Q5 Define power and state the unit it is measured in.

Q6 Write down the equation linking power to work done and time.

Q7 From this, show that power = force × velocity.

Exam Questions

Q1 The motor in a model train does 7.5 J of work to move the train 3.6 m in a straight line. Calculate the force applied by the motor. You may assume that frictional losses are negligible. [2 marks]

Q2 A traditional narrow boat is drawn by a horse walking along the towpath. The horse pulls the boat at a constant speed between two locks which are 1500 m apart. The tension in the rope is 100 N at 40° (both to 2 s.f.) to the direction of motion.

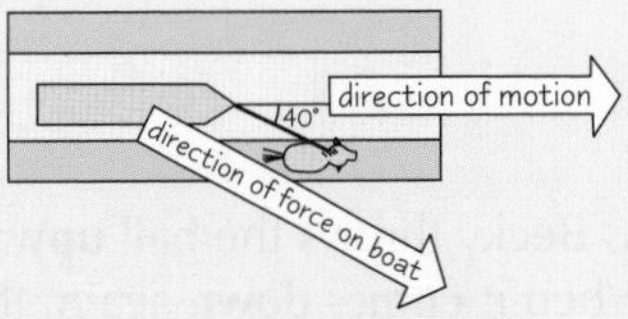

a) Calculate the work done on the boat. [2 marks]

b) The boat moves at 0.80 ms^{-1}. Calculate the power supplied to the boat in the direction of motion. [1 mark]

Q3 A motor is used to lift a 20.0 kg load a height of 3.00 m. *(g = 9.81 Nkg^{-1})*

a) Calculate the work done in lifting the load. [1 mark]

b) The speed of the load during the lift is 0.25 ms^{-1}. Calculate the power delivered by the motor. [1 mark]

Work — there's just no getting away from it...

Loads of equations to learn. Well, that's what you came here for, after all. Can't beat a good bit of equation-learning, as I've heard you say quietly to yourself when you think no one's listening. Aha, can't fool me. Aahahahahahahaha.

Conservation of Energy

Energy can never be lost. I repeat — energy can never be lost. Which is basically what I'm about to take up two whole pages saying. But that's, of course, because you need to do exam questions on this as well as understand the principle.

Learn the *Principle* of *Conservation* of *Energy*

The **principle of conservation of energy** says that:

> Energy **cannot be created** or **destroyed**. Energy **can be transferred** from one form to another but the total amount of energy in a closed system will not change.

You can talk about how well energy is transferred in terms of **efficiency**:

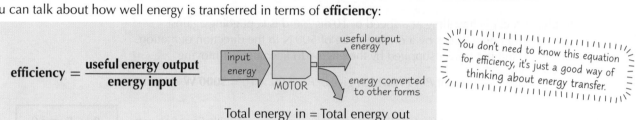

$$\textbf{efficiency} = \frac{\textbf{useful energy output}}{\textbf{energy input}}$$

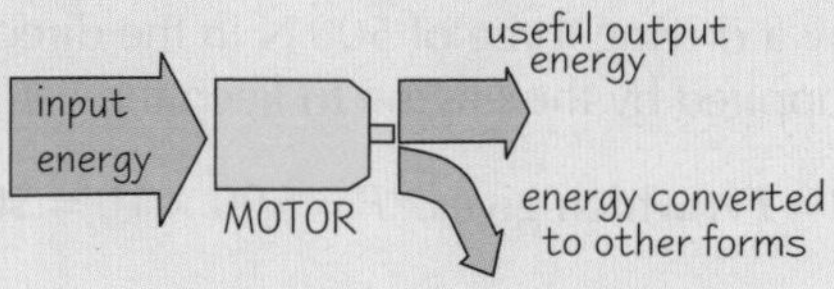

Total energy in = Total energy out

You don't need to know this equation for efficiency, it's just a good way of thinking about energy transfer.

You need it for *Questions* about *Kinetic* and *Potential Energy*

The principle of conservation of energy nearly always comes up when you're doing questions about **changes** between **kinetic** and **potential energy**. A quick reminder:

1) **Kinetic energy** is the energy of anything due to its **motion**, which you work out from:

   $$\textbf{kinetic energy} = \frac{1}{2}mv^2$$

   m is the mass of the object (kg) and v is its velocity (ms^{-1})

2) There are **different types of potential energy** — e.g. gravitational and elastic.
3) **Gravitational potential energy** is the energy something gains if you lift it up, where:

   $$\textbf{gravitational potential energy} = mgh$$

   g is the acceleration due to gravity, $g = 9.81\ ms^{-2}$ and h is the height (m)

Make sure you **know** the equations for kinetic and gravitational potential energy. You won't be given them in your exam.

4) **Elastic strain energy** (elastic stored energy) is the energy you get in, say, a stretched rubber band or spring. If the object obeys Hooke's law (see p.40), you work this out using:

   $$\textbf{elastic strain energy} = \frac{1}{2}kx^2$$

   x is the extension of the spring (m) and k is the stiffness constant (Nm^{-1})

These pictures show you three **examples** of changes between kinetic and potential energy.

1) As Becky throws the **ball upwards**, **kinetic energy** is converted into **gravitational potential energy**. When it **comes down** again, that **gravitational potential** energy is **converted back** into **kinetic** energy.
2) As Dominic goes **down the slide**, **gravitational potential energy** is converted to **kinetic energy**.
3) As Simon bounces upwards from the trampoline, **elastic strain energy** is converted to **kinetic energy**, to **gravitational potential energy**. As he comes back down again, that **gravitational potential** energy is **converted back** to **kinetic** energy, to **elastic strain** energy, and so on.

In **real life** there are also **frictional forces** — Simon would have to exert some **force** from his **muscles** to keep **jumping** to the **same height** above the trampoline each time. Each time the trampoline **stretches**, some **heat** is generated in the trampoline material. You're usually told to **ignore friction** in exam questions — this means you can **assume** that the **only forces** are those that provide the **potential or kinetic energy** (in this example that's **Simon's weight** and the **tension** in the springs and trampoline material).

If you're ignoring friction, you can say that the **sum of the kinetic and potential energies is constant**.

Conservation of Energy

Use Conservation of Energy to **Solve Problems**

You need to be able to **use** conservation of mechanical energy (change in potential energy = change in kinetic energy) to solve problems. The classic example is the **simple pendulum**.

In a simple pendulum, you assume that all the mass is in the **bob** at the end.

Example: A simple pendulum has a mass of 0.70 kg and a length of 50.0 cm. It is pulled out to an angle of 30° (to 2 s.f.) from the vertical.

a) Find the gravitational potential energy stored in the pendulum bob.

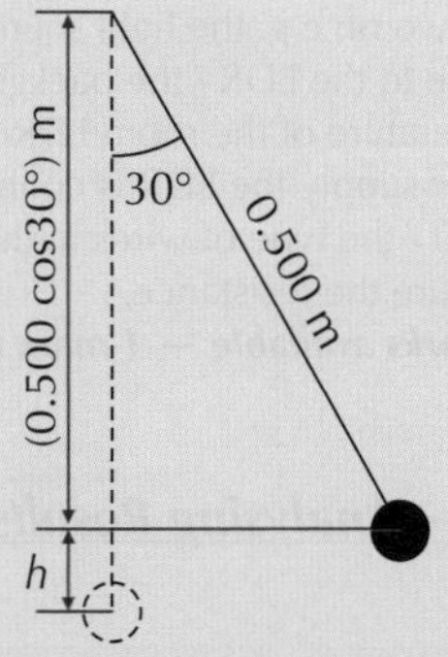

You can work out the increase in height, h, of the end of the pendulum using trig.

Gravitational potential energy $= mgh$

$= 0.70 \times 9.81 \times (0.500 - 0.500\cos 30°)$

$= 0.4600... =$ **0.46 J (to 2 s.f.)**

b) The pendulum is released. Find the maximum speed of the pendulum bob as it passes the vertical position.

To find the maximum speed, assume no air resistance.
The conservation of energy principle then gives $mgh = \frac{1}{2}mv^2$.

You can then work out the speed in two ways:

$\frac{1}{2}mv^2 = 0.4600...$

$v = \sqrt{\frac{2 \times 0.4600...}{0.70}}$

$= 1.1464... =$ **1.1 ms⁻¹ (to 2 s.f.)**

OR

Cancel the m's and rearrange to give:

$v^2 = 2gh$

$= 2 \times 9.81 \times (0.500 - 0.500\cos 30°)$

$= 1.31429...$

$v = 1.146... =$ **1.1 ms⁻¹ (to 2 s.f.)**

Practice Questions

Q1 State the principle of conservation of energy.

Q2 What are the equations for calculating kinetic energy and gravitational potential energy?

Q3 Show that, if there's no air resistance and the mass of the string is negligible, the speed of a pendulum is independent of the mass of the bob.

Exam Questions

$g = 9.81\ Nkg^{-1}$

Q1 A skateboarder is on a half-pipe. He rides the board down one side of the ramp and up the other. The height of the ramp is 2.0 m. Assuming there is no friction, calculate his speed at the lowest point of the ramp. [3 marks]

Q2 A 0.020 kg rubber ball is released from a height of 8.0 m. (Assume that the effect of air resistance is negligible.)

a) Find the kinetic energy of the ball just before it hits the ground. [1 mark]

b) The ball strikes the ground and rebounds to a height of 6.5 m. Calculate how much energy is transferred to heat and sound during the impact with the ground. [2 marks]

Q3 A 70.0 kg woman is bouncing on a trampoline and reaches a constant maximum height. When the woman is at the bottom of her bounce and the trampoline is fully stretched, it has gained 2750 J of elastic potential energy. Calculate her speed when she is at half the maximum height of a bounce. [3 marks]

Energy is never lost — it just sometimes prefers the scenic route...

Make sure you can recall the equations for kinetic and gravitational potential energy in a flash. They'll most likely be needed in a few questions. Remember to check your answers if you've got time — I always forget to multiply by the ½.

Answers

Module 1 — Development of Practical Skills in Physics

Page 5 — Planning and Implementing

1 a) Independent variable: light level / distance from the light source, dependent variable: resistance of the LDR ***[1 mark]***.

b) Any two of: e.g. the light source used / the angle of the light source to the LDR / the background lighting in the room / the temperature of the room/LDR/wires / the potential difference / the power supply the LDR is connected to / the length of wires in the circuit / the type of wires in the circuit / the multimeter used to measure the resistance.
[2 marks available — 1 mark for each correct answer.]

Page 7 — Analysing Results

1 a)

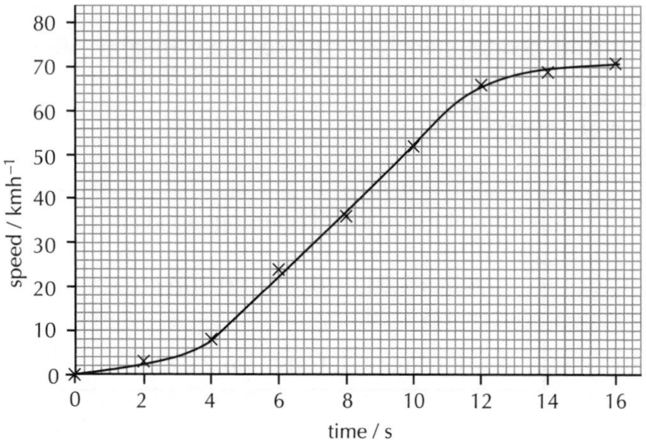

[1 mark for both axes drawn to a sensible scale and 1 mark for labelling both axes correctly, 1 mark for all the points drawn correctly, and 1 mark for a sensible line of best fit.]

b) The graph is linear between 4 and 10 seconds ***[1 mark]***.
Accept 11 seconds as the upper limit if the graph in part a) agrees.

c) The maximum acceleration is the value of the steepest gradient, which is the linear portion of the graph ***[1 mark]***:

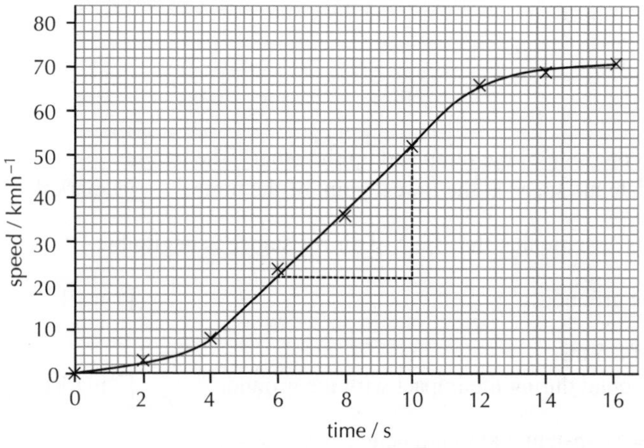

change in speed = 52 – 22 = 30 kmh^{-1} = 30 ÷ (60 × 60)
= 0.008333... kms^{-1} ***[1 mark]***

change in time = 10 – 6 = 4 s ***[1 mark]***

acceleration = 0.008333... ÷ 4 = 0.002083... kms^{-2}
= **0.0021 kms^{-2}** or **27000 kmh^{-2} (to 2 s.f.)** ***[1 mark]***

Accept an answer in the range 0.0020-0.0022 kms^{-2} or 26000-28000 kmh^{-2}.

Page 9 — Evaluating and Concluding

1 50 – (50 × 0.02 / 100) = 49.99 Ω, so the answer is **B**. ***[1 mark]***

2 a) t = 0.32 seconds, v = 2.0 ms^{-1} ***[1 mark]***

b) E.g. The results do not support this conclusion ***[1 mark]***, because the student has only collected data for a small range of times so he cannot draw conclusions about times longer than those he measured ***[1 mark]*** / because the student has only investigated one object so he cannot draw conclusions about other objects ***[1 mark]***.

Answers

Module 2 — Fundamental Data Analysis

Page 11 — Quantities, Units and Graphs

1 Work done = force × distance, and force = mass × acceleration. Velocity is distance ÷ time, so has units ms^{-1}. Acceleration is rate of change of velocity, so has units $ms^{-1} \div s = ms^{-2}$.
So the units of work are:
(units of mass) × (units of acceleration) × (units of distance)
[1 mark] = kg × ms^{-2} × m = $kg\,m^2s^{-2}$ ***[1 mark]***

2 a) You can tell the axes are logarithmic because the increments represent a change by an equal factor ***[1 mark]***.
The increments on the horizontal axis increase by a factor of 10 each time, whilst the vertical axis increments increase by a factor of 10^2 each time ***[1 mark]***.

b) A sound with a frequency of 100 Hz would need to have an intensity of at least 10^{-8} Wm^{-2} to be heard by a human ***[1 mark]***.

Page 13 — Measurements and Uncertainties

1 a) (0.02 ÷ 0.52) × 100 = 3.846... = **3.8 % (to 2 s.f.)** ***[1 mark]***

b) (0.02 ÷ 0.94) × 100 = 2.127... = **2.1% (to 2 s.f.)** ***[1 mark]***

c) acceleration = change in velocity / time = (0.94 – 0.52) ÷ 2.5
= 0.168 ms^{-2} ***[1 mark]***

Absolute error in change of velocity = 0.02 + 0.02 = 0.04 ms^{-1}
Percentage error in change of velocity:
(0.04 ÷ (0.94 – 0.52)) × 100 = 9.523...% ***[1 mark]***
Percentage error in time taken = (0.5 ÷ 2.5) × 100 = 20%
Percentage error in acceleration = 9.523...% + 20%
= 29.523...% ***[1 mark]***

Absolute error in acceleration = 0.168 × (29.523... ÷ 100)
= 0.0496 ms^{-2}

So the acceleration = **0.17 ± 0.05 ms^{-2} (to 2 s.f.)** ***[1 mark]***

Module 3: Section 1 — Imaging and Signalling

Page 15 — The Nature of Waves

1 a) $v = f\lambda$ and $f = 1 / T$
So $v = \lambda / T$, giving $\lambda = vT$ ***[1 mark]***
λ = 3.0 × 6.0 = **18 m** ***[1 mark]***

The vertical movement of the buoy is irrelevant to this part of the question.

b) The trough to peak distance is twice the amplitude, so the amplitude is 0.60 m ***[1 mark]***

2 $I = P \div A$ = 10.0 ÷ 0.002 = **5000 Wm^{-2}** ***[1 mark]***

Page 17 — Polarisation

1 a) They are at right angles to one another (90°, 270° etc.) ***[1 mark]***.

b) It would be half of the intensity ***[1 mark]***.
This is because at 45° the vertical and horizontal contributions are equal, so the intensity is halved between them.

c) E.g. Polaroid sunglasses or 3D film glasses ***[1 mark]***.

Page 20 — Forming Images with Lenses

1 a) Rays meeting the lens parallel to the principal axis converge at the focal point. / Waves parallel to the lens axis are given spherical curvature as they pass through the lens. This curvature is centred on the focal point. ***[1 mark]***

b) $\frac{1}{v} = \frac{1}{u} + \frac{1}{f}$ so $\frac{1}{v} = -\frac{1}{0.2} + \frac{1}{0.15} = \frac{5}{3}$ ***[1 mark]***,
so $v = \frac{3}{5}$ = **0.60 m** ***[1 mark]***

2 a) $m = \frac{\text{size of image}}{\text{size of object}} = \frac{47.2}{12.5}$ = 3.776 = **3.78 (to 3 s.f.)** ***[1 mark]***

b) $m = \frac{v}{u}$, giving $v = m \times u$ ***[1 mark]***
v = 3.776 × 4.0 = 15.104 = **15 mm (to 2 s.f.)** ***[1 mark]***

c) $P = \frac{1}{f} = \frac{1}{v} - \frac{1}{u}$ ***[1 mark]***, so $P = \frac{1}{0.015104} - \left(-\frac{1}{0.004}\right) = 316.20...$
= **320 D (to 2 s.f.)** ***[1 mark]***

Remember u is negative.

Page 23 — Information in Images

1 a) Number of bits = $\log_2(65\,536)$ = 16 ***[1 mark]***.
Number of bytes = number of bits ÷ 8 = 16 ÷ 8 = **2 bytes** ***[1 mark]***

b) total information = number of pixels × bits per pixel
= (1920 × 1080) × 16 = 3.3177... × 10^7
= **3.32 × 10^7 bits (to 3 s.f.)** ***[1 mark]***

c) width of square = 1920 × 0.25 = 480 pixels ***[1 mark]***
resolution = real size of object ÷ pixels representing object
= 1.5 ÷ 480 = 3.125 × 10^{-3}
= **3.1 × 10^{-3} m $pixel^{-1}$** ***[1 mark]***

2 a)

The diagram should show a fairly uniform mid-grey outside, with a lighter square in the centre. ***[1 mark]***

Answers

b) Noise can be removed by replacing each pixel with the median of itself and the eight pixels surrounding it. ***[1 mark]***

c)

100	99	100
97	100	98
101	101	98

[1 mark]

Page 25 — Digital and Analogue Signals

1 a) time period of shortest repeating part = (1.25 – 0.25) × 10^{-3} = 1.0 × 10^{-3} s

$f = \frac{1}{T} = \frac{1}{1.0 \times 10^{-3}}$ = **1000 Hz** ***[1 mark]***

b)

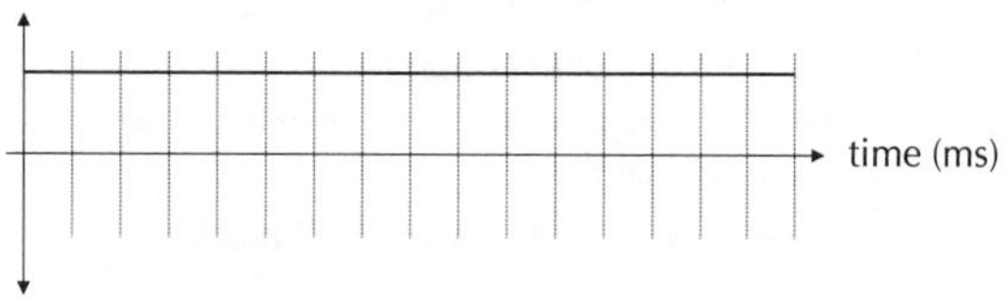

[1 mark for a straight line and 1 mark for the line being above the horizontal axis]

The graph is a straight line because the sample frequency is the same as the fundamental frequency.

Page 27 — Sampling and Transmitting Signals

1 $b = \log_2\left(\frac{V_{total}}{V_{noise}}\right)$ ***[1 mark]*** $= \log_2\left(\frac{160}{10}\right) = \log_2 16$ = **4 bits** ***[1 mark]***

You don't need to convert the variations from mV to V because the units cancel in the fraction.

2 a) Rate of transmission = samples per second × bits per sample
= 8000 × 8
= **64 000 bits per second** ***[1 mark]***

b) 1 byte = 8 bits.
So, 64 000 bits per second = **8000 bytes per second** ***[1 mark]***

3 a) rate of transmission = samples per second × bits per sample, so

samples per second = $\frac{\text{rates of transmission}}{\text{bits per sample}} = \frac{128 \times 10^3}{16}$
= **8000 Hz** ***[1 mark]***

b) rate of transmission = number of bits to transmit ÷ time taken

number of bits = (2.0 × 10^6) × 8 = 1.6 × 10^7 bits ***[1 mark]***

rate of transmission = $\frac{1.6 \times 10^7}{110}$ = 145 454 = 150 kbit s^{-1} (to 2 s.f.) ***[1 mark]*** **150 > 128, so yes** — the connection is sufficient to stream the radio station. ***[1 mark]***

Module 3: Section 2 — Sensing

Page 29 — Charge, Current and Potential Difference

1 a) $P = \frac{W}{t} = \frac{75}{6.0}$ = 12.5 = **13 W (to 2 s.f.)** ***[1 mark]***

b) $V = \frac{P}{I} = \frac{12.5}{0.18}$ = 69.44... = **69 V (to 2 s.f.)** ***[1 mark]***

2 Energy transferred to water = 0.88 × electrical energy input so the energy input will be 308 / 0.88 = 350 J ***[1 mark]***

$V = \frac{W}{Q}$ so $Q = \frac{W}{V}$

Q = 350 / 230 = 1.52... = **1.5 C (to 2 s.f.)** ***[1 mark]***

The heat energy that the kettle transfers to the water is less than the electrical energy input because less than 100% of the electrical energy is transferred to the water.

Page 31 — Resistance and Conductance

1 a) $R = \frac{V}{I} = \frac{1.5}{2.8}$ = 0.5357... = **0.54 Ω (to 2 s.f.)** ***[1 mark]***

b) $G = \frac{I}{V} = \frac{0.15}{1.5}$ = **0.10 S** (or 0.10 Ω^{-1}) ***[1 mark]***

c) The wires have a resistance that causes power dissipation ***[1 mark]***. The power that is dissipated is transferred to heat, making the wires warm ***[1 mark]***.

Page 33 — Electrical Properties of Solids

1 a) E.g.

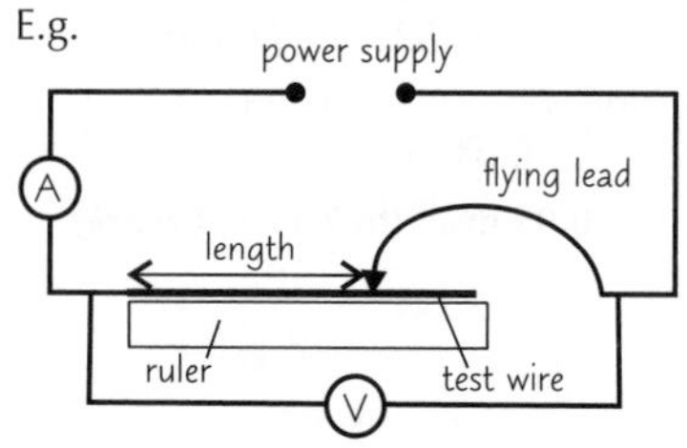

[1 mark for sensible circuit diagram]

Measure the diameter of the wire using a micrometer (to calculate the cross-sectional area) ***[1 mark]***. Connect the wire in a circuit as shown above. Use the flying lead to vary the length of wire connected to the circuit ***[1 mark]***. Take a measurement from the voltmeter and the ammeter for each length of wire used, and use these to calculate the wire's resistance at each length using the formula $R = \frac{V}{I}$ ***[1 mark]***. Plot a graph of resistance against length, then calculate the gradient of the line of best fit ***[1 mark]***. Multiply the gradient of the graph by the cross-sectional area to get ρ (as $\rho = \frac{RA}{L}$). ***[1 mark]***

Answers

b) E.g.

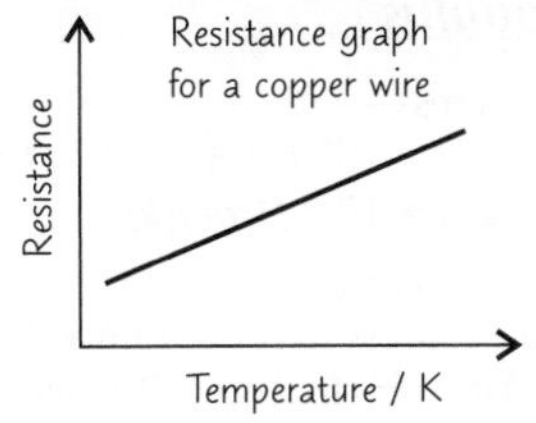

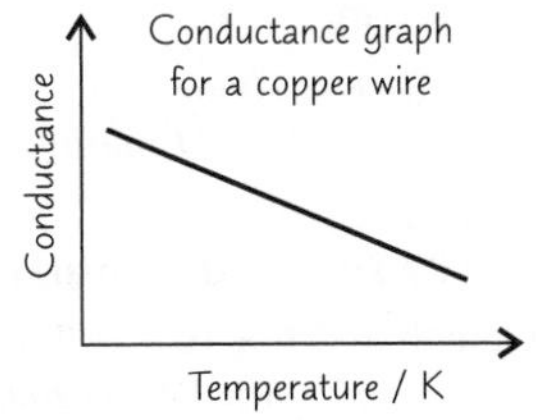

[1 mark for each correct graph]

The graphs of resistance and conductance against temperature for a copper wire are straight lines, the graphs for an NTC thermistor are curves in the opposite direction ***[1 mark]***. This is because copper is a metal and has a high number of mobile charge carriers. As temperature increases, the electrons become less free to move so resistance increases and conductance decreases ***[1 mark]***. An NTC thermistor is a semiconductor so has fewer free electrons to begin with, but as temperature increases more electrons are freed so conductance rapidly increases and resistance rapidly decreases. ***[1 mark]***

Page 35 — E.m.f. and Internal Resistance

1 a) $\varepsilon = I(R + r)$ so $I = \varepsilon/(R + r) = 24/(4.0 + 0.80)$ ***[1 mark]***
$= \mathbf{5.0\ A}$ **(to 2 s.f.)** ***[1 mark]***

b) $v = Ir = 5.0 \times 0.80 =$ **4.0 V (to 2 s.f.)** ***[1 mark]***
You could have used $\varepsilon = V + v$ and calculated V using $V = IR_{drill}$

2 **C** ***[1 mark]***
$\varepsilon = I(R + r)$, but since there are two cells in series replace r with $2r$, and ε with 2ε, then rearrange to find I.

Page 37 — Conservation of Energy & Charge in Circuits

1 a) Resistance of parallel resistors:
$1/R_{\text{parallel}} = 1/6.0 + 1/3.0 = 1/2 \Rightarrow R_{\text{parallel}} = 2.0\ \Omega$ ***[1 mark]***

Total resistance:

$R_{\text{total}} = 4.0 + R_{\text{parallel}} = 4.0 + 2.0 =$ **6.0 Ω** ***[1 mark]***

b) $V = I_3R_{total} \Rightarrow I_3 = V / R_{\text{total}} = 12 / 6.0 =$ **2.0 A** ***[1 mark]***

c) $V = IR = 2.0 \times 4.0 =$ **8.0 V** ***[1 mark]***

d) E.m.f. = sum of p.d.s in circuit, so $12 = 8.0 + V_{\text{parallel}}$
$V_{\text{parallel}} = 12 - 8.0 =$ **4.0 V** ***[1 mark]***

e) $I = V/R$, so $I_1 = 4.0 / 3.0 =$ **1.3 A (to 2 s.f.)** ***[1 mark]***
$I_2 = 4.0 / 6.0 =$ **0.67 A (to 2 s.f.)** ***[1 mark]***
You can check your answers by making sure that $I_3 = I_2 + I_1$.

Page 39 — The Potential Divider

1 a) $V_A / V_B = R_A / R_B$ so $V_A = V_B \times (R_A / R_B)$
$= 6.75 \times (35 \div 45) =$ **5.25 V** ***[1 mark]***

b) Input p.d. $= V_A + V_B = 5.25 + 6.75 =$ **12 V** ***[1 mark]***

c) $V_B = \frac{R_B}{R_A + R_B}V_{in} = \frac{45}{75 + 45} \times 12 =$ **4.5 V** ***[1 mark]***

2 a) $V_{AB} = \frac{R_2}{R_1 + R_2}V_{in} = (50 / (30 + 50)) \times 12 = 7.5\ \text{V}$ ***[1 mark]***
Ignore the 10 Ω — no current flows that way.

b) Total resistance R_T of the parallel circuit:
$1/R_T = 1 / 50 + 1 / (10 + 40) = 1 / 25$
$R_T = 25\ \Omega$ ***[1 mark]***

Use $V_{out} = (R_2 / (R_1 + R_2)\ V_{in}$ to find the p.d. over the whole parallel arrangement: $(25 / (30 + 25)) \times 12 = 5.454...\ \text{V}$ ***[1 mark]***

Use $V_{out} = (R_2 / R_1 + R_2)\ V_{in}$ again to find the p.d. across AB:
$V_{AB} = 40 / (40 + 10) \times 5.454... = 4.363...$
$=$ **4.4 V (to 2 s.f.)** ***[1 mark]***

current through 40 Ω resistor $= V/R$
$= 4.363... / 40 =$ **0.11 A (to 2 s.f.)** ***[1 mark]***
This question might look tricky, but it's basically just one potential divider on top of another.

Answers

Module 3: Section 3 — Mechanical Properties of Materials

Page 41 — Hooke's Law

1 a) First find the force constant:
$F = kx$ and so $k = F \div x$
$k = 10 \div (4.0 \times 10^{-3})$ = **2500 Nm^{-1}** ***[1 mark]***
Now find the extension when the 15 N force is applied:
$x = F \div k = 15 \div 2500$ = **6.0 × 10^{-3} m** or **6.0 mm** ***[1 mark]***
You could also find the new extension by using the fact that force is proportional to extension. The new force is 1.5 times the original force, so the new extension will be 1.5 times the original extension: 1.5 × 4.0 mm = 6.0 mm.

b) Any one from e.g. the string now stretches much further for small increases in force ***[1 mark]***. / When the string is loosened it is longer than at the start ***[1 mark]***.

2 If the rubber band obeys Hooke's law, then force will be proportional to extension ($F = kx$). 5.0 N is double 2.5 N, so increasing the load should mean the extension is doubled too.
The extension under the 2.5 N load is 10.4 – 6.0 = 4.4 cm.
The extension under the 5.0 N load is 16.2 – 6.0 = 10.2 cm.
10.2 is not double 4.4 ***[1 mark]***, so the rubber band does not obey Hooke's law ***[1 mark]***.
Or you could show that k is different for 2.5 N and 5.0 N.

Page 43 — Stress, Strain and Elastic Energy

1 a) strain = extension ÷ original length
= $4.0 \times 10^{-3} \div 2.00$ = **2.0 × 10^{-3} (to 2 s.f.)** ***[1 mark]***

b) stress = tension ÷ cross-sectional area
$A = \pi r^2$ or $\pi(d^2 \div 4) = \pi \times ((1.0 \times 10^{-3})^2 \div 4)$
$= 7.8539... \times 10^{-7}\ \text{m}^2$ ***[1 mark]***
stress = $300 \div (7.8539... \times 10^{-7})$
= **3.8 × 10^{8} Nm^{-2} (to 2 s.f.)** ***[1 mark]***

2 a) $F = kx$ so $k = F \div x = 50 \div (3.0 \times 10^{-3})$
= **1.7 × 10^{4} Nm^{-1} (to 2 s.f.)** ***[1 mark]***

b) $E = \frac{1}{2}Fx = \frac{1}{2} \times 50 \times 3.0 \times 10^{-3}$ = **7.5 × 10^{-2} J** ***[1 mark]***
You could also find E using $E = \frac{1}{2}kx^2$ with your value of k from part a).

3 $E = \frac{1}{2}kx^2 = \frac{1}{2} \times 40.8 \times 0.05^2 = 0.051$ J ***[1 mark]***
To find maximum speed, assume all this energy is converted to kinetic energy in the ball. $E_{kinetic} = E$
$E = \frac{1}{2}mv^2$, so $v^2 = 2E \div m$ ***[1 mark]***
$v^2 = (2 \times 0.051) \div 0.012 = 8.5$
So v = **2.92 ms^{-1} (to 3 s.f.)** ***[1 mark]***

Page 45 — The Young Modulus

1 a) E = stress ÷ strain, so strain = stress ÷ E
$= 2.6 \times 10^{8} \div 1.3 \times 10^{11}$ ***[1 mark]***
= **2.0 × 10^{-3}** ***[1 mark]***

b) stress = tension ÷ cross-sectional area, so:
cross-sectional area = tension ÷ stress = $100 \div (2.6 \times 10^{8})$
= **3.8 × 10^{-7} m^2 (to 2 s.f.)** ***[1 mark]***

2 Cross-sectional area = πr^2 or $\pi(d^2 \div 4)$.
So the cross-sectional area = $\pi \times ((0.6 \times 10^{-3})^2 \div 4)$
$= 2.827... \times 10^{-7}$ ***[1 mark]***
stress = tension ÷ cross-sectional area
$= 80 \div (2.827... \times 10^{-7}) = 2.829... \times 10^{8}$ ***[1 mark]***
strain = extension ÷ original length = $(3.6 \times 10^{-3}) \div 2.50$
$= 1.44 \times 10^{-3}$ ***[1 mark]***
E = stress ÷ strain = $(2.829... \times 10^{8}) \div (1.44 \times 10^{-3})$ ***[1 mark]***
$= 1.964... \times 10^{11}$ = **2.0 × 10^{11} Nm^{-2} (to 2 s.f.)** ***[1 mark]***

3 The Young modulus is the gradient of a stress-strain graph, so
$$E = \frac{10 \times 10^{8}}{15 \times 10^{-3}} = 6.66... \times 10^{10}$$
= **6.7 × 10^{10} Nm^{-2} (to 2 s.f.)** ***[1 mark]***

Page 47 — Mechanical Properties of Solids

1 Material C would be the best choice as it has a strength of 2000 MPa ***[1 mark]***. Support beams for bridges need to be strong enough to support heavy loads without deforming ***[1 mark]***. This is more important than toughness, so whilst other materials are tougher, they would be less suitable as their strength is much smaller than material C's ***[1 mark]***.

2 ***5-6 marks:***

The answer clearly explains three properties of materials and why they would be useful when creating riding helmets.
The answer is structured in a logical way, with relevant information supporting it throughout.

3-4 marks:

The answer either: describes two properties of materials and fully explains why they would be useful when creating riding helmets or correctly identifies three useful material properties with minimal explanation for why they would be useful when creating riding helmets. The answer has some logical structure, with mostly relevant information supporting it.

1-2 marks:

The answer describes two properties without explanation, or correctly describes one property with a brief explanation as to why it is useful when creating riding helmets.

The answer is basic, poorly structured and unsupported by relevant information.

0 marks:

No relevant information is given.

Here are some points your answer may include:

- The material would need to be stiff so that it would keep its shape and not crush the rider's head when a force was applied to it.
- It would also need to be tough so that it could absorb the energy of an impact without breaking.
- The material should be strong so that the helmet withstands the force of the impact without deforming or breaking.

Answers

Page 49 — Structures of Materials

1 a) Instead of increasing the space between the ions in the metal, the applied force causes planes of ions to slip across each other. This slipping is what causes the plastic deformation ***[1 mark]***. Dislocations or imperfections lower the stress needed to cause slipping, meaning that a lower stress is needed in order to cause plastic deformation ***[1 mark]***.

b) Alloying a metal is the process of adding ions from a second material into the crystal lattice ***[1 mark]***. These ions are placed inside dislocations to 'pin' them down ***[1 mark]***. This means a greater stress is needed to cause slipping, and so the chance of slipping is reduced ***[1 mark]***. Alloying the sample will make it harder and less ductile ***[1 mark]***.

2 C ***[1 mark]***

3 ***5-6 marks:***

The answer thoroughly describes two methods and how they measure the size and/or spacings of atoms. References may be made to other additional methods. The time frame has been referenced, showing an appreciation that increased knowledge has lead to the creation of new methods which can directly observe atomic size.
The answer is structured in a logical way, with relevant information supporting it throughout.

3-4 marks:

The answer correctly identifies two methods for calculating atomic size and/or spacing. Brief explanations of these methods are given. No reference to how changing methods over time have lead to direct measurements of atomic sizes/spacing. The answer has some logical structure, with mostly relevant information supporting it.

1-2 marks:

The answer attempts to identify experiments to measure atomic size and spacing, but doesn't describe them.

The answer is basic, poorly structured and unsupported by relevant information.

0 marks:

No relevant information is given.

Here are some points your answer may include:

- Rayleigh's oil drop method was used to estimate atomic sizes.
- This involved comparing the volume of an oil drop to the area and thickness of a thin sheet of oil floating on water.
- From this, the height of an oil molecule could be found.
- The size of an atom is roughly equal to the size of an oil molecule divided by the number of atoms in an oil molecule, so Rayleigh's measurements could be used to find an upper limit for the size of individual atoms.
- Modern day methods include X-ray crystallography, where X-rays are diffracted by a sample.
- The diffraction patterns are then analysed, in order to investigate atomic spacing.
- Scanning Tunnelling Microscopes are used to probe a surface of a sample.
- A voltage is applied to the microscope's fine tip. Electrons then tunnel from the sample to the tip, creating a current.
- The height of the tip is adjusted to keep this current constant, so the surface of the sample can be mapped to find atomic size and spacing.
- Scanning Electron Microscopes and Atomic Force Microscopes create a digital image of the surface, with 'blobs' representing each atom.
- By knowing the magnification of the image, atomic size and spacing can be calculated from the image.
- Modern day techniques are able to investigate the spacing of atoms as well as their size.
- The accuracy with which atomic size can be found has increased over time, as Rayleigh's oil drop experiment could only roughly calculate molecular not atomic sizes.

Answers

Module 4: Section 1 — Waves and Quantum Behaviour

Page 51 — Superposition and Coherence

1 a) $10.2 \div 0.6 = 17$. As the path difference is a whole number of wavelengths, constructive interference occurs ***[1 mark]***.

b)

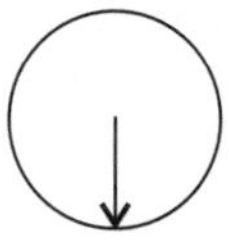

[1 mark for correct direction] The magnitude of the phasor is the same size as for the first sound wave ***[1 mark]***.

Page 53 — Standing Waves

1 a)

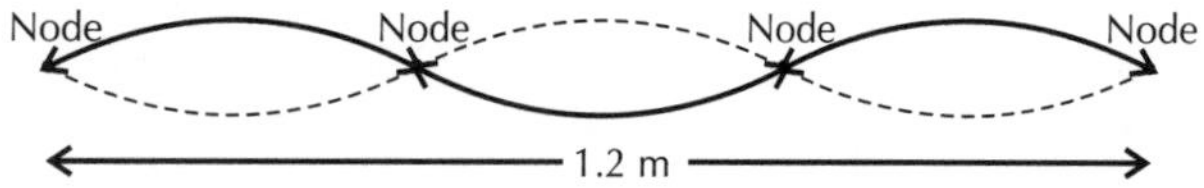

[1 mark for the correct shape, 1 mark for labelling the length]

b) For a string vibrating at three times the fundamental frequency, length $= 3\lambda / 2$
$1.2 \text{ m} = 3\lambda / 2$
$\lambda =$ **0.8 m** ***[1 mark]***

c) When the string forms a standing wave, its amplitude varies from a maximum at the antinodes to zero at the nodes ***[1 mark]***. In a progressive wave all the points have the same amplitude ***[1 mark]***.

d) $T = 4 \times 2 \times 10^{-3} = 8 \times 10^{-3}$ s ***[1 mark]***
$f = 1 / (8 \times 10^{-3}) = 125 =$ **130 Hz (to 2 s.f.)** ***[1 mark]***

Page 55 — Refraction and Refractive Index

1 a) $n_{diamond} = c / c_{diamond} = (3.00 \times 10^8) / (1.24 \times 10^8) = 2.419...$
$=$ **2.42 (to 3 s.f.)** ***[1 mark]***

b) $n_{diamond} = \sin i / \sin r$ ***[1 mark]***
$\sin r = \sin 50 / 2.419... = 0.316...$
$r = \sin^{-1}(0.316...) = 18.459... =$ **18° (to 2 s.f.)** ***[1 mark]***
Don't forget to write the degree sign in your answer.

2 a) $\dfrac{\sin i}{\sin r} = \dfrac{c_{1\text{st medium}}}{c_{2\text{nd medium}}} = \dfrac{c}{c_A}$

$c_A = \dfrac{c \sin r}{\sin i} = \dfrac{3.00 \times 10^8 \times \sin(27)}{\sin(40)} = 2.118... \times 10^8$ ***[1 mark]***

$c_A =$ **2.1×10^8 ms^{-1} (to 2 s.f.)** ***[1 mark]***
Remember, the speed of light in air is approximately c.

b) $n = \dfrac{c}{c_{\text{medium}}} = \dfrac{3.00 \times 10^8}{1.7 \times 10^8} = 1.764... =$ **1.8 (to 2 s.f.)** ***[1 mark]***

c) $n_1 \sin i = n_2 \sin r$
$1.4\sin(27) = 1.76...\sin r$ so $\sin r = \dfrac{1.4\sin(27)}{1.76...} = 0.3601...$ ***[1 mark]***
$\sin^{-1}(0.3601...) = 21.1... =$ **21° (to 2 s.f.)** ***[1 mark]***
The angle of incidence for B is the same as the angle of refraction for A.

Page 57 — Diffraction

1 When a wavefront meets an obstacle, the waves will diffract round the corners of the obstacle. When the obstacle is much bigger than the wavelength, little diffraction occurs. In this case, the mountain is much bigger than the wavelength of short-wave radio. So the "shadow" where you cannot pick up short wave is very long ***[1 mark]***.

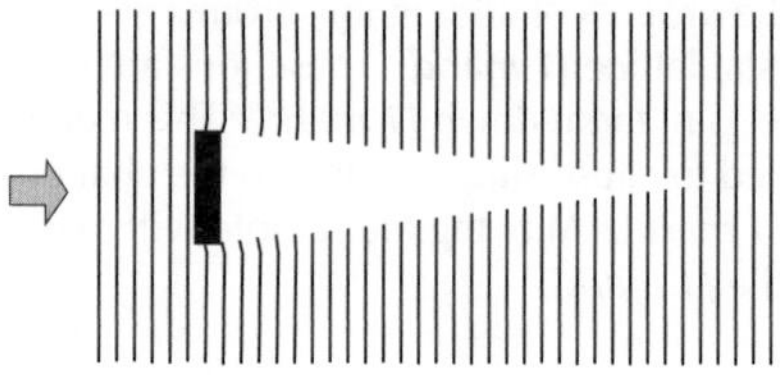

[1 mark]

When the obstacle is comparable in size to the wavelength, as it is for the long-wave radio waves, more diffraction occurs. The wavefront re-forms after a shorter distance, leaving a shorter "shadow" ***[1 mark]***.

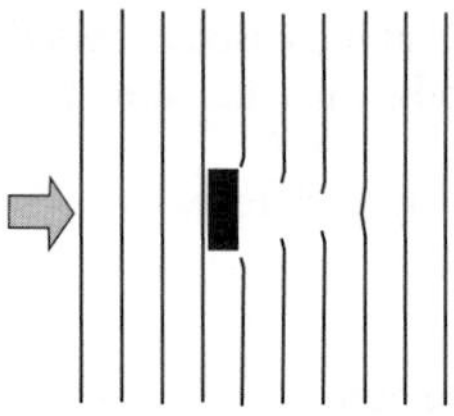

[1 mark]

Page 59 — Two-Source Interference

1 a)

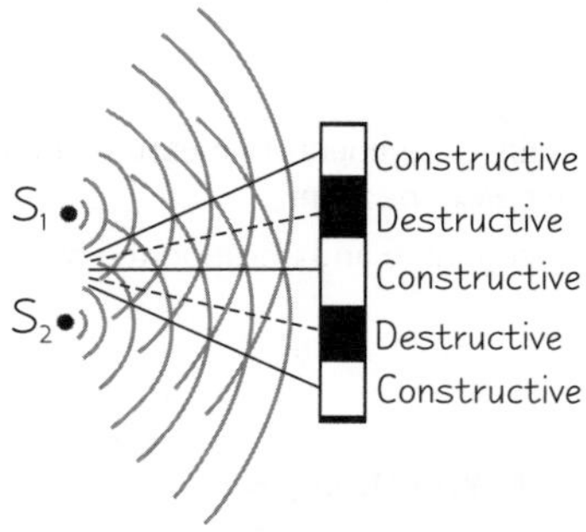

[1 mark for correct placement of constructive interference patterns, 1 mark for correct placement of destructive interference patterns]

b) The light sources must be coherent ***[1 mark]***.

2 a) $\lambda = v / f = 330 / 1320 =$ **0.25 m** ***[1 mark]***.

b) Separation $= X = D\lambda / d$
$= 7 \times 0.25 / 1.5$ m ***[1 mark]*** $= 1.166... =$ **1.2 m (to 2 s.f.)** ***[1 mark]***.

Answers

Page 61 — Diffraction Gratings

1 a) Use $\sin\theta = n\lambda / d$

For the first order, $n = 1$

So, $\sin\theta = \lambda / d$ ***[1 mark]***

No need to actually work out d. The number of lines per metre is $1 / d$. So you can simply multiply the wavelength by that.

$\sin\theta = 6.00 \times 10^{-7} \times 4.0 \times 10^5 = 0.24$

$\theta = \sin^{-1}(0.24) = 13.8865... =$ **14° (to 2 s.f.)** ***[1 mark]***

For the second order, $n = 2$ and $\sin\theta = 2\lambda / d$. ***[1 mark]***

You already have a value for λ / d. Just double it to get $\sin\theta$ for the second order.

$\sin\theta = 0.48$

$\theta = \sin^{-1}(0.48) = 28.685... =$ **29° (to 2 s.f.)** ***[1 mark]***

b) No. Putting $n = 5$ into the equation gives a value of $\sin\theta$ of 1.2, which is impossible ***[1 mark]***.

2 $\sin\theta = n\lambda / d$, so for the 1st order maximum, $\sin\theta = \lambda / d$
$\sin 14.2° = \lambda \times 3.70 \times 10^5$ ***[1 mark]***
$\lambda = 6.629... \times 10^{-7}$
$=$ **663 nm (or 6.63×10^{-7} m) (to 3 s.f.)** ***[1 mark]***.

Page 63 — Light — Wave or Particle?

1 a) At threshold voltage:
$E_{photon} = e \times V = 1.60 \times 10^{-19} \times 1.74 = 2.784 \times 10^{-19}$
$=$ **2.78×10^{-19} J (to 3 s.f.)** ***[1 mark]***

b) $E = \frac{hc}{\lambda}$ so $h = \frac{E\lambda}{c}$

$\lambda = 7.00 \times 10^{-7}$, $c = 3.00 \times 10^8$

So, $h = \frac{2.784 \times 10^{-19} \times 7.00 \times 10^{-7}}{3.00 \times 10^8}$ ***[1 mark]***

$= 6.496.... \times 10^{-34}$

$=$ **6.50×10^{-34} Js (to 3 s.f.)** ***[1 mark]***

c) $V = 1.74 - 0.0400 = 1.70$ V

$E_{photon} = e \times V = 1.60 \times 10^{-19} \times 1.70 = 2.72 \times 10^{-19}$ J ***[1 mark]***

$E = \frac{hc}{\lambda}$ so $h = \frac{E\lambda}{c}$

So, $h = \frac{2.72 \times 10^{-19} \times 7.00 \times 10^{-7}}{3.00 \times 10^8}$

$= 6.346.... \times 10^{-34}$

$=$ **6.35×10^{-34} Js (to 3 s.f.)** ***[1 mark]***

Page 65 — The Photoelectric Effect

1 $\phi = 2.9$ eV $= 2.9 \times (1.60 \times 10^{-19})$ J $= 4.64 \times 10^{-19}$ J ***[1 mark]***

$f = \frac{\phi}{h} = \frac{4.64 \times 10^{-19}}{6.63 \times 10^{-34}} = 6.99... \times 10^{14}$

$=$ **7.0×10^{14} Hz (to 2 s.f.)** ***[1 mark]***

2 a) The work function is the minimum energy needed to break an electron free from the surface of a metal ***[1 mark]***.

b) Energy is conserved so $E_{before} = E_{after}$
$E_{before} = \phi + E_{kin}$ so $\phi = 9.0$ eV $- 3.6$ eV $= 5.4$ eV ***[1 mark]***
$5.4 \times 1.60 \times 10^{-19} = 8.64 \times 10^{-19}$ J ***[1 mark]***

$f = \frac{\phi}{h} = \frac{8.64 \times 10^{-19}}{6.63 \times 10^{-34}} = 1.303... \times 10^{15}$

$=$ **1.3×10^{15} Hz (to 2 s.f.)** ***[1 mark]***

3 An electron needs to gain a certain amount of energy (the work function energy) before it can leave the surface of the metal ***[1 mark]*** and the electron can only absorb one photon ***[1 mark]***.
The energy of a photon is given by $E = hf$ so the energy an electron can absorb depends only on the frequency of the photon ***[1 mark]***.

Page 67 — Energy Levels and Photon Emission

1 a) The movement of an electron from a lower energy level to a higher energy level by absorbing energy ***[1 mark]***.

b) $-2.18 \times 10^{-18} - -2.04 \times 10^{-18} = -1.4 \times 10^{-19}$ which corresponds to the $n = 4$ level ***[1 mark]***.

c) 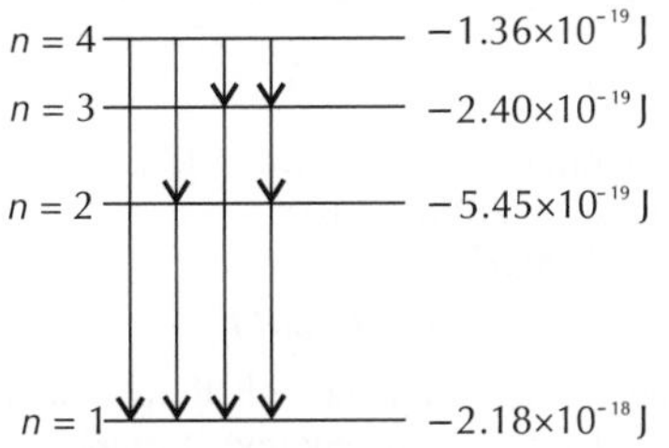

[1 mark per 2 correct transitions]

d) There would be 6 lines on the emission spectra ***[1 mark]***
The transitions from $n = 4$ to $n = 3$ and $n = 2$ to $n = 1$ are in two transition paths, but would only produce one line on the emission spectra (as they will always emit a photon of the same energy).

e) $\Delta E = E_3 - E_1 = hf$
$\Delta E = -2.40 \times 10^{-19} - -2.18 \times 10^{-18} = 1.94 \times 10^{-18}$ J ***[1 mark]***
$f = \Delta E \div h = (1.94 \times 10^{-18}) \div (6.63 \times 10^{-34}) = 2.926... \times 10^{15}$
$=$ **2.93×10^{15} Hz (to 3 s.f.)** ***[1 mark]***

Page 70 — The "Sum Over Paths" Theory

1 Probability $\propto$ (resultant phasor amplitude)^2
Probability of electron reaching point A $\propto (6.3)^2 = 39.69$ ***[1 mark]***
Probability of electron reaching point B $\propto (4.5)^2 = 20.25$ ***[1 mark]***
$39.69 \div 20.25 = 1.96$, so an electron is **1.96 times** as likely to reach point A as point B ***[1 mark]***.

2 The frequency of phasor rotation $= 6.0 \times 10^{14}$ rotations per second.
Use time (s) = distance (m) ÷ speed (ms^{-1}) to find the time taken for the photon to reach the detector.
$t = 0.12 \div c = 0.12 \div 3.0 \times 10^8 = 4.0 \times 10^{-10}$ s ***[1 mark]***
So the number of phasor rotations along this path is:
$f \times t = 6.0 \times 10^{14} \times 4.0 \times 10^{-10} =$ **2.4×10^5 rotations** ***[1 mark]***

3 Photons take every possible path. To find out the probability of a photon taking a particular path, the resultant phasors describing each individual path are summed ***[1 mark]***. Usually, these cancel each other out, with the quickest path (a straight line) having the largest resultant amplitude. The probability of a photon arriving at a certain point is proportional to the resultant phasor amplitude squared ***[1 mark]***. This means that light is most likely to take the quickest path, a straight line, as that is the path with the largest contribution to the resultant vector. As the detector is around the corner from the source, instead of in a straight line view of the source, the photons have a very low probability of reaching the detector ***[1 mark]***.

4 All of the phasors are pointing in the same direction, so the focal point is described by point B ***[1 mark]***.
The lens will focus the photons by ensuring the paths take the same time to reach the focal point.

Answers

Page 73 — Quantum Behaviour of Electrons

1 a) $E = hf$ so $f = (5.22 \times 10^{-19}) / (6.63 \times 10^{-34}) = 7.873... \times 10^{14}$
= 7.87 × 10^14 Hz (to 3 s.f.) ***[1 mark]***

b) $E_{kinetic} = \frac{1}{2}mv^2$ so $v = \sqrt{\frac{2E}{m}} = \sqrt{\frac{2 \times 5.22 \times 10^{-19}}{9.11 \times 10^{-31}}}$

$v = 1.07... \times 10^6$ ***[1 mark]***

$$\lambda = \frac{h}{mv} = \frac{6.63 \times 10^{-34}}{9.11 \times 10^{-31} \times 1.07... \times 10^6} = 6.798... \times 10^{-10}$$

So you need a spacing of **6.80 × 10^-10 m (to 3 s.f.)** to cause diffraction ***[1 mark]***

c) $v = \frac{h}{m\lambda} = \frac{6.63 \times 10^{-34}}{9.11 \times 10^{-31} \times 2.3 \times 10^{-10}}$

$= 3.164... \times 10^6$ ***[1 mark]***

From part b) you know the original velocity was $1.07... \times 10^6$.
$(3.16... \times 10^6) - (1.07... \times 10^6) = 2.09... \times 10^6$
= 2.1 × 10^6 ms^-1 (to 2 s.f.) ***[1 mark]***

2 a) The accelerating voltage was increased ***[1 mark]***.

b) As the accelerating voltage is increased, the only thing which changes is the electron's velocity (kinetic energy) ***[1 mark]***. As wavelength is inversely related to the velocity, the larger the velocity, the smaller the wavelength. This means the spread of the lines is smaller ***[1 mark]***.

Module 4: Section 2 — Space, Time and Motion

Page 75 — Scalars and Vectors

1

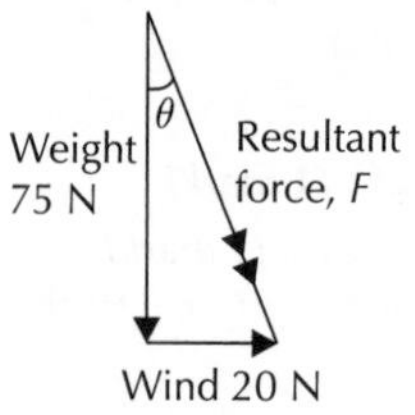

$F^2 = 20^2 + 75^2 = 6025$
So $F = \sqrt{6025} = 77.62... = 78$ N (to 2 s.f.)
$\tan\theta = 20 / 75 = 0.266...$
So $\theta = \tan^{-1} 0.266... = 14.93... = 15°$ (to 2 s.f.)
The resultant force on the rock is **78 N (to 2 s.f.)** ***[1 mark]*** at an angle of **15° (to 2 s.f.)** ***[1 mark]*** to the vertical.
Make sure you know which angle you're finding — and label it on your diagram.

2

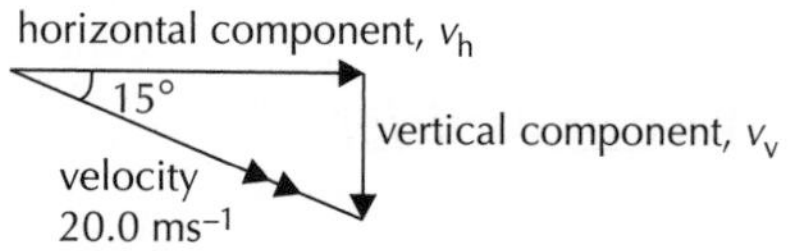

horizontal component $v_h = 20.0 \times \cos 15.0° = 19.318...$
= 19.3 ms^-1 (to 3 s.f.) ***[1 mark]***

vertical component $v_v = 20 \times \sin 15.0° = 5.1763...$
= 5.18 ms^-1 (to 3 s.f.) ***[1 mark]***

3 E.g.

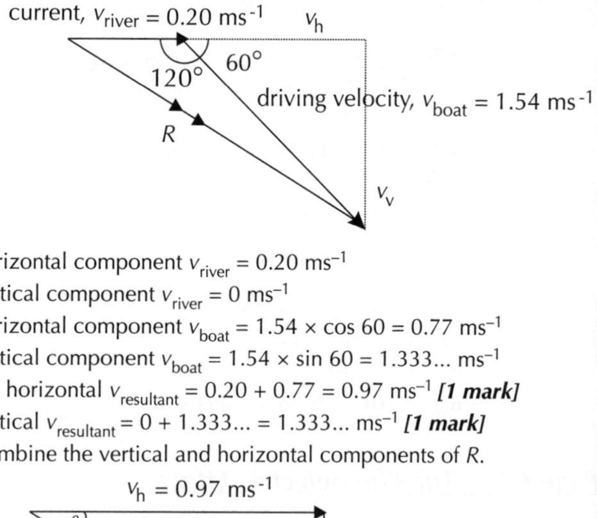

horizontal component $v_{river} = 0.20$ ms^{-1}
vertical component $v_{river} = 0$ ms^{-1}
horizontal component $v_{boat} = 1.54 \times \cos 60 = 0.77$ ms^{-1}
vertical component $v_{boat} = 1.54 \times \sin 60 = 1.333...$ ms^{-1}
So, horizontal $v_{resultant} = 0.20 + 0.77 = 0.97$ ms^{-1} ***[1 mark]***
vertical $v_{resultant} = 0 + 1.333... = 1.333...$ ms^{-1} ***[1 mark]***
Combine the vertical and horizontal components of R.

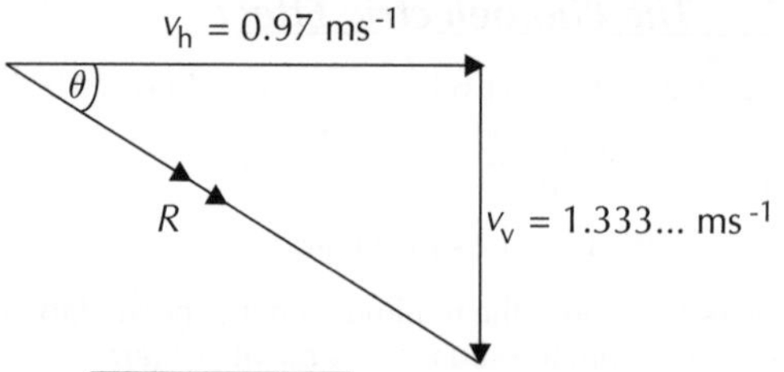

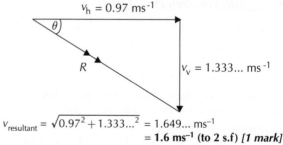

$v_{resultant} = \sqrt{0.97^2 + 1.333...^2} = 1.649...$ ms^{-1}
= 1.6 ms^-1 (to 2 s.f) ***[1 mark]***

$\tan\theta = 1.333... \div 0.97$ so $\theta = \tan^{-1} 1.374... = 53.97...$
= 54° (to 2 s.f) ***[1 mark]***

So the resultant velocity of the boat is 1.6 ms^{-1} at an angle of 54° to the current.

Answers

Page 77 — Motion with Constant Acceleration

1 a) Take upwards as positive.
$a = -9.81\ ms^{-2}$, $t = 5\ s$, $u = 0\ ms^{-1}$, $v = ?$
use: $v = u + at$
$v = 0 + -9.81 \times 5$ ***[1 mark]***
$v = -49.05 = $ **$-49\ ms^{-1}$ (to 2 s.f.)** ***[1 mark]***.
NB: It's negative because she's falling downwards and upwards was taken as the positive direction.

b) Use: $s = \left(\frac{u+v}{2}\right)t$ or $s = ut + \frac{1}{2}at^2$
$s = \frac{-49.05}{2} \times 5$ or $s = 0 + \frac{1}{2} \times -9.81 \times 5^2$ ***[1 mark]***
$s = -122.625$ m or $s = -122.625$ m
So she falls **120 m (to 2 s.f.)** ***[1 mark]***

2 a) $v = 0\ ms^{-1}$, $t = 3.2\ s$, $s = 40\ m$, $u = ?$
use: $s = \left(\frac{u+v}{2}\right)t$
$40 = 3.2u \div 2$ ***[1 mark]***
$u = 80 \div 3.2 = $ **$25\ ms^{-1}$** ***[1 mark]***

b) Use: $v^2 = u^2 + 2as$
$0 = 25^2 + 80a$ ***[1 mark]***
$-80a = 625$
$a = -7.81... = $ **$-7.8\ ms^{-2}$ (to 2 s.f.)** ***[1 mark]***
You could also have solved this using $v = u + at$.

3 a) Take upstream as negative: $v = 5\ ms^{-1}$, $a = 6\ ms^{-2}$, $s = 1.2\ m$, $u = ?$
use: $v^2 = u^2 + 2as$
$5^2 = u^2 + 2 \times 6 \times 1.2$ ***[1 mark]***
$u^2 = 25 - 14.4 = 10.6$
$u = -3.255... = $ **$-3.3\ ms^{-1}$ (to 2 s.f.)** ***[1 mark]***
The negative root is taken because the boat is moving upstream at the start, which was taken as the negative direction.

b) From furthest point: $u = 0\ ms^{-1}$, $a = 6\ ms^{-2}$, $v = 5\ ms^{-1}$, $s = ?$
use: $v^2 = u^2 + 2as$
$5^2 = 0 + 2 \times 6 \times s$ ***[1 mark]***
$s = 25 \div 12 = 2.083... = $ **2.1 m (to 2 s.f.)** ***[1 mark]***

4 a) Use $v = u + at$ with $t = 0$ as the starting time.
In the first second, $u = 3$, $v = 3 + a$
In the second second, $u = 3 + a$, $v = (3 + a) + a = 3 + 2a$
In the third second, $u = 3 + 2a$, $v = (3 + 2a) + a = 3 + 3a$
[1 mark]
For the third second, use: $s = \left(\frac{u+v}{2}\right)t$
$6 = \left(\frac{3 + 2a + 3 + 3a}{2}\right) \times 1 = \left(\frac{6 + 5a}{2}\right)$ ***[1 mark]***
$12 = 6 + 5a$
$6 = 5a$
$a = $ **$1.2\ ms^{-2}$** ***[1 mark]***
There's another way to work out acceleration — the cyclist travelled 6 m in the third second, so for the period 2-3 s his average velocity must have been $6\ ms^{-1}$. So at $t = 2.5$ seconds his speed must have been $6\ ms^{-1}$. You can use acceleration = change in speed ÷ time taken and get $a = 3 \div 2.5 = 1.2\ ms^{-2}$.

b) In the fourth second, $u = 3 + 3a$, $v = (3 + 3a) + a = 3 + 4a$
Use $s = \left(\frac{u+v}{2}\right)t$ for the fourth second:
$s = \frac{1}{2}(3 + 3a + 3 + 4a) \times 1 = \frac{1}{2}(6 + 7 \times 1.2) \times 1$ ***[1 mark]***
$=$ **7.2 m** ***[1 mark]***

Page 79 — Acceleration of Free Fall

1 a) The air resistance on a falling small steel ball will be less than that on a beach ball. The air resistance on the ball used in this experiment needs to be negligible in order to be able to calculate the value of g ***[1 mark]***.

b) E.g. the experiment might be affected by random error caused by the wind ***[1 mark]***. To remove this error, conduct the experiment indoors and close all windows ***[1 mark]***. The experiment might be affected by systematic error if the ruler is not aligned properly so would give slightly incorrect vertical height measurements ***[1 mark]***. To remove this, use a clamp to ensure the rule is straight and unmoving ***[1 mark]***.

c) Use: $s = ut + \frac{1}{2}at^2$ ***[1 mark]***
$u = 0$ and $a = g$, so $s = \frac{1}{2}gt^2$ or $\frac{1}{2}g = \frac{s}{t^2}$ ***[1 mark]***
So the gradient of a graph of s against t^2, $\frac{\Delta s}{\Delta t^2}$, is equal to half the acceleration, i.e. $\frac{1}{2}g$ ***[1 mark]***.

2 Change of height $\Delta h = 15.03 - 11.04 = 3.99$ m ***[1 mark]***
Frequency of 4 Hz means there are 4 frames per second, so each frame takes $1\ s \div 4 = 0.25\ s$ ***[1 mark]***
$v = \Delta h \div \Delta t = 3.99 \div 0.25 = 15.96\ ms^{-1}$
So $\Delta v = 15.96 - 13.51 = 2.45\ ms^{-1}$ ***[1 mark]***
$a = \Delta v \div \Delta t = 2.45 \div 0.25 = $ **$9.8\ ms^{-2}$** ***[1 mark]***

Page 81 — Projectile Motion

1 a) You only need to worry about the vertical motion of the stone.
$u = 0\ ms^{-1}$, $s = -230\ m$, $a = -g = -9.81\ ms^{-2}$, $t = ?$
You need to find t, so use: $s = ut + \frac{1}{2}at^2$
$-230 = 0 + \frac{1}{2} \times -9.81 \times t^2$ ***[1 mark]***
$t = \sqrt{\frac{2 \times (-230)}{-9.81}} = 6.847... = $ **6.8 s (to 2 s.f.)** ***[1 mark]***

b) You know that in the horizontal direction:
$u = v = 8.0\ ms^{-1}$, $t = 6.847...\ s$, $a = 0$, $s = ?$
So use velocity $= \frac{\text{distance}}{\text{time}}$, $v = \frac{s}{t}$
$s = v \times t = 8.0 \times 6.847...$ ***[1 mark]*** $= 54.781...$
$=$ **55 m (to 2 s.f.)** ***[1 mark]***

2 You know that for the arrow's vertical motion (taking upwards as the positive direction):
$a = -9.81\ ms^{-2}$, $u = 30\ ms^{-1}$ and the arrow will be at its highest point just before it starts falling back towards the ground, so $v = 0\ ms^{-1}$.
s = the vertical distance travelled from the arrow's firing point.
So use $v^2 = u^2 + 2as$
$0 = 30^2 + 2 \times -9.81 \times s$ ***[1 mark]***
$900 = 2 \times 9.81s$
$s = \frac{900}{2 \times 9.81} = 45.87...$ ***[1 mark]***
So the maximum distance reached from the ground $= 45.87... + 1 = $ **47 m (to 2 s.f.)** ***[1 mark]***

Answers

Page 83 — Displacement-Time Graphs

1 Split graph into four sections:

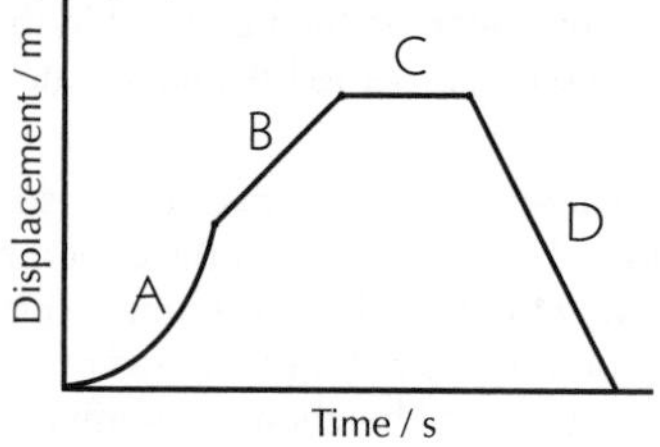

A: acceleration ***[1 mark]***

B: constant velocity ***[1 mark]***

C: stationary ***[1 mark]***

D: constant velocity in opposite direction to A and B ***[1 mark]***

2 a)

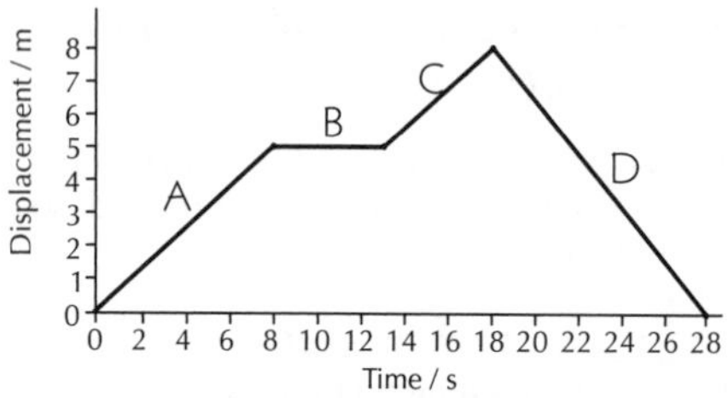

[4 marks — 1 mark for each section correctly drawn]

b) A: $v = s \div t = 5 \div 8 = 0.625 =$ **0.63 ms^{-1} (to 2 s.f)**

B: $v =$ **0 ms^{-1}**

C: $v = 3 \div 5 =$ **0.6 ms^{-1}**

D: $v = -8 \div 10 =$ **–0.8 ms^{-1}**

[2 marks for all correct or just 1 mark for 2 or 3 correct]

Page 85 — Velocity-Time Graphs

1 a)

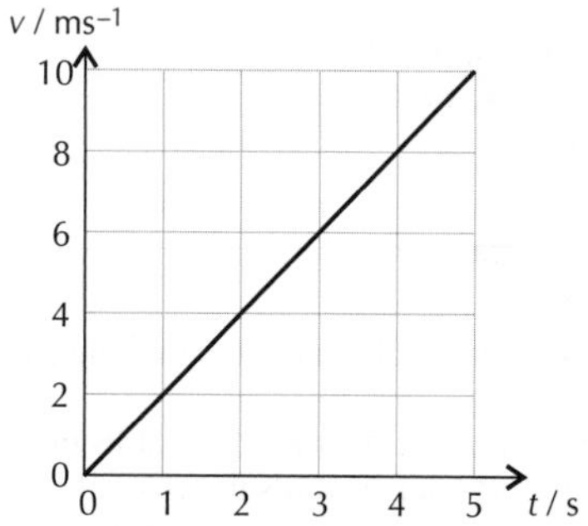

[1 mark for correct axes, 1 mark for correct line]

b) Use $s = ut + ½at^2$

$t = 1$, $s =$ **1 m**

$t = 2$, $s =$ **4 m**

$t = 3$, $s =$ **9 m**

$t = 4$, $s =$ **16 m**

$t = 5$, $s =$ **25 m**

[2 marks for all correct or 1 mark for at least 3 pairs of values right]

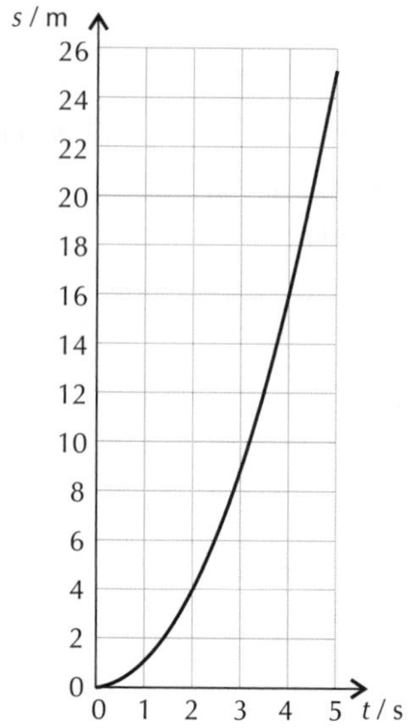

[1 mark for correctly labelled axes, 1 mark for correct curve]

c) E.g. another way to calculate displacement is to find the area under the velocity-time graph ***[1 mark]***.
E.g. displacement after 5 seconds = ½ × 5 ×10 = **25 m** ***[1 mark]***

Page 87 — Motion Experiments and Models

1 a) If it takes 1 frame to pass the reference point,
$t = 1 \times \frac{1}{26} = 0.03846...$ s ***[1 mark]***

$v = L \div t = 0.15 \div 0.03846...$ ***[1 mark]*** = **3.9 ms^{-1}** ***[1 mark]***

b) E.g. any one of: Use a camera with a higher frame rate ***[1 mark]*** so the time can be measured more precisely, which decreases the overall uncertainty of the velocity ***[1 mark]*** / Use longer trollies marked with distances ***[1 mark]*** to make sure the trolley takes at least one frame to pass the reference point so more accurate time assumptions can be made ***[1 mark]***.

2 Acceleration is 10 ms^{-2} so Δv = 10 ms^{-1} every second.
E.g.:

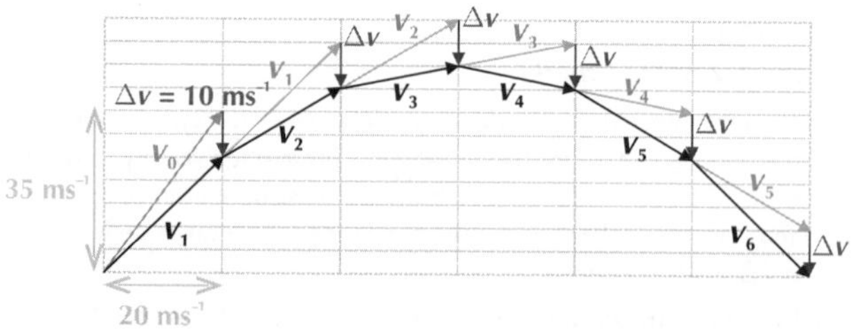

[1 mark correctly drawing vector v_0 and Δv nose-to-tail and correctly drawing resultant vector v_1, 1 mark for correctly using v_1 as the starting velocity for the second internal, 1 mark for correctly drawing full symmetrical parabola.]

Answers

Page 89 — Forces

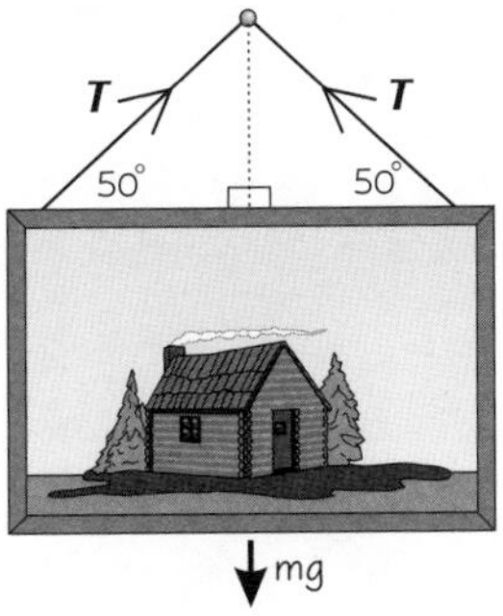

The picture is in equilibrium, so the forces are balanced.
Resolving vertically:
Weight = vertical component of tension × 2
$8 \times 9.81 = 2T \sin 50°$ ***[1 mark]***
$78.48 = 0.7660... \times 2T$
$102.448... = 2T$
$T = 51.224... =$ **50 N (to 1 s.f.)** ***[1 mark]***

2

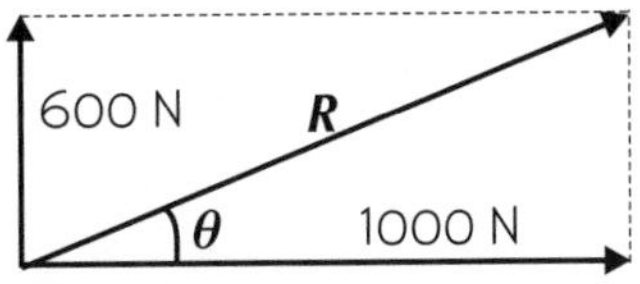

By Pythagoras:
$R = \sqrt{1000^2 + 600^2} = 1166.19... =$ **1170 N (to 3 s.f.)** ***[1 mark]***
$\tan \theta = (600 \div 1000)$
so $\theta = \tan^{-1} 0.6 = 30.96...° =$ **31.0° (to 3 s.f.)** ***[1 mark]***

Page 91 — Newton's Laws of Motion

1 a) When the parachutist first jumps out of the plane, the only vertical force acting on her is due to gravity, so there is a net downward force ***[1 mark]***. Newton's 2nd law states that, for a body of constant mass, the acceleration is proportional to the net force, so she will accelerate downwards ***[1 mark]***.

b) $F = ma = 78 \times 9.81 = 765.18 = 765$ N (to 3 s.f.) ***[1 mark]***

2 Force perpendicular to river flow = 500 – 100 = 400 N ***[1 mark]***
Force parallel to river flow = 300 N
Resultant force = $\sqrt{400^2 + 300^2} = 500$ N ***[1 mark]***
$a = F \div m = 500 \div 250 =$ **2 ms^{-2}** ***[1 mark]***

Page 93 — Momentum and Impulse

1 a) total momentum before collision = total momentum after
$(0.145 \times 1.94) + 0 = (0.145 \times -0.005) + 0.148v$ ***[1 mark]***
$0.2813 + 0.000725 = 0.148v$, so $v = 1.90557...$
$=$ **1.9 ms^{-1} (to 2 s.f.)** ***[1 mark]***

b) Kinetic energy before the collision =
$(½ \times 0.145 \times 1.94^2) + (½ \times 0.148 \times 0^2) = 0.272861$ J
Kinetic energy after the collision =
$(½ \times 0.145 \times 0.005^2) + (½ \times 0.148 \times 1.90557...^2) = 0.26871...$ J
[1 mark]
The collision is not perfectly elastic / is inelastic ***[1 mark]***, as the kinetic energy is greater before the collision than after it ***[1 mark]***.

c) $F\Delta t = \Delta mv = (0.145 \times 0.005) - (0.145 \times 0) = 0.000725$
so $F = \Delta mv \div \Delta t$
$= 0.000725 \div 0.15$ ***[1 mark]***
$= 0.00483... =$ **4.8 ×10^{-3} N (to 2 s.f.)** ***[1 mark]***

Page 96 — Terminal Velocity

1 a) The velocity increases at a steady rate, which means the acceleration is constant ***[1 mark]***.
Constant acceleration means there must be no atmospheric resistance (atmospheric resistance would increase with velocity, leading to a decrease in acceleration). So there must be no atmosphere ***[1 mark]***.

b)

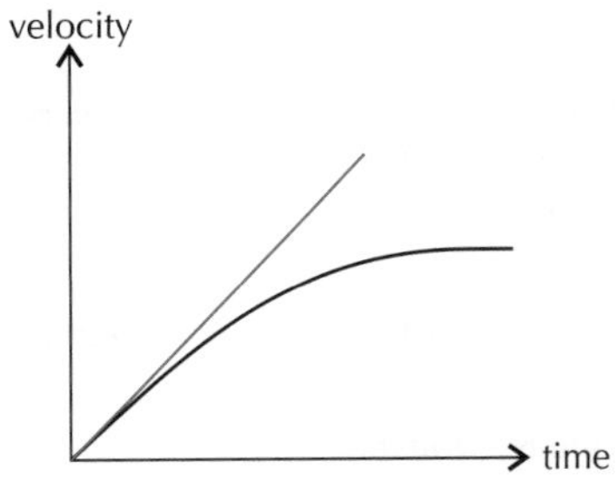

[1 mark for a smooth curve that levels out, 1 mark for correct position relative to existing line]
Your graph must be a smooth curve which levels out. It must NOT go down at the end.

c) (The graph becomes less steep)
because the acceleration is decreasing ***[1 mark]***
because air resistance increases with speed ***[1 mark]***
(The graph levels out)
because air resistance has become equal to weight ***[1 mark]***
If the question says 'explain', you won't get marks for just describing what the graph shows — you have to say why it is that shape.

2 a) The 15 cm cone will have the lowest terminal velocity ***[1 mark]*** because it has the largest surface area and therefore the largest drag ***[1 mark]***.

b)

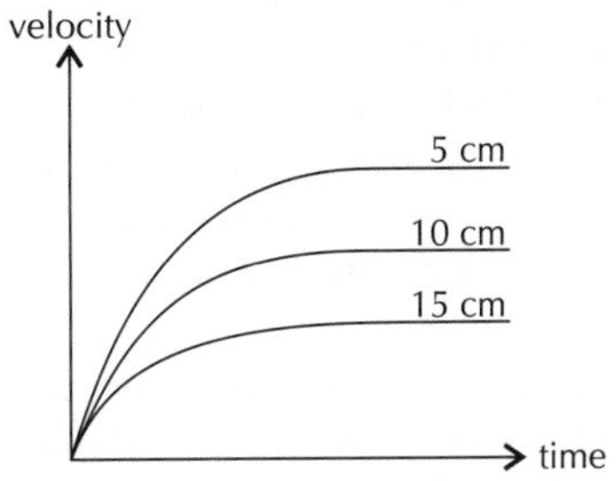

[3 marks, 1 mark for each correct line.]

c) E.g. The shape/slant/height of the cone because it would affect the amount of air resistance ***[1 mark]***.

d) The curve for the largest cone would reach a higher terminal velocity ***[1 mark]*** because the shape is more streamlined ***[1 mark]*** so the air resistance would be lower at a given speed ***[1 mark]***.

Answers

Page 99 — Work and Power

1 $\Delta E = F \times \Delta s$ so $F = \Delta E \div \Delta s = 7.5 \div 3.6$ ***[1 mark]***
$= 2.083... =$ **2.1 N (to 2 s.f.)** ***[1 mark]***

2 a) 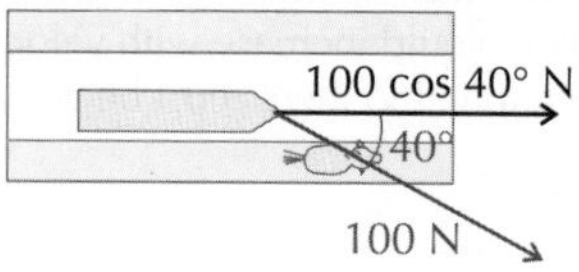

Force in direction of travel = 100 cos 40° = 76.60... ***[1 mark]***
$\Delta E = F\Delta s = 76.60... \times 1500 = 114\ 906.6...$ J
= **110 000 J (to 2 s.f.)** ***[1 mark]***

b) Use $P = Fv$
= 100 cos 40° × 0.80 = 61.28... = **61 W (to 2 s.f.)** ***[1 mark]***

3 a) Use $\Delta E = F\Delta s$
= 20.0 × 9.81 × 3.00 = **588.6 J** ***[1 mark]***
Remember that 20.0 kg is not the force — it's the mass. So you need to multiply it by 9.81 Nkg^{-1} to get the weight.

b) Use $P = Fv$
= (20.0 × 9.81) × 0.25 = 49.05 = **49 W (to 2 s.f.)** ***[1 mark]***

Page 101 — Conservation of Energy

1 a) Use kinetic energy = $\frac{1}{2}mv^2$ and g.p.e. = mgh
$\frac{1}{2}mv^2 = mgh$ ***[1 mark]***
$\frac{1}{2}v^2 = gh$
$v^2 = 2gh = 2 \times 9.81 \times 2.0 = 39.24$ ***[1 mark]***
$v = 6.264... = 6.3\ ms^{-1}$ **(to 2 s.f.)** ***[1 mark]***
'No friction' allows you to say that the changes in kinetic and potential energy will be the same.

2 a) If there's no air resistance, k.e. = g.p.e. = mgh
So kinetic energy = 0.020 × 9.81 × 8.0
= 1.5696 = **1.6 J (to 2 s.f.)** ***[1 mark]***

b) If the ball rebounds to 6.5 m, it has gravitational potential energy:
g.p.e. = mgh = 0.020 × 9.81 × 6.5 = 1.2753 J ***[1 mark]***
So 1.5696 – 1.2753 = 0.2943 = **0.29 J (to 2 s.f.)** is transferred to heat and sound ***[1 mark]***

3 At half of the maximum height, half of the elastic potential energy of the trampoline has been converted into gravitational potential energy and half into kinetic energy.
So kinetic energy = 2750 ÷ 2 = 1375 J ***[1 mark]***
$\frac{1}{2}mv^2 = 1375$ so $v^2 = (2 \times 1375) \div 70.0 = 39.28...$ ***[1 mark]***
$v = \sqrt{39.28...} = 6.2678... =$ **6.27 ms^{-1} (to 3 s.f.)** ***[1 mark]***

Index

Index

Index

Index